Praise for "Survivor"

"*Survivor*'s sociological, pseudo-Machiavellian aspect makes it the antithesis of traditional quiz shows.... On *Survivor*, it's as much who you know, and what they think of you... The psychological rigors of twoscore days in the rain forest—and the potential humiliation of being booted by fifteen comrades on national television—are as worrisome as the jungle fauna." —*Time*

"Cinéma vérité with an Orwellian aura is finding a home on American television..... *Survivor* breaks the mold of comedies, dramas and news programs.... This is Peeping Tom to the max." —*The New York Times*

"What's being tested here isn't whether any of these people can survive on an uninhabited island but whether they can survive one another, and how they negotiate the conflict between their selfish, competitive instincts and their need to preserve group strength."
—Nancy Franklin in *The New Yorker*

"*Survivor*, the well-produced, irresistible, inessential and insanely successful hybrid of fantasy and reality, has changed television."
—*Inside TV*

"The summer television sensation *Survivor* is quickly working its way into American pop culture." —*USA Today*

"*Survivor* is summer's unofficial water-cooler show."
—*Minneapolis Star Tribune*

"Not only is *Survivor* the biggest-ever launch of a summer series, but it beats all the time-slot competition combined." —Inside.com

"*Survivor* now ranks as the most watched summer primetime series in modern televison history." —*Hollywood Reporter*

"Fascinating entertainment, the kind that people will be talking about."
—*New York Post*

"The hottest show in America." —*TV Guide*

By Mark Burnett

with Martin Dugard

NEW YORK

SURVIVOR

The Ultimate Game

The Official Companion Book
to the CBS Television Show

CBS
Consumer Products

LIBRARY OF CONGRESS CATALOGING-IN-PUBLICATION DATA
Burnett, Mark.
 Survivor / Mark Burnett with Martin Dugard
 p. cm.
 Companion book to the CBS show "Survivor."
 ISBN 1-57500-143-8 (pbk.)
 1. Survivor (Television program) I. Dugard, Martin.
II. Title.
PN1992.77.S865 B87 2000
791.45'72—dc 21

                                        00-057689

TV Books, L.L.C.
1619 Broadway
New York, NY 10019
www.tvbooks.com

Interior design by Rachel Reiss
Manufactured in the United States of America

Dedicated to
adventure seekers everywhere

Contents

Prologue

In the first week of October 1999, CBS announced a nationwide casting call for a most intriguing new adventure show. "Survivor" would shipwreck sixteen men and women on the island of Pulau Tiga, twenty miles off the coast of Borneo. Cameras would film them day and night as the "castaways" built shelter, foraged for food and water, and, most important, learned to get along with each other. The point of the show was this: Once every three days the castaways would vote one of their own off the island. The last person left would win a million dollars.

For several years I had been producing Eco-Challenge, arguably the world's toughest expedition race. More than fifty four-person teams of adventurers would gather annually to race for eight to ten nonstop days across the world's most brutal landscapes—places like Morocco, the Australian Outback, and Patagonia. Less than one-half the teams finished. The elite Navy SEALS fielded teams for five years before one managed to officially finish.

The major lesson I learned from Eco-Challenge was that success depends far more on team dynamics and interpersonal skills than any other attribute. It was this understanding that led me to search for a new and clever "nature based" way of providing men and women with an opportunity to discover who they really were.

"Survivor" was the outcome of that search. After years of negotiating to buy American and Canadian rights from Charlie Parsons, a British friend of mine, I then spent an even longer period convincing various television networks that it would be a great show.

My persistence paid off.

In the fall of 1998, I was offered the opportunity to pitch the idea at CBS. I met with a young executive named Ghen Maynard, a man with the vision to see that such cutting-edge programming had a place on the Tiffany network. Ghen immediately took the idea to Leslie Moonves, head of CBS Television. The deal was soon done—thirteen prime-time hours of "Survivor" would splash into American households in the summer of 2000. All that remained was find the castaways, hence, a call for men and women with the guts and audacity to participate.

"Two parts adventure contest and eight parts surviving the peer group," is how I was quoted in the press release. As the show's executive producer, I envisioned something akin to "Gilligan's Island" meets *Lord of the Flies* meets *Ten Little Indians* meets "The Real World." "Survivor" marks a return to a core element of adventure: staying alive. The only real difference between stranding sixteen people on a deserted island with cameras and wealthy individuals paying six-figure sums to be guided up Everest with cameras was the size of the safety net.

Pulau Tiga is perched almost atop the equator. The average temperature and percent humidity are the same: 95. Sand flea nests pock the beaches, making a barefoot stroll an exercise in endurance instead of a romantic interlude. The deceptively serene-looking blue waters around the island are home to stinging jellyfish and the world's highest concentration of deadly sea snakes. The jungle interior is choked with pythons, kraits, adders, monkeys, monitor lizards, and white-bellied sea eagles. Nothing that could eat a person, but definitely enough to make life interesting.

Over six thousand were brave enough to apply. Of those, eight hundred were interviewed in sixteen cities. Forty-eight finalists were selected. After intense background checks and psychological evaluations, the final sixteen and two alternates were picked just after New Year's. They came from all around the United States, representing all ages and demographic backgrounds. Occupations ranged from CEO to Navy SEAL to single mother. There was a Gilligan, a Skipper, a Mary Ann. They had only two characteristics in common: All were extroverts, and all swore that even if money weren't involved, they would spend six weeks on Pulau Tiga just for the sake of the adventure—a fact I already knew from the psychological evaluations.

The castaways were flown to Los Angeles on March 7, 2000. The next day they boarded a plane for the Bornean city of Kota Kinabalu, from where they'd take a boat to Pulau Tiga. In the interest of building alliances only in the island environment, castaways weren't allowed to speak to each other in Los Angeles, on the flight over (where they were seated separately), or even during the two days and nights at Kota Kinabalu's Magellan Sutera Resort—their last bit of paradise before the abrupt descent into deprivation.

Meanwhile, their island was being prepared. Roughly the shape of a boomerang, Pulau Tiga is three miles long by one mile wide. It is a jungle island in the harshest sense. A coral reef surrounds the island a quarter-mile offshore. Then the thinnest strip of white sand beach marks the advent of land before giving way to the tangle of vegetation and rot draping Pulau Tiga like a humid green shroud. A rise in elevation at the island's center gives the island a three-dimensional feel. Bubbling mud from methane gas pockets reveal Pulau Tiga's volcanic origin. The Japanese operated a small refueling dock on Pulau Tiga during World War II, leaving behind a single steel boat cleat. In the early 1970s a Malaysian university tried building an oceanographic institute there, but the island is too isolated and wild for even the most adventurous student. The bungalows were soon reclaimed by the jungle and its inhabitants.

The abandoned institute is on the inside of the boomerang's open "V." This is the leeward side of the island. It faces west, and the South China Sea sunsets turn the sand orange-purple each evening at 6:30. On these shores we built a dock for offloading equipment, then living quarters with cold-water showers for sixty-five personnel—the camera crews, the production staff, and the assorted other individuals vital to producing thirteen hours of prime-time television. This makeshift "Survivor Resort" offered a television and one phone line. Floodlights illuminating the main compound at night cut the intense dark of a world far from civilization, unused to street lights, headlights, flashlights, Christmas lights—indeed, any illumination save sunlight.

Just two hundred yards away from the crew compound, but swallowed entirely by jungle, was the most vital piece of construction. The "Tribal Council" set would be the arena for voting members off the island. Just thirty feet by thirty feet, the platform without walls would be the only traditional shooting stage on the island and was a reminder to all involved of "Survivor"'s surreal nature.

Faux-Mayan columns surrounded a communal fire lava pit. Tiki torches lit the rope bridge marking the entrance. There was an area known as the Confessional to one side for those castaways wishing to vent emotions alone into a camera. A pirate's treasure chest sat open, revealing a million dollars in fake cash. (The winner would actually receive a check.) Every three days a gathering of the Tribal Council would be led by the show's host and the island's de facto chief, Jeff Probst.

This appropriation of elements from cultural anthropology, religious ritual, and Robert Louis Stevenson mines the common subconscious ideal of island life. All jungles have ruins and fire and lava and rope bridges and buried treasure and a chief. Without that built-in comfort factor the audience would surely cringe as they realize how truly terrifying life on Pulau Tiga will be for the castaways.

Their walk through the jungle at night to the Tribal Council will be an hour trek punctuated by stops to wait for six-foot–long snakes to writhe off the trail. Their bodies will be covered with bug bites as they sleep on the sand or in the jungle. They will catch rats to supplement the diet of rice and water provided. There will be nothing entertaining or fabricated in those moments. The barriers between TV and survival, between what's real and what's not real, will be blurred in the total immersion into a quest to outwit, outlast, and outplay one's fellow castaways.

For in the end, "Survivor" is less about an Outward Bound class gone terribly wrong than about Machiavellian politics at their most primal. Human dynamics mean everything. The goal is to avoid getting voted off the island. Some will avoid this through alliance, some through hard work resulting in non-expendability, some through sympathy. But in the end, all but one must go. Even the best of friends will eventually vote against each other. Only one can win the million, and secret pacts to split the loot are strictly forbidden. Just because you may be the fittest and strongest and best survivor, if you treat people badly and act like a jerk you will be kicked off. Conversely, if you're a very, very congenial and nice person but are completely useless and can't provide any meaningful contribution to island life, you'll also be kicked off. "Survivor" is about how you can manipulate complicated team dynamics under pressure.

To encourage those team dynamics, the castaways will be divided into two tribes of eight just before being sent ashore. Every few days the tribes will compete against each other in specially designed challenges. One type of challenge will reward the victors with creature comforts such as matches, a beer, use of a cell phone to call home. The second and more nerve-wracking sort of challenge rewards the victors by excusing them from a session of the Tribal Council, which is held every three days. For only one of the tribes votes a member off in each Tribal Council. The tribe that wins immunity doesn't have to vote, doesn't have to tear down the precarious walls of new friendship by sending one of their own home. After the castaways have been winnowed to just ten, the tribes will merge into one hyper-competitive group of Survivors. The former enemies will be teammates. And the castaway dynamic will change in two dramatic ways: The challenges will reward the individuals instead of the team, and every individual makes that long walk to the Tribal Council every three days.

But that social Darwinism will be a long way off as the castaways get to know each other during the four-hour boat ride from Kota Kinabalu— KK. The speaking ban will be lifted the moment they leave civilization.

They'll make small talk. As the island comes into sight, in my last formal interaction with the castaways before Chief Jeff takes over, I will separate them into tribes. One will be assigned to Pagong Beach, the other to Tagi. The tribes will take the names of their beaches. Their first impression when they land will be just beach and jungle. As the shock that this is an actual, real-world adventure instead of something pretend wears off, the tribes will take a harder look at their new home. They'll ferret out water holes, a sleeping area. They'll build quarters. They'll learn where to sit without being swarmed by sand fleas and where to sleep without rats crawling over them (answer to the last two: nowhere).

What they won't see are the hidden microphones and infrared cameras at the watering hole and along the beach. In addition to the hand-held cameras and boom mikes that will be in their faces, this array of unseen recording devices will document their every move. To make sure each and every camera works properly, crews of sound engineers and camera men arrived three weeks before the March 13 "shipwreck" to begin the camouflage and testing process. The castaways won't have a moment's privacy, even in the jungle. And although they knew that going in, they have no idea how invasive television can be. For every hour of television broadcast, over a hundred hours of tape will be edited down. The inevitable nervousness and reluctance to reveal their true selves on camera will disappear as the cameras become as familiar to their daily lives as breathing. Only then can the true range of human personality dynamics—the love and hope and sex and dreams side of life—come forth.

In Meeting Room 10 at the air-conditioned, five-star Magellan, the castaways fired questions at me. Will physical relationships be allowed? Absolutely. The island is a microcosm of real life. If romance blooms and two (or three or four) people want to act on it, they may.

What kinds of "challenges," physical or mental? Both.

When a castaway is voted off the island, does that person have to leave immediately? Yes. A short good-bye, then a quick escort back to civilization.

Then I showed them a documentary about Pulau Tiga and nearby Snake Island, where sea kraits flock by the thousands to breed. They peered at the television screen intently, not so much watching the snakes or the eagles that feast on them, but studying the island—THEIR island. They stared at the images of beach and jungle—which revealed nothing at all—for clues about comfort and food and whether or not they have what it takes to coexist with fifteen strangers on an island. They all looked so well-fed and wholesome and clean and polite and incredibly urban-American that it was hard to believe they were actually one night's sleep away from spending, possibly, six and a half weeks fighting for their existence, their mental health, their self-respect. Their money. If ever a device were invented to help men and women gauge the caliber of their character, "Survivor" is it.

Then they returned to their rooms. Around midnight I visited each room in turn with a few of my key staff and removed all but essential clothing from each castaway's small island-bound pack. Then they were left alone to try to sleep. Day One of "Survivor" began with a 4:30 A.M. wake-up call.

The Castaways

Tagi Tribe

Name:	Kelley Wiglesworth
Age:	22
Hometown:	Las Vegas, Nevada
Marital Status:	single
Profession:	river guide
Quote:	"I do get irritable when people get in my way, but I don't have the rage I used to."

Name:	Dirk Been
Age:	23
Hometown:	Spring Green, Wisconsin
Marital Status:	single
Profession:	farmer
Quote:	"I feel pornography is a sin, but when I was mad at God I did look at some."

Name:	Rudy Boesch
Age:	72
Hometown:	Virginia Beach, Virginia
Marital Status:	married, three daughters
Profession:	US Navy SEALS (retired)
Quote:	"I don't need none of that affection."

Name: Sean Kenniff
Age: 29
Hometown: Carle Place, New York
Marital Status: single
Profession: neurosurgeon
Quote: "The party doesn't go on without me. I like it
               that way."

Name: Stacey Stillman
Age: 27
Hometown: San Francisco, California
Marital Status: single
Profession: lawyer
Quote: "My directness is often misunderstood as bitchi-
               ness."

Name: Richard Hatch
Age: 38
Hometown: Newport, Rhode Island
Marital Status: single
Profession: corporate trainer—conflict management
Quote: "I am bright, logical, and rational (with hardly
               any ego!)."

Name: Sonja Christopher
Age: 63
Hometown: Walnut Creek, California
Marital Status: single
Profession: retired investment counselor
Quote: "I can do anything for seven weeks!"

Name: Susan Hawk
Age: 38
Hometown: Palmyra, Wisconsin
Marital Status: married
Profession: truck driver
Quote: "John Wayne in *True Grit* is a hero for me."

Pagong Tribe

Name:	Greg Buis
Age:	23
Hometown:	Plano, Texas
Marital Status:	single
Profession:	journeyman
Quote:	"I'm not tied to any outcome either way."

Name:	Jenna Lewis
Age:	22
Hometown:	Franklin, New Hampshire
Marital Status:	single, mother of twin girls
Profession:	student
Quote:	"My dad and I didn't get along because he wanted me to act like a girl. I wanted to play baseball and act like a boy."

Name:	Gervase Peterson
Age:	30
Hometown:	Willingboro, New Jersey
Marital Status:	single, father of three
Profession:	unemployed
Quote:	"Since my dad died when I was fifteen I've been an adult. Nobody has told me what to do."

Name:	Joel Klug
Age:	27
Hometown:	Sherwood, Arkansas
Marital Status:	single
Profession:	financial services, health clubs
Quote:	"Bottom line, I can be very persuasive to get my way."

Name: Colleen Haskell
Age: 23
Hometown: Miami Beach, Florida
Marital Status: single
Profession: student
Quote: "I have a strict set of morals. Nobody in my family is divorced. I wouldn't commit adultery, ever."

Name: Ramona Gray
Age: 29
Hometown: Edison, New Jersey
Marital Status: single
Profession: chemist
Quote: "You can just call me G.I. Jane & McGuyver, what else needs to be said?"

Name: B.B. Andersen
Age: 64
Hometown: Mission Hills, Kansas
Marital Status: married, four children
Profession: retired CEO
Quote: "I have a great intolerance for people not working for what they are paid."

Name: Gretchen Cordy
Age: 38
Hometown: Clarksville, Tennessee
Marital Status: married, two children
Profession: pre-school teacher
Quote: "I have a lot of patience and like to make things fun."

EVOLUTION ONE

Survival of the Fittest

DAY ONE

Richard Hatch was destined to be the first castaway voted off, and being gay had nothing to do with it. A Falstaffian figure with a neatly trimmed salt-and-pepper beard, the corporate conflict management trainer was so much larger-than-life than his fellow castaways that it seemed they were of a different species. From the moment the castaways were allowed to speak, his every broad action and pronouncement confidently broadcast that he was sure he was going to win the million dollars. That he did so without apology or guile was of no matter. It was annoying. So, of course, his fellow castaways began marking him as the first man to go.

Richard's self-confidence had been barely kept under wraps as the castaways were led from the Magellan and bused to a small Filipino fishing village north of KK. In the tranquil cove lay the *Matahari*. Bright yellow, with olive-drab sails and an orange rising sun painted on the stern, the authentic Indonesian sailing ship had been hand-built by her French skipper. The wooden hull was of a very durable construction to support loads in the hold and support the weight of the ship when she was beached for cleaning. No glue or screws were used in *Matahari*'s construction. Instead, dowels known as trunnels were hammered through the timber then secured in place with wedges of wood. In preparation for the castaways, two bamboo rafts were lashed to the ship, one on each side of the stern.

Her decks were littered with wicker fish traps, seine nets, wooden crates, and even a pair of machetes.

The castaways seemed wary of everything—the island, each other, the TV cameras—as they walked single-file through the fishing village. The giddiness of the previous afternoon was gone. But once they'd been motored out to the *Matahari*, all that pent-up energy poured out in laughter and easy conversation. They were united in having been selected for the show. Two months of curiosity about their fellow castaways could finally be satisfied, and they wasted no time in getting to know each other. Where you from? What do you do? How many kids? What's it like living there? No one else on earth knew their apprehensions and expectations, so to finally be able to share was an emotional release. Perhaps their greatest relief was unspoken: Everyone looked so normal. No supermen. No supermodels.

Their differences were equally obvious. Sonja looked frail but enthusiastic, Jenna ran around like a manic princess, Ramona looked strong and proud, and everyone else did their best to mingle. It was like a cocktail party without the drinks, where the ability to make small talk was the only skill that mattered.

B.B. Andersen and Rudy Boesch stood to one side, patriarchs waiting to be enthroned. "I'm going to be in trouble if one of these kids starts talking about MTV," Rudy allowed. A stoic and judgmental man, the art of small talk was something the seventy-two-year-old retired Navy SEAL didn't value much. Even talking to B.B.—at sixty-four, Rudy's nearest peer—was a difficult duty. Rudy had long ago embraced the ideal of keeping his mouth shut. He'd joined the navy at seventeen, in the waning days of World War II. It was the only job he ever held. At twenty-two he'd become one of the first SEAL (Sea, Air, Land) commandos. Over the next forty years Rudy became the most senior noncommissioned officer in the Navy. Blue-collar, with a gray flattop, Rudy was the stereotypical old swabbie. When the Navy offered him the chance to become an officer, he turned it down. It just wasn't him, and if there was a defining characteristic about Rudy it was that he knew who he was and remained true to himself. He wasn't changing for anyone.

Whereas another man—Richard, for instance—might speak a thousand words about a single emotion, Rudy liked to sum up an entire thought process with a one-line zinger. He didn't like homos. He didn't

know what MTV was. The only entertainers he valued were Frank Snot-
grass and Perry Homo.

"Er . . . Como," B.B. corrected.

"Right."

Everyone had a greatest fear: Gervase and swimming, for instance.
Rudy's was homosexuals. He knew a gay would be on the island and didn't
like the thought of one rubbing up against him one bit. He had his "gay-
dar" up, as Richard later joked, but couldn't figure out who it was. Richard
was mildly effeminate and very over-the-top, but was quick to explain to
all that he was married and had a son. So that ruled out Richard. As the
island drew closer, Rudy spent less time worrying about the homosexual
and more about survival. But finding the offender—it was like he was back
in the SEALs, ferreting out weakness in his men—never strayed far from
his priority list.

Then all talk ceased as Pulau Tiga drew nearer, first as a lump on the
horizon, then as a clearly defined forest rising from the ocean. The castaways stood about the deck, clustered in twos and threes. The island
didn't scare them so much as awe them and fill them with relief—they
were finally there. All that waiting and wondering and worrying was finally about to be set aside. It was time to begin surviving.

I gathered them, then quickly split them into tribes. Tagi was handed
orange bandannas, Pagong, yellow. They were to put them on immediately so their fellow tribe-members could recognize them. I pointed out
Tagi Beach and Pagong Beach, a mile apart from each other, their new respective homes. Then Chief Jeff took over. "Now, you have two minutes
to grab everything you need and get off this boat. Starting . . . now."

There was the briefest instant of stunned silence. Then, pandemo-
nium. B.B. took charge of Pagong, grabbing a machete and cutting loose
one bamboo raft. Rudy followed his lead and cut the Tagi raft. Paddles,
fish traps, crates, nets, and, finally, people were thrown overboard, until
either side of the *Matahari* resembled an actual shipwreck—flotsam bobbing atop the bottomless green water. Gervase had learned to swim just a
month before and should have been the most afraid of leaping, but he
didn't hesitate. Two minutes later, Jenna was the only castaway left on
deck, running around trying to find those last items that would make survival easier. Her new chief, Jeff Probst, marched to her side and commanded her to either leap now or get thrown. Jenna leapt.

Overboard, men and women struggled to their rafts, bonding under fire with the only friends they had in the world. For the next six weeks, the slate would be wiped clean: no phone calls, no bills, no jobs. Just survival. They began the job of paddling the cumbersome rafts to shore. The Tagi preferred to hang on to the sides and propel the raft by swimming. The Pagong did a mixture of paddling and swimming. Neither method, however, was efficient. The only reason Tagi reached their beach an hour sooner was a friendly current.

Leaders—real leaders, not just those who assume command but who earn it through a mixture of hard work, intelligence, and charisma—emerged the moment the womb of *Matahari* became a memory. Gretchen Cordy, the mother and former Air Force survival instructor, led Pagong. She and Joel Klug paddled at the front of the raft most of the time, navigating it away from shore when rocks loomed close and calling out words of inspiration for the tired—Ramona (who swallowed sea water and vomited), Gervase, B.B. Greg played like an otter alongside the boat, refusing to wear a life jacket. Colleen said nothing, merely paddled. Jenna sang "Welcome to the Jungle" at the top of her lungs and declared it should be their theme song. If Jenna were auditioning for the role of team cheerleader she couldn't have done a better job.

As soon as Tagi landed, Rudy put them to work. A latrine was built first and the process of building shelter begun. As others began collecting driftwood and palm fronds, Richard called out in a loud voice that he was calling a meeting. In his best corporate trainer mode, Richard declared that he wanted them all to communicate their feelings and find a common goal.

Susan Hatch, the truck driver from Wisconsin whom the crew had nicknamed "Fargo" for her distinctive Midwest twang, kept working. "I thought that's what we're doing here—working together to make our lives a little easier."

Richard persisted. His voice was paternal, soothing, as though he were talking to the employees of a grossly dysfunctional corporation. "But we need to decide the point of our being here. You know, our goals."

"Oh," Susan laughed. She is an earthy woman. She and her husband go bear hunting in Siberia for a good time. "I knew that the moment I signed on for this. I'm surprised you didn't."

"I understand that you know what you want. And I know what I want. But WE need to learn what the group wants. We need to communicate . . .

to establish our goals. I am a corporate group trainer and this is the correct way to maximize our success."

Susan stopped. She turned—but only until she stood three-quarters, so as not to be too confrontational so early in their time together. Her tone, though, was sharp. Her words were spoken through a pained smile. "The only trouble is that this is not the corporate world. This is an island. We are all trying to survive."

Susan resumed her labor. She was looking for bits of driftwood to make a fire. She added over one shoulder as she walked away, "Action, Richard. Action. Action is what we need."

Richard stood alone on the beach. His plan thwarted, he climbed into a tree and pouted for the next hour. His fellow tribe members didn't know him or each other well enough to make pointed comments about his lack of work. Richard tried to atone later, joining the driftwood collection and crowing that the tribe could relax in the future. With his might, he explained, Tagi would win all the Tribal Council immunities

Stacey Stillman, the firecracker from San Francisco, wasn't so good at concealing her emotions. She rolled her eyes at Richard's comments but didn't say anything.

To break the tension, Sonja Christopher serenaded Tagi on her ukulele. She was already the emotional heart and soul of the tribe. Betrayal was a common theme running through her life—her body betraying her with breast cancer—but she had the pluck to put that behind her and so became a real-life survivor. With her gray hair trimmed short and her body lean, she always had a kind word. No one disliked Sonja. If it weren't for Sonja the Tagi would be a fractured, contentious bunch. Protecting her brought them together. So the atmosphere that began with the crazed leaping from *Matahari* and grueling ninety-minute swim to shore and degenerated into pettiness with Richard's vain attempt to demand power softened as dusk approached. Sonja was playing the part of the lovable, benevolent grandmother. She entertained them, hugged them, made the island more like home—and they loved her for it. To say the Tagi were becoming one big, happy family would be an overstatement, but not by much.

Culture shock fading, their new home proving livable, Tagi's only frustration was that the quest for fire had been unsuccessful. There was only blackness as the sun set on Pulau Tiga. The rats began to creep out of the jungle, and the sea kraits slithered up onto the shore for their nighttime hunting. The cold, wet, tired, hungry, and miserable castaways lay down to sleep. Some were on the bamboo raft along the shoreline, others huddled at jungle's edge. None would sleep more than an hour. Rats scurried over, under, around, and through their camp. Two six-foot-long sea kraits, with their telltale, striking, black and yellow bands, spent the evening on the sand at the edge of camp.

DAY TWO

As Day One turned into Day Two, it became clear that being in charge was very important to the individuals with leadership tendencies. Among the Tagi that was Richard and Rudy and Susan; among the Pagong, it was B.B. Andersen and Gretchen Cordy. B.B. was a wealthy contractor from Kansas. He was used to having authority over large groups of people, giving commands and having them followed. Gretchen was a mother of two from Clarksville, Tennessee. Before leaving the Air Force to have children she had been an instructor at their SERE (Survival, Evasion, Resistance, Escape) school. She had taken time off from her job as a pre-school teacher to travel to Pulau Tiga. So Gretchen brought a two-pronged attack to the island: survival skills learned from the Air Force and management skills learned in the greatest learning ground anywhere, dealing with children.

Though Gretchen did hard physical work paddling to shore, she got sick from dehydration, seasickness, heat, and her anti-malaria prescription once they hit the beach. B.B. took charge, barking orders like a commandant, much to the amusement of his younger cohorts. The tone of the Pagong camp was much lighter than that of the Tagi, perhaps owing to the greater number of young castaways. But when B.B. attempted a coup upon seeing Gretchen retching, then attempted his coup, that light tone turned to jokes at his expense. Jenna, the cheerleader, called him Mr. Viagra. So did Greg, Joel, Sean, and Gervase, mimicking him behind his back. The mockery would have been appalling if B.B. had made any effort to be likeable. But instead he kept chastising the others for not working hard enough. He'd been brought up a strict father in South Dakota. Hard work and self-sufficiency were all he knew. To see these young people without such a vital core value angered him. Still, he eased up on the commands and began to work alone, framing a shelter on the beach while Colleen and Joel went swimming. That night the Pagong had a long talk about sex and their personal backgrounds. B.B. slept alone on the raft at the waterline, ostracized for his age and his power grab. Kansas had never seemed so far away.

But what a difference a night made. On the morning of Day Two B.B. became an indispensable tribal member. First, he built a shelter—a really *great* shelter—with palm fronds on the sides and roof, a sturdy bamboo frame, and a doorway. Gretchen suggested that it was too close to the shore and might be vulnerable to the incoming tide, but nobody paid much attention. B.B. was the man. B.B. was the hero.

Then he got them fire. Using B.B.'s prescription glasses as a magnifying beam to direct the sun, Gretchen started a small cooking fire. It took just one night without hot food for Pagong to realize what a wondrous thing such meals truly were. Fish, for instance, caught in the fish traps, tasted a whole lot different with a little fire under them. As the others congratulated B.B. he smiled and said to no one in particular, "If anyone thinks this island living is bullshit, they're wrong." He was talking to himself, verbalizing the doubts he'd had back home when the "Survivor" gig seemed a trifle. Now he was here and the difficulty was beyond anything he'd imagined. He sighed. "This is the real thing."

The castaway's bodies showed it. They were all pretty smart about staying out of the sun, but bug bites already flecked their arms, legs, and backs. Much worse was the mental pressure. They were really isolated. That crew compound on the other side of the island was off-limits. The whole of their world consisted of their beaches. Their only relationships were with the men and women around them.

Before flying to Borneo they never imagined that having to constantly stay together with the same seven people could be so grating. But it was. Even little things, like the way Greg was always clowning or Jenna always cheerleading wore thin quickly. Worse, there were no distractions. No telephone, e-mail, television, books, Nintendo, gym, mall—nothing. Sometimes it got boring, sometimes it got tense. But those other people never went away, and their presence was always felt in what they expected of each other—work, conversation, comfort, or just being in plain sight. No one could retreat into deep thought; it was too early in the game for that. Deep thoughts needed privacy, and to be seen wandering away from the group could easily be mistaken for pouting or disdain. The only member of either tribe willing to risk such communal ire was Greg Buis of Pagong. The free-spirited Brown grad liked to wander the jungle alone for hours. He never told anyone where he was going or where he had been. Yet for a million dollars, the castaways put up with each other's eccentricities, and even learned to embrace them. In the back of everyone's mind was the fear that they might be voted off the island.

The castaways received messages about upcoming challenges through a "message center," a bamboo mailbox on the edge of the jungle. Camera crews slipped the messages in, and the castaways checked their "mail" several times a day. On the morning of Day Two, Pagong and Tagi received their first message. It told of a water-based challenge that would take place on a section of the island known as the Sand Spit. Perhaps the most beautiful part of Pulau Tiga, this sand peninsula was only thirty yards wide, but curved away from land in a lazy "S" almost a mile long. The Malaysian name was Pulau Kalampunian Besar ("Little Durian"), but Sand Spit was easier to say and remember. High tide obscured the Sand Spit, but low tide made it seem a pristine slice of paradise. The water was warm and clear aquamarine. It remained chest-deep for several hundred yards before tapering into the South China Sea depths. The bottom was sandy and free of rocks.

The tribes would assemple for the challenge on the Sand Spit at dusk. The winning tribe would receive immunity from the Tribal Council the next evening; the losers would take that long walk to the Council through the jungle in the dark, with low-hanging vines looking like snakes and the snakes looking like nothing at all because they were impossible to see until it was too late. Then, after that hour of trauma, they would appear before Chief Jeff and vote someone off.

The Tagi and the Pagong appeared at the Sand Spit simultaneously. The surrealism of their world could again be seen clearly. They were haggard from no sleep, dressed in the same clothes they'd worn for a day— Jenna preferred a stunning hot pink bikini, while Greg mocked her by lowering the back of his shorts into a permanent moon. On the other side, the camera crews waiting for them were showered, in clean clothes, carrying the very latest in high-tech audiovisual equipment. Divers in the water carried cameras to record underwater and offshore action. And, most importantly, pyrotechnical specialists were putting the finishing touches on a fifteen-foot-high Fire Spirit. Made of wood, with a scarecrow's outstretched arms, this marvel was built to be burned. At the end of each arm, in upturned palms, was a low metal bowl filled with kerosene and kindling. A saturated wick draped from the bowl.

The confusing thing was the dual line of tiki torches arrayed before the (unlit) Fire Spirit. The torches were also unlit, and they led straight down the Sand Spit. Past the last torch another dual row began ... thirty yards out into the water. At the very end of this row floated a crucible filled with flames. Next to the crucible were two bamboo rafts.

The castaways looked at each other as if they'd stepped into the Twilight Zone. This ... THING ... they'd signed on for was getting more grueling and demanding every moment. The locale was bizarre, but the games even more so. If the "Quest for Fire," as this challenge would be known, was the standard by which other games were measured, the ante had just been upped. Island life would be about days and nights of survival, studded with frenzied games designed to test character, physical strength, and mental fortitude.

Chief Jeff explained the rules: Both teams would swim out to their rafts. Every member must keep hold of their raft at all times. On top of each raft was an unlit torch. On his command they would light the torch in the crucible and, guiding their raft as a group, light every torch between the crucible and shore. Once they reached the beach they would lift their raft from the water and heave it down the second line of torches to the burning man.

"OK, Tagi," Wisconsin farm boy Dirk Been enthused in his gangsta voice, which sounded most affected coming from a rural twentysomething. "Let's do it, bad boy. Let's lay it on the line." The Pagong huddled. Led by Jenna, they engaged in a loud group cheer.

Rudy and Richard walked back down the beach side-by-side. Rudy liked the former West Point officer. He had even said as much that morning. "I don't usually like fat guys, but that Richard is OK. He's a leader."

And surprisingly, Richard was. He'd continued his gentle sparring with Susan Hawk, but he'd begun to mold himself to the island. He was still loud, and he played up his outrageousness by wandering the beach shirtless throughout the day, not caring if anyone was offended by his spare tire. His demands for attention—the same acting out that had gotten him in trouble with his family as a child and led him away from a military career—had been tempered. He was becoming more interested in the group than himself. And Rudy, who'd known a thousand commanders, thought Richard was one of the good ones.

"Let's win this one, Rudy."

"Sure."

They took their places. Jeff stood at the Fire Spirit, a hundred yards up the spit from the castaways. He raised a torch in the air. That was the signal. The Tagi and the Pagong had each selected one individual to do all their torch lighting—Richard and Jenna, respectively—and as the rafts were pushed toward shore, the line of bobbing torches were lit one by one. Tagi took the lead as the beach drew near. They weren't as young or athletic as the Pagong, but they worked better as a team. That was their maturity speaking.

Tagi's final tiki torch before shore wouldn't light. Pagong caught up as Richard desperately tried to ignite the wet wick with his hand-held torch. Finally, the flame burst to life. Tagi rushed to stay even with Pagong as both teams carried their heavy raft up the beach.

Then Sonja slipped. A hole in the sand was the culprit—just a depression carved by some errant wave, but she stepped wrong and fell flat on her face. Her teammates dragged the older woman as she clung desperately to the raft, afraid of losing her grip because it would mean her team's disqualification. Tagi slowed. Pagong surged further ahead. Tagi stopped entirely. Sonja struggled to her feet, looking very frail. Then Tagi was moving again. The entire process, from Sonja's slip to Tagi resuming forward movement, took just two seconds, but the damage was done. Pagong went on to win.

Chief Jeff stepped forward and handed Pagong a piece of Philippine mahogany two feet tall and just a few inches around. At first glance it looked like a miniature Bornean version of a Native American totem pole. Faces were carved into the wood, some grotesque and some merely startling. Primary colors outlined lips, eyes, teeth. The wood had heft, but was light enough for Jeff to lift overhead with one hand.

"This is the Immunity Idol," Jeff announced. Possession of the idol signified immunity from Tribal Council. That piece of wood had just become Pagong's most important possession.

Greg Buis, the Ivy League mountain man from Plano, Texas, lit the Fire Spirit.

As night fell on the Sand Spit, that outrageous scarecrow lit the world. Pagong danced in its glow, relieved victors. They'd all just earned another three days.

DAY THREE

"Quest for Fire" illuminated the biggest difference between Tagi and Pagong: age. Pagong, in my mind, was turning into MTV's "Beach House." They were all young and single, with the exception of B.B. and Gretchen. Their bodies were sleek and hard. Discussions centered around sex. Greg and Colleen were pairing off already, disappearing into the jungle together for an hour or more at a time. Ramona, Gervase, Jenna, and Joel stayed on the beach, flirting. B.B. was always to one side, working, congratulating himself on working so hard. But he feared being cast out.

As the shelter grew sturdier, his building expertise was needed less. Youth would reign, and with it, arrogance. Speaking of that night's inaugural Tribal Council, Joel didn't bother being politically correct in predicting Richard's demise: "The boy named Sue is going home."

Tagi, on the other hand, was the older, more mature tribe. The Tagi embraced their age and imperfect bodies, skinny-dipping together at dawn (except for Dirk and Rudy). When they sat down in small groups for discussion, topics like God and love and relationships came up. Dirk had brought his Bible and read it, well, religiously. Susan once led a pointed

discussion on abortion. Sonja listened intently to everything. Whereas either Gretchen or B.B. could easily have been voted off Pagong first because of their age, Tagi embraced their older demographic. When Sonja expressed her fear that she would be voted off because of age to Stacey, Susan, and Kelly, they made a secret pact to form an alliance at the Tribal Council. The women would vote off one of the men.

And of course the obvious choice (though Stacey was in favor of dumping Rudy) was Richard. It was only Tagi's third day on the island. And though they'd all worked hard to transform their beach into a new home with a fire area, lean-to, and clothes-drying area, seventy-two hours wasn't long enough for Richard to have recovered from his boastfulness of the first day. His physical strength was a definite asset—the man was a bull—and he'd dragged that raft and the entire team through "Quest for Fire." But he was overbearing in an environment where overbearing gets old fast. Kelly told him as much after "Quest for Fire."

The tribe had returned from the Sand Spit in low spirits. While the rest of the tribe lay down to sleep, Kelly and Richard sat on the bamboo raft. Kelly Wiglesworth was the rebel of Tagi, a twenty-two-year-old river guide who spent winters with her mother in Las Vegas. Her tongue was pierced, a tattoo of the rising sun spread across her lower back, and she hated losing more than anything in the world. Losing bent her jovial disposition towards rage. Just the briefest flash of that burned Richard as they sat on the bamboo raft in the South China Sea darkness, rats scampering across their legs. Then the rage died and revealed its source: fear. The Tribal Council was gnawing at her. "It's going to be so weird to vote one of our own off the island," she sighed.

"Let's talk about that," Richard said. He was trying, really trying, but that corporate trainer side of his kept wanting to take control.

This time, however, Kelly went along with it. They talked. And in their talk Richard admitted that his cover story was a sham. He wasn't really married. His son was adopted. He was, he disclosed to her, gay.

She knew. It wasn't a great stretch of the imagination. Kelly sympathized with him, though. His admission enabled her to open up and chastise him for being so overbearing. Richard vowed to change. And so they bonded, Tagi's first real alliance.

The next day Richard came out to the whole group except Rudy. Not that Rudy was being excluded, he just didn't happen to be there when

Richard got the itch to share. After a brief discussion of homosexuality, Richard's group encounter shifted the topic to religion. By strange coincidence, Rudy walked over then. Politely, he excused himself from the "Jesus talk" and walked away. The conversation flowed naturally back to sexuality.

The intimacy was shadowed by the Tribal Council looming just hours away. In small groups and as individuals they'd grappled with the decision. Richard's admission made him more likeable—part of the family—and it pained them to vote even one Tagi off. Their future as a tribe was at stake, though. Gathering Rudy, they set off single file through the jungle for the Tribal Council. Even during that dark walk's most terrifying moment, when a sea krait (one other must have been close; kraits always hunt in pairs) slithered through the group, that dilemma haunted them all.

Should they vote off Rudy, whose SEAL background brought valuable survival skills, but whose social detachment ("I don't know their names and I don't want to know their names") reminded everyone of a crotchety grandfather? Or should they vote off Richard, with his loud calls to discussion and reluctance for action?

Those were the only two candidates. Sonja was protected by the women. Kelly was tough. Both Sean Kenniff and Dirk Been were young, strong, and likeable. The team needed their athleticism for future challenges. Without athletic talent there was a good chance Tagi would lose every immunity challenge, which would mean that they would attend the Tribal Council eight consecutive times while Pagong flourished, untouched by that emotionally jarring experience.

Stacey Stillman, the San Francisco attorney, was safe. She was bitchy, once bashing Rudy behind his back by asking rhetorically, "What kind of Navy SEAL are you if you can't make fire?" She rolled her eyes at other's weaknesses and annoying quirks. And she'd even said she wouldn't mind going home, because she missed her bed. But so early in the game, the most visible competitors were going to be the ones to go. Stacey had stayed below the radar for that very reason.

Susan Hawk definitely wasn't going. Her accent camouflaged both sarcasm and affection, but the words were always spoken with a smile, so she came across as likeable. And she was a hard worker. Her fellow castaways even looked down on her slightly, as if she were dim—though she was anything but.

By the time the Tagi took their last few steps out of the darkness, each had made his or her decision.

The Tribal Council set loomed bright, a beacon in the jungle. They'd never seen it before. With its carved stone columns, tangle of vines, and look of a primitive amphitheater nearly reclaimed by the jungle, they were experiencing Mowgli's confusion when he stumbled into ape-King Louis' *Jungle Book* domain. How could civilization rise so abruptly from the jungle? Suddenly there were people, lots of people. A camera boom hovered above the set. Film reels were loaded, batteries checked. Around the set, like Romans awaiting a gladiator duel to the death, "Survivor"'s crew eagerly awaited the first-ever "Survivor" vote. The two opposite sides of island living had become one. And, as the crew were not only fellow inhabitants of Pulau Tiga but also knew as many details about the castaways' lives as the castaways themselves, the moment an islander would be voted off was cause for emotion. No longer merely a sound stage, the thirty-by-thirty patch of jungle was a place where lives would change forever. Surrealism had merged with television to produce reality.

Chief Jeff welcomed them and bade them to bang the gong to announce their entrance, then cross the rope bridge over to the communal fire. Arranged around the fire were logs for sitting. Behind the logs were eight unlit torches. Before allowing them to sit, Jeff instructed the Tagi to dip their torches in the communal fire. "Fire symbolizes your life on the island," he explained. As long as a person's torch was symbolically lit, they were still playing the "Survivor" game. After being voted off, a castaway's last island duty would be to extinguish his/her flame.

When each torch was lit, the Tagi sat down.

Other than the voting's outcome, the moment of the Tribal Council that resonated with everyone present was the moment Rudy discovered Richard was gay. He was stunned. "What do you think of him now?" Chief Jeff asked.

"I like him," Rudy blurted out. The revelation that he could actually like a gay person floored him. He smiled.

Then the vote. One by one the Tagi left the fire and walked to the voting booth. They wrote their decisions in bold letters on slips of white paper. Then, speaking into a camera before them, they gave the reasons for their decisions. When it came to Susan's turn she wrote her decision and said, "I'm removing the weakest link from the tribe."

And so it was that the compassionate arrangement was broken. Sixty-two-year-old Sonja Christopher had been betrayed. The votes were held up one by one for all the castaways to see. A few minutes later Sonja's torch was extinguished and Chief Jeff informed her solemnly, "It's time for you to go."

She walked the lonesome log pathway into the jungle, troubled by her betrayal. "It must have been whoever spelled my name S-O-U-N-A. Who could that be?"

Later, Rudy summed up Sonja's expulsion with his latest Rudy-ism. "It's like when you've got a great dog that's sick. You don't want to put it to sleep, but you know you have to."

EVOLUTION TWO

Power Can Only Be Granted

DAY FOUR

A prominent CEO was once asked why he never sat at the head of the table during meetings in the corporate boardroom. "Wherever I sit," he replied, "is the head of the table."

For years, B.B. Andersen knew that sensation. His word was law. Every utterance was treated as a command, not a suggestion. Tall, white-haired, always in motion, he is a handsome man with a presence. But as words like "Monday," "Tuesday," and "Wednesday" became quaint reminders of another time and place to the residents of Pulau Tiga, presence wasn't enough. Hard work wasn't enough. Money, his other form of commanding respect, meant nothing. What mattered was the ability to get along. That was proving a most slippery task for B.B. Andersen.

Age wasn't the only reason. B.B. could only see his way. In his mind, Joel was a divisive force, a pretender to the tribal throne B.B. assumed was rightfully his. Joel could be diplomatic, but he also kept up a lively barrage of wisecracks behind B.B.'s back which served only to widen the generation gap. B.B., in Joel's words, was a grandfather, Mr. Viagra. In reality, B.B. was Pagong's alpha male. It was a role Joel wanted very badly. B.B., through trying to hold the young tribe members to his self-imposed standards, wore himself down. As early as Day Two B.B. had decided to quit. "If I had a satellite phone I'd call in a helicopter to pick me up right now," he said wistfully. His voice was tired, his manner resigned.

There was nothing in the rules against a castaway leaving the island on his or her own volition. But B.B. was the last castaway for whom quitting should have been an option. Quitting was synonymous with failure. And failure was abhorrent to B.B. This was beaten into him at a young age by his father, who wanted his sons to be men of achievement and backbone. To make the old man proud, B.B. had driven himself to the very limits of his abilities as he grew older, developing a nonstop work ethic that didn't allow for things like hobbies—"My work is my hobby"—or even relationships. By the time B.B. reached Pulau Tiga, he was on his third marriage.

But the ethic had brought results. B.B.'s construction company in the greater Kansas City metropolitan area was immensely successful. He had become wealthy. But that still wasn't enough. As if his father still stood at his side, prepared to beat him for the least indiscretion, B.B. drove himself to greater and greater heights. Somehow he would make the old man proud. Ideally, B.B. would usurp his father, becoming above criticism and the metaphorical beatings—becoming more of a man.

So B.B. devoted himself to manly achievements. He earned his private pilot's license and bought a pair of jet aircraft—a 707 and an Australian fighter—to test his new skill. He bought a Harley Davidson, and, leathers and all, B.B. rode trips to Mexico from his Mission Hills, Kansas, home. Finally, he applied to be a castaway—the ultimate hardcore adventure. The million dollars had nothing to do with it. He planned to give the money to charity. Even in his sixties, B.B. was still proving his manhood to a father for whom even the best wasn't good enough.

As part of his psychological evaluation, B.B. had a session with Dr. Gene Ondrusek, chief psychologist for the Center for Executive Health at Scripps Hospital in La Jolla, California. Ondrusek interviewed all the castaways, but B.B. was closest to the type he saw in his everyday practice. He pointed out to B.B. that most CEOs come from a volatile family background, just as did B.B. Their defense mechanism—their survival tool in that hostile childhood world—was control. By controlling their environment—cleaning their room, doing their homework perfectly, becoming captain of the football team—they reduced the chance of critical parents attacking them and tearing them down.

Ondrusek suggested that B.B. take a hard look at his relationship with his father. B.B. needed to understand that relational dynamic, then learn that his worth as a person wasn't about achievement but about character. Most importantly, he needed to get to a point in his life where not being the best and brightest was OK.

B.B. flew back to Mission Hills, thinking about what Ondrusek had said. A few weeks later he shook his wife awake at 3 A.M. "I need to talk to you," he told her urgently, "about my father. I'm not mad at him any more." They sat in bed and talked about his feelings for that silent, invisible, omnipresent force in his life.

Something was freed up in B.B. from that moment on. Winning "Survivor" was no longer vital to his ego. He would travel to Pulau Tiga solely for adventure. Once on the island, with the rest of Pagong taking his hard work for granted and mocking him, B.B. could read the writing on the wall. He was sure to get voted off, not because he was a bad person but because he was a threat to the younger slackers. In his mind, Ramona was lazy. Joel was lazy. Gervase was lazy. Colleen was lazy. Greg worked hard but disappeared into the jungle at night to sleep alone. Jenna worked hard but talked too much. Gretchen worked hard but was warm and fuzzy at the core. Whether or not this was a liability was too early to tell.

So through Joel's barbed comments, hard-working—but cantankerous and self-congratulatory—B.B. became the target of Pagong wrath. Through it all B.B. tried to keep his temper in check by remembering a comment from Ondrusek: research overwhelmingly confirms that success in the workaday jungle depends more on your interpersonal skills and ability to get along with people than on your technical competence. B.B. could build the shelter, get fire, build a seawall to stem the tide, whittle eating utensils and bowls from coconuts, all things he'd accomplished in four days of hard work, and it meant nothing. Ondrusek's words ran through B.B.'s brain on an ever-repeating tape loop.

So B.B. wanted out. There was no guarantee Pagong would ever go to the Tribal Council. Even without Sonja, Tagi wasn't nearly as athletic. But B.B.'s talk of quitting was because he feared being voted off. He'd built the shelter and prepared his tribe for island life. No need to stick around one day longer. Being best and brightest no longer mattered. What mattered was home and family and being comfortable within his own skin. At least, that was B.B.'s rationalization.

B.B. called a "come to Jesus" meeting for Pagong. "I've declared myself the winner," he told them. Then B.B. paused, looked at his fellow

tribe members. "I've built the camp. From here on out this is a mainte-nance situation. I want off." B.B. continued, saying he was passing the mantle of leadership to Gretchen. He looked hard at the group. Left to their own devices, B.B. was sure they were incapable of making proper de-cisions. "You can't make it without her."

Joel seethed. He knew that B.B. considered him a dumb slacker. B.B. even admitted disliking him. Joel thought it quite obvious that *he* was the tribe's strongest member. That alone should give him authority.

But another reason for Joel's anger was that he didn't want B.B. getting off so easily. B.B., to Joel, was authoritarian, his very presence a source of anger. What made Joel angriest was when B.B. got proprietary about the camp and everything in it. Like the day before, when B.B. had chosen to wash his shirt in some of Pagong's limited drinking water instead of the ocean. Joel could see through B.B. He was sure B.B. was trying to manipulate the tribe so he wouldn't look like a loser on national television.

What neither could see was that they were similar. Joel made his living as a financial advisor for a chain of Arkansas health clubs. He was very good at it, as Joel told anyone on the island who would listen. Very successful. Women always wanted him. He believed his body was strong and was a magnet to women. He rarely wore a shirt on the island. Among the Pagong he was a hard worker, but only on his own terms, and rarely when B.B. wanted him to be. Hence, B.B. thought him a slacker.

Like silverback gorillas in the mountains of Rwanda, where one alpha male oversees a harem of women and a herd of lesser young males, Joel was rising up to challenge the authority of the aging leader. That this dictatorial Pagong silverback was suggesting a woman take charge was galling beyond words. A woman! To Joel, women were fun to look at and even more fun to rock and roll with, but they certainly weren't leaders.

But Joel was so wrapped up in achieving alpha male status that he wasn't paying attention to the slowly-emerging rules of "Survivor." Being alpha male wasn't necessarily a good thing. Power made someone a threat. Any threat had to be dealt with. Joel didn't realize that all around him were castaways scheming his demise. Pagong was outwardly loving, but they were a duplicitous bunch. Jenna, for instance, sweet-talked Ramona one minute, then, as soon as the biochemist walked away, Jenna would grumble that Ramona was weak and lazy and should be voted off instead of B.B.

Jenna was eagerly looking two weeks into the future when eight or nine people had been voted off and life would be turning cutthroat. "Things are going to get really nasty," she exclaimed, as if nastiness in its purest form was a very good thing.

Colleen, the shy bookstore employee from Miami, was the emotional one. Her strategy was to stay quiet and shy so no one would dislike her, which was smart. It had been working just fine until her flirtation with Greg turned serious. The two snuck into the jungle alone, always followed, at a discreet distance, by a camera crew. There was nothing like being trailed by a camera crew to blow the quiet-and-shy strategy.

In a phrase: They were all leaders. Pagong was no tribe of gorillas, where physical force meant power. Joel needed to see that if he was to survive. All he knew was that B.B. was going. Ideally, it would be a public outing instead of that quitter business. Then, in his mind, Joel Klug would be king.

• • •

Day Four had begun with another challenge at the Sand Spit. Instead of immunity, this challenge offered as first prize the map to a new and much closer watering hole. Unlike "Quest for Fire," this challenge was a complex act of strength. Each tribe selected their strongest man: Richard went for Tagi, silverback Joel for Pagong. They were placed on pedestals thirty feet offshore, then a bamboo pole was slung across their shoulders. The goal was to load up the other team's strong man with water-filled coconut shells, slinging them across the pole. The first strong man to be overcome by the weight and fall in the water would lose. After twenty excruciating minutes, Joel was suffering but it was Richard who toppled into the South China Sea with almost four hundred pounds of coconuts slung over his vast, freckled shoulders. Once again, Pagong's athleticism had defeated Tagi's maturity. Joel had shown his strength publicly and was looking more and more like the silverback.

Before the challenge Richard had crowed about his strength. "We're going to win, guys. I guarantee it. I won't let you down." Then standing atop the pedestal, coconuts and bamboo bending him over, he had taunted Pagong. Slinking back to their beach, though, his tribe members' mood at rock bottom after losing yet another challenge, Richard let forth a mighty whoosh of air. His shoulders sank. "It's better if I keep my mouth shut from now on. I've got to start coming through or I'm the next one to go."

As the sun set on Tagi that night, Richard was trying hard to rein himself in. The possibility of getting voted off haunted him every minute of every day. Meanwhile, as the sun set on Pagong, silverback Joel led his tribe on a fishing expedition. B.B. sat on the beach alone, wishing for a helicopter.

DAY FIVE

The South China Sea was in turmoil, with a monsoon threatening to the east. Weather has a lethal beauty on Pulau Tiga and there had been moments or hours like this before. But nothing so far had prepared the castaways for this blow. The sky and ocean turned black at noon. Sheet lightning hurled from one side of the horizon to the other. Rain fell in drops as fat as acorns. Raging winds bent the banyans and palms. Warm air shoved breakers onto Pagong and Tagi, ripping away chunks of beach. As the castaways gazed out from their beaches, Snake Island—usually visible straight ahead—was swallowed in rain. The view engendered hopelessness—and increased self-sufficiency. The storm was a reminder that Pulau Tiga was a tiny speck of land in the middle of the tempestuous South China Sea.

The castaways were joining a long roster of maritime observers of South China Sea weather. Seafarers and smugglers and traders had literally sailed over Pulau Tiga's location for centuries, first from India in the third century, then from the Majapahit Empire of Java, which claimed control of the waters in the fourteenth century. Traders from China and the Philippines sheltered their junks in Pulau Tiga's coves in times of storm. Then it was the Dutch and their Dutch East India Company calling the sea theirs between the seventeenth and nineteenth centuries, with power extending all the way to Japan. In 1888, Borneo and all her waters were made a British protectorate. In all that time, however, Pulau Tiga was nothing more than an underwater mountain.

Shortly after, on September 21, 1897, a mighty earthquake shook the Philippine Island of Mindanoa. The northern coast of Borneo was geologically unstable, but what happened next surprised even the hardened local fishermen. Out of nowhere, a group of three islands—Pulau Tiga, Sand Spit, and Snake Island—literally rose from the sea. They were small at first. Pulau Tiga, for instance, was only two hundred yards in diameter and sixty feet high in 1899. But it slowly grew, with seeds and animals from passing ships slowly populating this new wasteland. Pine trees known as casuarinas soon covered the side of the island closest to Borneo. The island slowly grew to its present size. During World War II the Japanese laid claim to Pulau Tiga, though it was too wild to occupy. But at least it was an island.

As the storm smashed into the beaches of Tagi and Pagong, the castaways became part of this ancient tradition of mariners privileged—if that is the word—to witness the sea exploding. But of all those who had passed that way before them, the castaways bore one unique distinction: They were the first to make Pulau Tiga home.

And a home it had truly become, especially for Tagi. Their shelter was spacious, nestled in the shade, and on the very fringe of the sand. Palm

fronds draped the roof of the lean-to, and it sat off the ground, on bamboo. Several felled trees, gray and pocked by the salt air, lay to either side.
The sand around the shelter was swept daily with Tagi's makeshift broom.
Whereas B.B. had built Pagong's shelter too close to shore, making it susceptible to stormy weather, former SEAL Rudy had selected just the right
site for Tagi's. Life was actually quite cozy, even in a storm. The Tagi
worked constantly to improve their way of life. The shelter had everything but a wine cellar.

Instead of getting tougher for the Tagi, life on the island was getting
easier. Susan said it felt like a vacation. Stacey was surprised to learn that
jungle walks were relaxing. Kelly led yoga on the beach each morning,
when the tide was all the way out. Dirk went off alone to read his Bible for
an hour each morning, taking heart in mentions of fishing that he considered relevant parallels to island life. Pulau Tiga had become their
island retreat, where their rice cask was enough to get by on, and water
was plentiful at a specially-placed well in the jungle known as Far Water.
Other than the disappointment of losing two consecutive challenges and
having to vote Sonja off, the Tagi had few complaints.

Most touching was the slow bonding of the Odd Couple, Rudy and
Richard. The homophobic Navy SEAL and the gay corporate trainer
were forming a small alliance. True, Rudy didn't much care for Richard
strolling up and down the beach nude every morning, as had become his
habit. But Rudy had spent considerable time on islands just like Pulau
Tiga for SEAL maneuvers. He knew the anarchy inherent in such a tangled world. The need for leadership was paramount. Rudy admonished
Tagi to follow Richard's leadership, saying, "He's got some good things to
say. If we'd all just shut up and let him lead we'd be OK."

But most of all, Rudy had publicly accepted Richard's sexuality at the
Tribal Council. Richard was touched, and later thanked Rudy. When
Richard pushed things further, asking Rudy to slather sunscreen on his
bare back, Rudy didn't hesitate. Even when Sean goaded Rudy, saying,
"You'd better have a beer in your hand when you watch this one on TV
with your Navy buddies," Rudy didn't stop rubbing in the lotion. Rudy
and Richard's friendship was tentative but growing. Of the men on the
island, their bond was strongest—the bond of greed.

The women were already tightly bonded. Yet Stacey Stillman, the new-
minted nature girl, felt unsure about her presence on the island. She'd

been insecure her first few days ashore. Rather than come out and admit that, she became contrary. A roll of the eyes was the San Francisco attorney's response to every request for assistance. She even mentioned that she wouldn't mind going home. But then came the Tribal Council. The winding, oppressive walk through the jungle in the dark terrified Stacey. The bigger scare, however, came during the voting. Four votes were cast for Sonja and three for Rudy. The last vote cast was for Stacey.

That bugged her. Leaving the island voluntarily was one thing, but being told she wasn't good enough was something else entirely. One reason Stacey had been selected for the show was her volatility. Her nicknames were Boom Boom and Slambona, hardly monikers for the docile. She remembered hurtful comments, didn't speak with her mother.

But she was intelligent, too. Born and raised in New York, Stacey attended the State University of New York at Binghamton, the same school Sean had attended (they even lived in the same dorm, but two years apart). Her time there was interrupted by thyroid cancer. She survived. Returning to school, Stacey completed a double major in physics and the philosophy of law, displaying a rare kind of genius—both right- and left-brain thinking. Her juris doctorate came from NYU. The move to San Francisco was law-related and had come just eighteen months before "Survivor." On her "Survivor" application she listed her hobbies as noting other people's absurdities and prying into the details of friends' and coworkers' lives; at the same time she noted that she often prefers to vacation alone and feels herself unlucky at love, calling her most recent breakup "yearlong and horrendous."

Finally, although the crew found Stacey manipulative and too eager to overhear crew dialogue about other castaways' behavior, she thought of herself as shy. "I was raised on 'Gilligan's Island,'" she noted. "People think I'm arrogant but I'm not. I'm just shy. If this was 'Gilligan's Island' I'd be Mary Ann."

Mary Ann would never go for a nickname like Boom Boom unless "Gilligan's Island" was doing one of their dream-sequence episodes. And Mary Ann was a simple woman. She wouldn't have ruminated long and hard about a vote being cast against her. That single vote changed Stacey's attitude toward being a castaway. The self-preservation instinct honed while kicking cancer—the same instinct that held her apart from people and made relationships messy and made her a wonderful attorney—began sharpening itself. The battlefield was different and the stakes not as final, but Stacey had come to Pulau Tiga to win what she called "the ultimate adventure." She would find a way to survive.

Stacey began to insinuate herself into conversations, hoping to find her enemy. (She never did find out who cast it—it was Richard, who cast his vote for "subtle reasons" he "couldn't explain.") To avoid a recurrence of the Tribal Council vote, if only for the length of her stay, Stacey changed. She curbed the eye-rolling. She developed a sudden fondness for manual labor. She smiled more. And when everyone sat down for one of Richard's chats, she participated instead of silently listening and noting other's absurdities. When Richard put on his corporate trainer hat to ask, "Who is the real you?" Stacey actually opened up. She talked about her parents' divorce and the distance between her and her mom. She smiled that big perfect smile of hers. A nervous smile. Uncomfortable. But it was real, and betrayed more than a little vulnerability. The Tagi were glad to see that smile instead of a scowl, and decided that Stacey Stillman really must be shy—either that or the transparency was a wonderfully performed act to win them over.

The storm ended with Tagi putting new shingles on the roof to keep out the next rain. Stacey was being accepted, if only warily. She still needed to do something to prove herself to Tagi.

DAY SIX

The table was long, like a dinner table, but low, like a coffee table, made of dark brown dipterocarp wood. Luminescent orange, yellow, and blue silk sitting cushions were arranged along both sides. In the manner of a traditional Malaysian feast, guests would remove their shoes and arrange themselves on the cushions. The feast would be served only when the guests and their host were all seated.

Of course, this being "Survivor," the dipterocarp table was smack in the middle of the jungle. A two-hundred-foot-tall banyan tree rose directly behind the head of the table. The screech of cicadas was abrasive background music, sounding like a host of car alarms gone amok. The host was Chief Jeff. The guests were the Tagi and Pagong. The main course was beetle larvae. And the feast was not merely a meal, but an Immunity Challenge, losers to make the long jungle walk to Tribal Council that night.

It was midafternoon, the most sweltering time of the equatorial day, when the human body sweats ceaselessly and physical exertion can lead to collapse. A perfect time, then, for a sumptuous repast. Jeff waited for the tribes as they entered from opposite jungle trails—Tagi from his left, Pagong from his right. The tribes had received the invitation to dine, but the table was empty, save a small bowl and a bamboo cup of water for each diner. They made small talk as they sat down, greeting one another like long-lost relations. The tribes were getting more competitive with every passing day, but that hadn't gestated into full-blown animosity. They liked one another. Their concern for each other's welfare was touching. Also, they couldn't afford to get too mean. A lucky few from each tribe would someday join forces. It wouldn't pay to have animosities when that day came.

"Welcome, tribes," Jeff began, then explained the rules of the challenge. There would be two courses. Basically, whichever team ate the most bugs would win. Then Jeff brought out the first course, much to the contestant's amusement. The beetle larvae—"butod" to the Malaysians—had been deep-fried. The contestants ate in pairs, with one Pagong and one Tagi facing each other as they consumed their bugs. Only when each

had swallowed fully could they take a drink of water. Then the next pair went. Gervase and Dirk led off. The last to eat for Tagi was Susan, who would have to eat twice because they'd lost a member. She would square off against B.B.

In a conversation with Gretchen that afternoon, B.B. had suggested throwing the challenge. He was already talking with the others about upgrading his return plane ticket to First Class for the long flight back to Mission Hills. To ensure leaving the island that night he needed Pagong to attend the Tribal Council. Throwing the challenge wasn't quitting, but it was a lame way for a proud man to exit. When he broached the subject to Gretchen, B.B. was sitting on a log on the beach. Gretchen stood before him. The instant he mentioned intentionally losing, she walked away without answering. The look of disgust on the thirty-eight-year-old mother's face was crystal clear. Quitting was never an option to her.

To make sure that B.B. didn't throw the bug-eating challenge, Gretchen kept a close eye on him, especially when it came his turn to eat. He didn't return the gaze. Instead, B.B. popped the mahogany-colored beetle into his mouth. When he swallowed without making a face, Gretchen cheered warmly. It was as though B.B. was one of her kids, instead of the tribal silverback. She wouldn't let him give into his weakness. Instead, she encouraged him with eye-contact and spoken communication to perform to the best of his ability.

"OK," Jeff announced, removing a glass globe from a small chest near his seat. Bulbous white bodies, three inches long with dark brown heads, squirmed inside. "This," Jeff said gravely, "is what you've just eaten, only before it's cooked." He paused. "What the hell, let's make that the second course."

The globe was passed. One by one the contestants pulled their own white squirmy morsel from inside and laid it in the bowl before them. Stacey, who had swallowed the first course without chewing, smiled grimly. Gervase was repulsed. B.B. sat at the end of the table quietly, Gretchen leaning into him for support. Then Gervase and Dirk began the round, lifting the bug from their bowl. They didn't know that butod explode into a brown juicy mess when bitten into, or that they tasted somewhat like shrimp. All they knew was that the plump butod wiggling between their thumb and forefinger was alive, and that it was a bug. Put that together—live bug—and it added up to a singular dining experience civilized people only discuss in the abstract. As in, "I'm not sure I could ever eat a live bug, but I probably would if it was for a million dollars."

This was for a million dollars. Dirk ate his with a flourish. Gervase couldn't. He shouted loudly, his narrow face howling into the jungle sky. He slapped his forehead repeatedly, like pain would bring courage. "I CAN'T DO IT!"

Jeff let him wail, then began a countdown. "Five...four...three... two..." Gervase ate the bug.

Everybody ate their bugs, even B.B. A tie-breaker was needed. Each tribe was to pick the most squeamish member from the other team for a bug-off. The squeamish person eating *two* lives bugs fastest won for their tribe.

Tagi's choice was easy: Gervase. Pagong pointed across the table to the most urban, high-maintenance, civilized woman they could think of: Stacey.

It was a poor choice. Pagong had no idea Stacey hated to lose. Giving her the right to win it all for Tagi was the greatest gift they could have given her. And although Gervase performed amazingly, overcoming his squeamishness to munch down two robust butods, he was no match for the amazing Stacey. She lifted her two bugs into the air, tilted her head back, then dropped the squirming critters straight into her mouth and swallowed them in two seconds. Done.

As Pagong accepted their fate, Tagi erupted in jubilation. They'd finally won a challenge. What was more, they didn't have to vote a member off Pulau Tiga that night. They danced back to their campsite, their self-belief strong and their team unity even stronger. Maybe Richard's boasting that they'd win every challenge would come true from that day forward.

Meanwhile, Jeff arched an eyebrow calmly at Pagong. "You've got a date with me tonight," Jeff informed them in soothing tones. They seemed relieved and curious. How bad could it be?

As they rose from the table, struggling to extricate themselves from the thick pillows, B.B. moved to Gretchen's side and mumbled into her ear: "See? I told you I'd do whatever it took to win the challenge." She smiled and gave him a small hug, for B.B. had truly done the right thing.

When B.B. next emerged from the jungle and stood before Chief Jeff it was night, and time for the Tribal Council. B.B. led Pagong. He carried a staff, and needed it. The long walk through the jungle had left him stooped. With his staff and week-long growth of snow-white stubble he looked like what he was, an older man in a harsh environment.

With great ceremony—ceremony befitting his efforts to make the island livable for his MTV Beach House tribe members—B.B. was voted off.

The process, however, was anything but solemn. Several things conspired to make the second Tribal Council an awkward turning point for island life. First, Pagong had daubed charcoal from the communal fire on their faces before coming to the Tribal Council. Except for B.B., their faces were covered in war paint. That only served to accentuate the age gap. The reason for the charcoal was that Pagong wanted to "vote behind masks" at their first Tribal Council.

Then, as they sat around the fire pit at the Tribal Council, Greg and Colleen started cutting up. Despite Joel's designs on leadership and B.B.'s wishes for Gretchen, Greg Buis was the most powerful member of Pagong. He was offbeat, preferring to make a bed of leaves and fronds on the jungle floor each night rather than sleep in the hut. And Greg refused to play by either the tribe's or television's rules, never giving a straight answer and always finding a unique way to tweak island life. While B.B. was working so hard on the shelter, Greg could be found hosting a Pulau Tiga version of the "Dating Game." Greg was funny and kept his true emotions hidden. This combination of humor and mystery endeared him to all the women. "The women of Pagong," one of the camera crew exclaimed about Greg, "adore that man. They simply adore him."

What ensured his popularity was that the men of Pagong found him non-threatening. They were all sure he was just on Pulau Tiga for a few laughs, but that he had no designs on winning it all. Which, of course, played right into Greg's strategy. "Don't lose sight that this is a game," Greg constantly reminded them.

And so in his offbeat, counterculture way, Greg controlled the tribe's actions. He encouraged them to think differently and not be afraid of island life. It was his idea to look for the mud volcano he'd heard was on the island. Refusing to accept the gravity of the Tribal Council or the notion that he might someday be the castaway hearing Jeff say, "The Tribe has spoken," Greg mocked it. To come from the reality of castaway life to the other side of the island, with its comforts and faux-Mayan ruins, seemed absurd to him. And he wasn't afraid to say so.

Only he said so while sitting around the fire pit as the voting was taking place. As usual, he expressed his thoughts as jokes. His nonstop schtick was designed to make him the center of attention instead of Jeff, for Greg didn't want to just take over Pagong, he wanted to manipulate the entire island.

Finally, mercifully, the voting and the Greg's banter came to an end. B.B. began the long walk. The solemn moment was broken by Greg seeking one last moment in the spotlight. He called out a good-bye to B.B. in a loud pirate voice. "Arrr... and a good captain you were." Then MTV Beach House applauded. And though they would all explain later that the applause was out of respect for B.B., it sounded a whole lot like young punks disrespecting a fine older man.

The second Tribal Council ended on that strange note. It was fitting for B.B.'s departure, of course. Ambivalence ran through the air. More than that, though, the fourth wall—that unseen barrier between television crew and castaways—was falling.

Jeff Probst, normally the calmest man on the island, seethed as he walked off the set once Pagong was gone. Greg's clever manipulation had gotten under Jeff's skin. "I don't ever—EVER—want that to happen again," he said carefully, keeping his emotions in check. "That's not what this is about." Jeff failed to see that his anger was exactly the emotion Greg sought. Greg, in other words, was winning.

EVOLUTION THREE

Embracing Reality

DAY SEVEN

At dawn an urgent meeting was called in the production compound. The dozen or so core production personnel sat around a long table (in chairs) arguing about a new direction for "Survivor." There was a fear it was getting too easy, that the castaways were not suffering enough. In reality, the castaways were proving much tougher than I or anyone had predicted. They were all proving, truly, to be survivors.

And while that was all well and good, "Survivor"'s essence was challenge. Adjustment was a by-product, but challenge was the core. Something had to be done immediately to make life more difficult—especially for the Beach House—or the lunatics would start running the asylum. The final television show wouldn't resemble reality on a deserted island so much as a peek into the lives of a dozen spoiled Americans.

That the meeting was taking place at all was testimony to the fact that Greg Buis was achieving his goal of controlling life on the island. He had no interest in allowing Chief Jeff or television to be the arbiter of reality. Greg was handsome and likeable and kind, but lacked a vital kernel of self-confidence, so he believed his greatest strength lay in mocking authority. To stop the mocking just for the sake of television would steal Greg's power. In his mind he would become vulnerable—both as a human being and to being voted off.

Immediately after the second Tribal Council, Chief Jeff didn't just wish

Greg was off the island, he would have volunteered to drive the boat himself. But Jeff gained perspective through a good night's sleep. Adjustments would have to be made for Greg, but otherwise his high jinks wouldn't be a problem. The reality of "Survivor" would grow deeper and deeper, no matter how hard Greg tried to pretend it was absurd.

More than any other island inhabitant, Jeff Probst was clearly aware of the fine line between reality and scripted make-believe. His job, though, was to keep it real. His on-camera delivery had to be just-so—neither too faux-epic, like the voice of NFL Films ("Like warriors marching across the frozen tundra...") nor too much like a game show host, but somewhere in between. Yes, "Survivor" was a television production. Yes, one side of the island did have generators for electricity, cold beer, and running water. And, yes, Jeff was not actually chief of Tagi and Pagong, but a professional host paid to interact with their lives on-camera.

But the cold, hard fact was that the castaways were trying to make a life on the fringes of a tropical hellhole. Their bodies were covered with real insect bites. The humidity drenched them in real sweat when they tried to sleep at night. Very real six-foot banded sea kraits slithered about the surfline to hunt. They lingered near the camps because their main food source—Malaysian field rats—were attracted to the castaway's food and waste. And even that Tribal Council set was real. That it had been specially constructed in the jungle and that television cameras and lighting surrounded it did not make the Tribal Council set any less real. Its reality stemmed from the Tribal Council's brutal, unscripted truth. A tribe walked in, destroyed a member's pride, then traipsed back through the jungle to their seaside palm-frond-and-bamboo hut. The banished member walked alone down a dark jungle path. Sixty yards down the path a "confessional area" allowed them one last chance to vent on-camera. Then they walked five minutes more down the path into the production compound. After a psychological debriefing and physical examination, they boarded a boat the next morning for the Magellan Sutera. KK. Home. All experienced very real pain from their banishment. Once home, they would experience real questions from co-workers and loved ones about their failure. Then, when the show finally aired, their every weakness and character flaw would be exposed on national television. Complete strangers would pick them apart, discuss them over coffee, exult in their banishment.

No wonder the castaways dreaded the Tribal Council and competed ferociously in the Immunity Challenges. Even as they adapted to island life and began to find it easy, the Tribal Council was discussed with words like "execution" and "judgment day." Chief Jeff was compared to an executioner, which was ironic because Jeff's likeability was key to his being selected host. Without amiability, I feared the television audience would turn against whomever presided over the Tribal Council.

Jeff initially heard about "Survivor" like everyone else, through that lone initial press release in early October. He was professionally adrift at the time, being offered a great deal of work as an on-air personality but turning it all down. He was tired of projects lacking emotional depth—game shows, confrontational talk shows—and had taken a mental vow not to accept anything that didn't speak to him. In his thirties, casting about for meaning in his life, the deep-thinking on-air personality wanted to do something that mattered.

When his agent called about "Survivor," Jeff knew he wanted the job. Wanted it, in fact, badly enough to fight for it. Interviewing, drawing a subject out, getting inside people's heads—those were Jeff's strengths. His wife Shelley was a psychotherapist, and Jeff was also a student of the human condition. He eagerly applied.

Two weeks passed with no answer from either me or CBS. Jeff was aware that "Survivor" was a hot ticket, and several other top anchors were applying for the position. He was a relative unknown, coming off stints on "Access Hollywood" and VH1's "Rock and Roll Jeopardy." Before that he'd done corporate videos in Seattle. The odds of his selection, Jeff knew, were slim.

Figuring bold action was called for, he put together a "corny" scrapbook of reasons he should be host and sent it to my office. Inside was a love letter to his Shelly, a fake press release talking about the "likeable host" Jeff Probst being responsible for "Survivor"'s incredible ratings, and a mock psychological evaluation saying how suited he was for island living.

The scrapbook wasn't why Jeff eventually got the job, but it got my attention. I looked at dozens of audition tapes before deciding on Jeff. Among the tapes were submissions from the agents of some of the most famous actors and television personalities in America.

But I wasn't looking for famous faces. I felt that they would be a liability. A known persona brought baggage in the shape of public expectations. Whoever hosted "Survivor" would need to spring fully-formed into the public consciousness, displaying complete professionalism, polished interviewing skills, and a strong improvisational ability ("Survivor" would be entirely unscripted). They would have to be believable and unruffled in the outdoors. My gut told me that Jeff Probst was the man for the job.

I presented a short-list of ten hosts to Leslie Moonves, the affable and extremely powerful president and CEO of CBS Television. Moonves narrowed the list to two—Jeff and a host with extensive outdoor experience. Ironically, the other candidate was a friend of Jeff's.

Moonves and I met with the final two at CBS in Los Angeles. Afterwards, Moonves asked my opinion. In hindsight, I see that as a moment of truth—Moonves trying to see if I had the confidence to step up and offer a bold answer. "Jeff Probst," I stated emphatically.

"Done. Let's make the deal," Moonves agreed. And, just like that, Jeff Probst had his dream assignment. Finally selected, Jeff heeded advice learned once from Bryant Gumbel to "do your homework and be yourself," immersing himself in the castaways' audition videos and personal biographies. He learned about Borneo and picked my brain about my vision and about Pulau Tiga. On March 5 he flew from Los Angeles International Airport to his new island home. Facing the biggest professional challenge of his life, he was revved but confident. He was comfortable in the outdoors, and comfortable before the camera. He'd done his homework; now it was time to be himself. His hope wasn't to suspend reality in his time on-camera, just to be the conduit through which it was blurred. "Survivor" was in the word of "Survivor"'s supervising producer, Scott Messick, "dramality," drama and reality. If Jeff didn't get it right the show might descend into parody, or worse, anarchy.

The key would be the Tribal Council. Tense before the first one, he had been loose and confident before the second. Our only concern was B.B. suddenly standing up and announcing he was quitting and that a vote wasn't necessary, thereby denying us the final dramatic moment needed to conclude hour two of our TV show. That didn't happen. But Greg's sudden, ambiguous outburst caught Jeff off guard. When shooting finished and Pagong began the trek home, Jeff had stormed off the set. Well, "stormed" is perhaps too forceful a word to describe Jeff's walk. He was totally under control, but tense, as if preparing for a fight. His eyes focused straight ahead.

He walked quickly back to Pulau Tiga's production compound. Closing the door on the audio room—the compound's *de facto* war room—he paced, still too angry to talk. Then he began regaining perspective, seeing Greg's action for what it was, the passive-aggressive actions of an insecure young man. It was also obvious that Pagong would have to be handled differently than Tagi at future Tribal Councils. They were younger, more prone to acting out. The Gen X mantra of cynicism and disdain were writ large in their behavior. Why should a group that dubbed their patriarch Mr. Viagra within hours of coming ashore show any more respect for Jeff or the television process? Only time on the island, as their defense mechanisms were slowly switched off by the decrease in food and comforts, would curb Pagong's arrogance. It was just a matter of time before reality—not television's reality nor fact and fiction blurred, but actual, full-blown reality of a sort Pagong couldn't mock away—would set in. Then they would be truly fighting for survival.

His usual calm self again, Jeff decided to stand back and let the island do its work. At the production meeting the following morning, I seconded that notion. As for Greg . . . well, Jeff would keep an eye on him. He was the chief, after all.

DAY EIGHT

With every passing day the crew began sinking deeper into island living. Real world names were dropped in favor of nicknames—Sandman, Ninja. Long pants were long forgotten; the same for anything resembling a jacket.

In all but the most torrential downpours raincoats weren't used. Shoes were ignored unless absolutely necessary, and never worn in the dining hall, per Malaysian custom. Deep tans and bug bites defined complexions. The crew often wore T-shirts reading "Don't Vote Me Off." Otherwise, men were frequently bare-chested and the women wore tank tops. Sarongs replaced shorts on the lower body, both for freedom of movement and ventilation. In a land that made Miami in August look arctic, every little breeze helped.

Every morning at six, then again at six in the evening, crew boats carried a producer, production assistant, and a pair of two-person (sound engineer and camera man) camera teams with their hundreds of pounds of gear to Tagi and Pagong. These men and women existed side by side with the tribes, peripheral tribe members. They watched as island life became normal and each day filled with trivialities for the castaways, just like a day back home. The camera team's insinuation into this everyday reality allowed them to film those defining moments—the off-the-cuff remark, petty theft, sloth—which would make or break a castaway's fate. Both Tagi and Pagong knew their camera crew's and producer's names, with familiarity breeding off-camera asides and jokes. Because of this intimacy, whenever the crew boat arrived back at the production dock from the Other Side, the crew finishing their shift was deluged with questions about their tribe's activity. Although the compound television could pick up CNN and ESPN, and Malaysian newspapers made their way in twice a week, the hottest gossip revolved around tribal activity.

Everyone had a theory about who would go next and who would be the ultimate winner. There were sentimental favorites with unsteady futures (Gretchen, Rudy, and Richard) and perceived villains the crew was sure hadn't yet revealed their true colors (Jenna, Susan). Like an onion, the layers of castaway life were being peeled back day by day.

Judging which castaways would stay and which would go was definitely getting harder. Sonja and B.B. had been longshots to begin with, so their departures weren't surprising. For the fourteen remaining castaways—seven in each tribe—there were reasons each should be voted off and reasons they should be kept. Of Pagong, Greg, Colleen, Jenna, and Gervase were safest. Of Tagi, the safest were Kelly and Susan and Sean.

The gossip among the crew was that Dirk from Tagi and Ramona from Pagong were in trouble. This marked a sea change in tribal thinking. Both Dirk and Ramona were young, athletic, and likeable. Both were formidable during challenges, rallying their teams with their physical talents and enthusiasm. But the castaways had begun searching for reasons to dislike their fellows. The leisurely pace of beach life gave them plenty of time to ponder exactly why they wanted someone gone. That pondering would fester into a gripe, then into a confidence with another castaway about why the offending person should go. The conspiring then began, with one or more additional castaways convinced to vote against that person. Tagi's Susan was the Great Conspirator, first joining the bloc for Sonja, then changing her vote at the last minute. On Day Eight, should Tagi vote next, Rudy was in her sights. If all three women plus just one man could be persuaded to vote against him, the crusty vet was gone.

Dirk's demise was probably a few Tribal Councils off. But it was sure to come, for he was beginning to annoy Tagi. The reason was his Christianity. There seems to be something threatening about a devout person of any faith to non-believers. It's as though a mirror is being held up to their faults. They feel judged. Whenever an individual closer to life's ideal state comes in contact with those drifting further away—a physically fit person in a room of smokers, a mentally balanced person speaking with someone fragmented and dysfunctional—that person is quietly scorned as a reminder of imperfection. Thus the universal dislike for those seeking a higher plane. Mankind, by its very nature, is an imperfect animal. It's easier to revel in imperfection and mock those taking the bold step towards improvement than to actually attempt the step. On an island that mockery can translate into an easy vote.

And while Dirk wasn't in-your-face, there was definitely an enthusiasm to his faith. He didn't condemn Richard, for instance, for coming out. But Dirk buried his head in his hands as if tortured while Richard was speaking—as though he were praying for the strength to keep his mouth shut.

From the point of view of psychologist Ondrusek—seeing the world through different lenses than Dirk—there was also a strong subcurrent of suppression in Dirk's faith. Whenever Dirk began horsing around with say, Kelly, and it got too physical, he backed off immediately. When others made comments about sex or craving sex, he listened, absorbed every word, laughed along with them, then fled.

Because Dirk grew up on a farm in Spring Green, Wisconsin, popular opinion on the island held he was just an innocent farm boy who had never been exposed to real-world temptations. Hence, his virginity at

twenty-three. Dirk didn't enhance perceptions of his intelligence by publicly stating he was the Gilligan of Pulau Tiga.

But Dirk had spent five years in Seattle while in college, where he also
made captain of the basketball team. The ghetto speech patter was added
then. If he couldn't do worldly things like drink and have sex, he would at
least adopt a worldly tone to fit in. Otherwise he was just a white farm boy
in the big city. A rube. And Dirk was no rube. One of his heroes was Martin Luther King Jr., because he was a man of action. And it's not that Dirk
didn't think about sex, he just tried not to. Thinking too much about getting naked with a woman was tormenting, especially for a handsome
young man who listed "dancing and blind dates" as a hobby. Avoiding the
topic altogether was easier.

Dirk had a tendency to look lost at times, waiting for leadership instead
of charting a path. As for all those people who somehow equated virginity and a devout nature with stupidity, Dirk had learned to ignore their
sarcastic asides. In his mind those characteristics were as much a part of
him as being loud and goofy and more than a little annoying sometimes.
He came to Pulau Tiga vowing to win, toting his Bible for inspiration. It
was, Dirk said, his guide to daily life.

Ramona, on the other hand, oozed worldliness, or, more appropriately,
world weariness. She wasn't evil, she wasn't building alliances. She was still
feeling sick and just wanted to get by. That made the twenty-eight-year-
old vulnerable, even at the laid-back Beach House. The sickness-induced
fatigue, however, surprised many. With her background in martial arts
(fourth-degree black belt), powerful body, professional background as a
chemist, and head held high as the island's only African-American woman,
she seemed a cinch to challenge all involved. Mentally, physically, and
emotionally Ramona Gray was the equal or better of any castaway.

The problem was sickness. Ramona had swallowed great mouthfuls of
salt water during the paddle over from the *Matahari*. She vomited. Unable
to swallow water or food after that, she became seriously dehydrated. The
definitive Ramona image from Pagong's first days ashore was Ramona
lying on the beach, congratulating her teammates for working so hard.
She was too exhausted to move or work. Further conflict came when she
thought protein might make her feel better. Pagong had one canned good
with them, a tin of beans. Ramona spent an entire night craving protein,
dreaming of the luscious beans she would have for breakfast. But when

the sun rose and Ramona scampered over to the beans, Gretchen stopped her cold. "The beans," she told Ramona, "should be rationed. We can't eat our only source of protein just a day into a six-week ordeal."

Ramona argued. Then she pouted. Then she was too exhausted to do anything but sleep. Ramona contributed what she could to the development of Pagong's shelter, but she'd already earned a reputation as lazy. There was nothing she could do to turn it around. Even when she rallied to perform wonderfully in "Quest for Fire," Ramona was on the bubble.

On the evening of Day Eight Ramona saw very clearly that she was in trouble. The body language and tone of voice her fellow tribe members used towards Ramona was condescending, distant. Ramona was convinced that if they lost their next Immunity Challenge she was gone. Once Pagong drifted off to sleep—Greg and Colleen making a bed in the jungle, while everyone else stayed in the shelter—she lay awake, praying. She prayed for hours, asking God to give her an opportunity to show her worth. That crucial Immunity Challenge was scheduled for first thing in the morning.

Meanwhile, in the production compound, scuttlebutt confirmed Ramona's plight. If they lost the Immunity Challenge, a physically demanding race titled "Rescue Mission," she was gone. Then the conversation shifted away from Ramona to Pagong's precarious shelter. The moon was almost full and the tide was getting higher. Would it be carried off?

Overall, however, the mood was subdued. The communal area was clear by nine, with everyone save crews on the Other Side preparing for a big tomorrow.

DAY NINE

"Go to one," came the command from the Tribal Council stage. It was 8 P.M. and the third Tribal Council was about to get underway. First assistant director Jamie Schutz had logistical responsibility for the entire set. Supervising producer Scott Messick was in the "sound booth" (a rotting wooden shed thirty yards offstage, filled with monitors and sound equipment). I and my co-executive producer, Craig Piligian, moved back and forth between booth and set. My style is quiet micromanagement—a change of dialogue for Jeff, suggestions for a dramatic camera angle, a quick, unexpected compliment. The good cop.

Craig was the bad cop, marching around the set barking commands, exhorting the troops in very precise—and sometimes highly profane—

language to make sure every single individual did his or her job perfectly. The Tribal Council was shot entirely live. There was no room for error. Details were everything.

Craig and I complemented each other perfectly. Craig's bluster was effective in the island's compressed working environment because it ultimately offended no one. His rants were followed an hour later by a heartfelt apology for anything untoward he might have said.

As one technical glitch after another slowed preparation time for the third Tribal Council, Craig's impatience grew. His tone got increasingly agitated. Then the wind picked up. A sudden storm was bearing down on Pulau Tiga. Piligian strode from camera to camera—there were six—wondering loudly why things weren't ready to go. Throughout, I stood off to one side, trying to anticipate any minor problems that might stem from shooting in the rain. Eco-Challenge had given me unparalleled experience in producing reality-driven adventure shows. I've shot through sandstorms in Morocco, cyclones off the Great Barrier Reef, and blizzards in Patagonia. Before flying to Borneo, I'd done my homework on the severity of the South China Sea's weather, and knew of the raging winds, heavy rains, and horizontal lightning likely to define area storms. I also made sure to have local experts on set constantly to analyze how serious things were likely to get.

In my mind there was never a question of stopping due to this storm. "Survivor" was real. Period. Real meant shooting until it was unsafe, not stopping because it was merely uncomfortable. "I stop shooting when the storm gets to a ten, on a scale of one to ten," I told a camera man who asked if filming would shut down. "This is a three."

The cameras were wrapped in trash bags to keep them dry. Ninja (Mark Lynch) and Fed Wetherbee, the operating team for the jib arm, were most exposed to the weather. Their twenty-four–foot pole camera was actually located off the set, then extended into and over it. At one end of the boom was a camera; at the other, a complicated arrangement of batteries and a monitor. In case of rain those pieces of precision electronics would be ruined. Worse, if lightning struck the set—or more precisely, struck the boom, which was entirely metal and made a fine lightning rod—Ninja and Fed would most definitely get a shock. Amazingly, neither was ruffled. Ninja had once spent a night during Eco-Challenge with his boom atop an Andes peak, lightning striking all around him. He knew the parameters of safety; when to push forward creatively and when to step aside for nature.

The wind picked up, blowing a cover off one of the lights. Drops of rain splattered the set seconds apart, increasing in frequency.

"Tribe members are five minutes out," Jamie yelled from the stage. He was in contact with a remote producer by walkie-talkie. He looked to me for the OK, I nodded, and Jamie went to work. "Let's go, everyone. First positions." "First position" meant an individual's battle station for filming.

Craig immediately reinforced Jamie's command. "Now. People. First positions. Now. I want to see movement."

Tagi was Chief Jeff's guest that night. They'd lost that morning's "Rescue Mission" Immunity Challenge by the narrowest of margins. The goal of the challenge was for each team to build a stretcher, then rescue a member from deep in the jungle. That team member—Colleen for Pagong, Kelly for Tagi—would be carried out of the jungle and back down to a "first aid" station on the beach. Once again, the challenges were mirroring island living's bent towards survival in all its guises—in this case, not the need for fire or water or food, but empathy.

A narrow path wound through the jungle, but that wasn't the fastest way in to where the "victims" dangled from a tree by a chest harness and carabiners. Unafraid of the once-fearsome jungle after nine days on Pulau Tiga, the tribes dragged the stretchers off-trail, crashing over rotting logs, ducking under inch-thick vines, crying out as razor-sharp rattan branches combed deep gashes in their arms and backs. Their stretchers were made by the teams of bamboo and rope, with fishing net slings.

Each team had sent one member ahead to mark a path. For Tagi, that was Stacey. Instead of bending twigs or drawing arrows in the soil, she stripped off items of clothing and set them on the ground or hung them on tree braches. They were impossible to miss.

But Susan, who had agreed on the choice of Stacey as the perfect pathfinder, exhorted Tagi to ignore Stacey's trail. Susan was sure she knew a quicker way to Kelly's location. Just as she had at the first Tribal Council, Susan was breaking a pact for her personal gain. In this case, the gain was to show her leadership skills and vast woodland experience.

She was wrong. If Tagi had followed Stacey's path they might have won. As it was, they got lost, wandering off the proper trail. Their lead over Pagong had been significant until then, so the mistake wasn't fatal.

But as Tagi collected Kelly, strapped her in, and began the mad dash back to the beach, Pagong was already racing back to the First Aid station with Colleen lashed into their stretcher.

It was hot inside the jungle canopy, with a stifling wall of humidity trapped between the ground and treetops. Passing through it was a tortuous process that didn't end until the beach. Even a slow jog inside the canopy would bring exhaustion in minutes, as the body expended more energy keeping cool than on the physical act of movement. But carrying a loaded stretcher on the dead run, over uneven terrain, after subsisting on a protein-less diet of rice and water, was a physical act of will. By the time the tribes finally crashed out of the jungle onto the narrow rocky beach, their wet shirts clung to their bodies like second skins. Arms and legs were filthy, bleeding, and bruised. Both tribes were exhausted.

With one hundred yards of soft-sand sprinting before them, Pagong had a twenty-yard lead over Tagi. And Pagong's youth gave them an insurmountable edge. The race was as good as over.

Pagong celebrated by walking out to a small pile of rocks known as Bird Island. A lone tree stood on the island's crown. Pagong's newly won Immunity Idol hung from a branch. Picking over the slippery rocks of low tide that lay between the beach and Bird Island, Pagong strutted out to claim their prize.

Tagi couldn't bear to watch. They skulked over to a log near the beach and sat down with great dejection. The Tribal Council was no longer a novelty. Tagi wasn't exactly a tight unit, so they weren't sad about losing one of their members. They were sad because that member could be them. No one was safe on Tagi.

"You," Chief Jeff told Tagi softly, "have a date with me tonight."

The wind was up to twenty-five knots, blowing out the torches lining the rope bridge. Tagi took their final steps onto the Tribal Council set. Lightning flashed hard. The rain came down in great torrents. It would maintain that intensity until past midnight, flooding the production compound. Ground around the set was already deluged. Individuals standing off set, most of whom hadn't expected a storm and wore just T-shirts, shorts, and boots (at night in the jungle, boots made more snake-resistant footwear than sandals), stood like statues as filming began and the rain poured down until their clothes were saturated and the cold rain had turned warm from their body heat. It ran down the inside of their clothing, along the contour of their torsos and legs, finally pooling inside their boots, where it began working its way back up again, covering first the toes and then the tops of feet and then spilling out of their boots onto the ground to join the rest of the flood.

Lightning flashed again. Jamie gave the order for Ninja to lock the boom down—select a camera angle, cinch the adjustment knob tight, then walk away. In Jamie's mind the chance for a lightning strike was very real. Jamie was young, only twenty-seven, but he'd already shown a tremendous amount of professional poise and capability. Though I had confirmed that it was only horizontal heat lightning and could not possibly strike the set, I gave Ninja the nod to comply. He locked down boom down and stepped back. All the other camera men kept their eyes locked to their viewfinders. Shooting continued.

From that point on, no one moved, for what was transpiring on the Tribal Council set was as real as it got. Rain and wind shoved across the set horizontally, soaking the Tagis' backs as they sat facing the fire. Chief Jeff maintained composure, calmly noting the rain then launching into a series of pointed questions about Tagi's group dynamics.

Their first visit to the Tribal Council had been an initiation for Tagi. Everyone had been loose and warm, joking about their new life. Only Rudy and Sonja had been vulnerable then. But that was six long days and nights ago. Tagi had lived together, slept together, bared quirks together. No one was perfect and no one was normal. Everyone was expendable. The strong, like Sean and Dirk, were proving less than super-survivalists. The annoying, like Richard, had become endearing and even a hard worker. Rudy was still vulnerable, mostly because of his age. Yet for a man of seventy-two he was remarkably athletic. And Tagi desperately needed athleticism.

With every member of Tagi vulnerable, and a fierce South China Sea blow whipping across the set, something clicked in the minds of Tagi. Their protective veneers dropped. One by one, they began pleading to stay on the island. With Rudy it was about ageism—he didn't like that only old people were being voted off. Then Sean, face calm but his eyes betraying deep inner panic, reminded everyone that he was funny and athletic. His job was to keep everyone laughing, and the island needed laughter.

Chief Jeff was dumbfounded. Sean had been picked by most observers to last until almost the end. Top Ten for sure. Top Five almost definitely. Now, before the same cutthroat brigade that could seal his fate, Sean was admitting insecurity. Insecurity equated to weakness, and any weakness was guaranteed to be ridiculed. Sean was playing his best hand too early.

Stacey spoke next. The time for talking was winding down, because the storm was moving from rainstorm to baby monsoon. The wind shoved across the set and Chief Jeff had to lean forward to hear Stacey's words. Even then, every third or fourth syllable was drowned out by the rain.

First, Stacey said, the tribe should remember that she'd won them a key victory at "Bugging Out." Her face, as she spoke, was anxious. For all the eye-rolling and defiance, she truly was the shy woman she saw herself as. Speaking up was hard for her. But Stacey really wanted to stay on the island. She wasn't too worried about her fate—she and Susan and Kelly had pledged an alliance that afternoon, with Rudy as the man they would vote off. But like the crackerjack attorney she was back where a job title mattered, Stacey knew the value of arguing her case—just to be on the safe side. And so she continued.

She wished she could have done more to help carry the stretcher during "Rescue Mission." She thought the upcoming challenges would be more mental than physical. Her intellectual ability would be an asset. Then she flashed that insecure-shy-Mary Ann smile one more time. The defense rested.

It was time to vote.

But before they could begin, Sean chimed in one more time. Chief Jeff was flabbergasted. Sean's desperation was painful to watch. But the affable young neurologist from Long Island couldn't stop talking. He'd come on "Survivor" with the secret ambition of launching an acting career. Soap operas interested him, mostly because they shot in New York, close to his home. To prove he was a little on the wild side, he wore his baseball cap backwards and had his left nipple pierced with a silver hoop. He shaved his chest. And he was intelligent enough to sense a growing alliance in Tagi, an alliance he was not part of. So he argued his case: He was funny. He was athletic. Tagi needed Sean Kenniff.

With that, the voting began. Halfway through, the generator died. The set went totally black. Voting resumed when the lights came back on, but only for a minute. Then the power went out again. Darkness and frenzy defined the set. From somewhere in the night Craig Piligian commanded the lights to go back on. And somehow, they did.

And so it was that the voting concluded. Chief Jeff wandered off the set into the jungle to do a pre-count and got soaked to the skin. When he returned to announce the newest castaway to be sent home, his shirt was plastered to his chest, his hair was pressed flat on his head, and he was still, somehow, poised. Later he would swear he had never felt so naked or vulnerable in his professional life.

Stacey's impassioned speech, the final voting showed, had done no good. Somehow Rudy had survived another three days, getting just one vote less than Stacey. As with the first council, one swing vote made all the difference. Stacey, sharp in defeat, knew exactly who it was.

As she got up to leave she turned to Susan Hawk. The others needed to know there was a Judas in their midst. "I guess you changed your vote again," Stacey said, looking into Susan's remorseless eyes.

Stacey didn't say another word. Didn't even attempt a good-bye to the men and women she'd spent nine uncomfortable days and nights with. She turned to walk the path back to civilization. "Time for you to go," Chief Jeff said softly.

"Go where?" she answered tartly. She could see the path straight ahead easily enough, but the wind had blown out the torches leading to the confessional. The lit portion of path effectively ended ten feet into the jungle. Beyond that, there was nothing but total blackness.

Of all the lonely walks any castaway would take, Stacey's was the most brutal. Just after the confessional lay a bridge and a swamp, then the fringes of the production compound. As though she was blind, Stacey felt her way along the slick path in the pitch dark, too scared to think about how she felt. The whole "Survivor" process begun back in October—the application, the homemade video featuring her co-workers, the flight to Los Angeles for interviews, the final selection, the flight to KK, the boat ride on the *Matahari*, the shipwrecking, all that time trying to forge a life on a beachhead—was done.

Back on the set, Jamie strode from offstage to center stage. "That's a wrap," he declared. With that, the night of dramality was done. No matter what, from that moment on "Survivor" would have the stamp of authenticity.

A party broke out in the production compound that night. While Stacey Stillman underwent a short psychological counseling session and took a well-earned shower, the covered deck where the crew took their meals and received their brutal schedules and caught ESPN now and again was a mad-house. The rain hadn't stopped. The puddles beneath the deck were six inches deep. Everything electrical, save the sound system, had been moved into a closed room. There was no announcement of the party, no word passed or notice posted. It began as a gathering over beers, with quiet music. An hour later the volume was amplified tenfold, the dancing had begun, and a dozen shirts bore the luminescent green of a glow-stick attack.

The party was a release, a ritual praising the rain for its heft and the show for its guts. These men and women who had bitched and moaned about how the castaways were eating better, and for whom sleep was stolen, were congratulating themselves for being the cream-of-the-crop type of individual invited to Pulau Tiga to film "Survivor." They grabbed the release frantically at first, as if drowning. The dancing was harsh, dis-jointed. Sweaty. The music was techno, alternative, country—Johnny Cash, Bruce Springsteen.

Two hours later it was over. A boat was leaving for the beaches in four hours and many of the revelers had to be on it.

Lost amid the hoopla, Jeff Probst leaned on the hand-carved ma-hogany table forming the deck's centerpiece. He had a beer in one hand, and a very tired grin on his face that wouldn't go away. "Now that," he said quietly before going to bed, "was reality."

EVOLUTION FOUR

Play the Game

DAY TEN

The gale hadn't destroyed Pagong's shelter, but they began tearing it down the next morning anyway. They wanted to start fresh. Under Gretchen's leadership—she bridled at the word, but that's what it was—Pagong moved off the beach. The previous location on the surf line, she'd fretted more than once, would make her the laughingstock of the military survival community. "I don't care if you vote me off for this," she told Pagong in her normal, calm tones, "but changes need to be made in this camp. We need to be more aware of our supplies. We cannot waste anything. We need to be organized. But above all else, I am not sleeping in that shelter the way it is one more night."

Pagong's new abode was a lean-to in the jungle instead of the frame house they'd had previously. For pillows, they stuffed coconuts shavings inside burlap bags. For mattresses, palm fronds were laid in thick piles atop the spongy dead leaves already cloaking the ground. Additional palm fronds were laid thickly on the roof to keep out leaks. Pagong's greatest criticism of their former shelter location wasn't, in fact, fear of being washed away, but the nagging discomfort of being constantly wet. Sea spray, rain, and the incumbent humidity from adult bodies sleeping close together in a closed space were the causes. Moving off the beach and fixing the roof solved two of the problems.

Greg solved the third by continuing to sleep alone in the jungle. "It's just like building a nest," he explained to Pagong. Greg's nesting began at dusk with a short hike off the beach. One night he would sleep just fifty yards into the jungle, the next it was a few hundred. Either way, the motivation was solitude to recharge his mental batteries. Greg considered the "Survivor" experience the most elaborate form of game. He was eager to stretch the limits of the game as far as he could, considering it mildly absurd. Even after Colleen took to sharing his nest, Greg admitted that their alliance was bound to end badly. "It's like a kitten you find along the side of the road. You pick it up, you take it home, you pet it. You give it a name, like Fluffy. A week goes by and you haven't eaten so you're starving. So you look right in the kitten's eyes and break its neck. Nothing personal."

The kitten, Greg continued in case anyone misunderstood, was Colleen. "And I hope she would break my neck if it came down to just the two of us. That's all part of the game."

And Greg was playing the game brilliantly. The tribes were entering into true survival mode, and a man with his knowledge of the jungle was a definite asset. He also possessed the physical strength to shine during challenges. Whether or not he would remain nonthreatening to Joel or the other Pagong remained to be seen. For as well as Greg was playing the game—and the term "game" was used widely at Pagong, though not at all by the Tagi—he was hardly the playful otter who'd first come ashore a week and a half earlier. Greg wouldn't admit it, but hunger was setting in and he was losing weight he couldn't afford to lose. His face was drawn and stomach muscles defined under the thinnest layer of body fat. The diet of rice and water left him often tired. Pagong hadn't been able to catch fish, and the few rats they caught and cooked provided just a subsistence level of protein. Gervase, for instance, with his fast metabolism, was burning more calories than the rice's complex carbohydrates could provide. The low-fiber diet, however, had made him so constipated he hadn't enjoyed a bowel movement on Pulau Tiga. So food was changing the lives of all Pagong.

When Chief Jeff called for an ambassador from each tribe to hear that pillows and hammocks went to the winners of the next Reward Challenge, a famished Jenna was appalled. "We have pillows. We don't need pillows. What we need is food or a spice rack."

The lack of food made Greg susceptible to disease, and he developed an external ear infection. Sleeping in the jungle exposed Greg to more in-

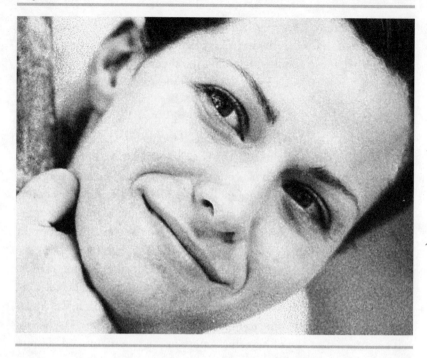

sect bites than his tribal members, especially after a rain, when the bugs sought out human flesh with the zeal of drunkards stumbling upon free beer. The scars on his legs and elbows grew larger every day. His body odor was palpable several feet away. But most importantly, he'd ceased to maintain a distance between himself and his tribe members. The human emotions he'd hidden with a smile and a quick joke in the early days—pride, anger, disgust—had wormed their way to just below the surface. For instance, he had taken to mocking Joel's persona, calling him "The Strongest Man in America" (Joel, taking it at face value—which Greg knew he would—thought it a compliment). The mocking was contempt delivered in an easily digestible package.

Greg was like a patient undergoing a very long psychotherapy session. The session had begun with jokes and banter to hide deep fears and issues. Now the jokes were growing further apart and the hard work of diving inward to touch his soul had begun. "Survivor" was his slow journey to the truth. He called it a game only because calling it anything else would have been too painful. When asked if he would make any lifelong friends on the island, Greg—the man everyone considered their best friend—

laughed scornfully. "Are you kidding? With the exception of your cell-mate on death row this is the weirdest place on earth to meet new people. I mean, I like these people. I wouldn't mind getting together with them again, but this is all just a game. These people aren't my friends, they're fellow contestants."

That sort of honesty surprised many, but if they had known Greg's background it would have been obvious. His hero was the archetypical loner-achiever, Chuck Yeager. Greg's favorite movie was Clint Eastwood's *The Outlaw Josey Wales* about a societal outcast seeking vengeance against the men who tried to kill him. One by one Josey Wales offed his opponents, just as Greg was doing to his adversaries on the island. At twenty-four, Greg was a year out of college and working manual labor in Colorado when he applied for "Survivor." And although his psychological profile diagnosed Greg as a "warm, fuzzy mountain man," he was definitely not soft. Lacrosse was his favorite sport. For a personal challenge, he put himself through a twenty-seven–day solo survival test in the Montana Rockies. So Greg came to Pulau Tiga prepared. On Day Ten he was still seventeen days shy of his achievement in the mountains and, despite the physical changes, still within his comfort zone.

If Greg were a lone man surrounded by team players, the Pagong would have been collectively stronger. But they were a fragmented assemblage of individuals. Gretchen had the depth that came from raising two children, but she was growing less verbal with every passing day because her age and outspokenness made her vulnerable. The others had all come to Pulau Tiga with almost cold-blooded expectations of winning. While the Tagi were bonding and working as a family unit, Pagong circled one another warily. They made a great show of unity at Reward Challenges and Tribal Challenges, and they hiked occasionally to one of the mud volcanoes to slather each other with therapeutic mud. But they were pretenders. Greg argued with Gretchen. Gretchen argued with Joel. Joel was annoyed by Jenna because she was a cheerleader. Gervase was annoyed by Jenna. Everyone except Greg had one eye on Colleen, whose friendship with Greg constituted an alliance. And Ramona worked furiously to ingratiate herself after a poor first week. When Greg thought aloud that the person he would vote off "if we voted right now changed from one minute to the next," he spoke for all the tribe members. No one person annoyed Pagong. Rather, all of Pagong annoyed Pagong.

That might have been enlightening if the tribe displayed some gen-uine emotion like rage or hatred. But they liked to pretend they were a happy-go-lucky clan, even though their camp consisted of just a lean-to and latrine, they'd caught only one small fish after dozens of attempts, and everyone was slowly starving. When Chief Jeff visited with them one day and said, as a joke, that he'd been talking on the phone with a friend that morning, a bag of M&Ms in one hand and a Diet Coke in the other, Pagong gasped—a phone call, chocolate, and a soft drink sounded otherworldly.

Even salt and pepper sounded otherworldly. Their rice diet was taste-less and unchanging. Dinner hour conversation invariably included a sen-tence beginning with, "Wow, if only I had something to spice this up..."

Yet they were so caught up in pretending to be happy that they were unable to drop their disingenuousness long enough to actually earn their coveted spices. The next day's Reward Challenge—the one for which Jenna said pillows and hammocks were worthless as prizes, what she wanted was food—asked each team to prepare a distress signal on their beach. The winning team would be the one with the most distressful sig-nal, the kind of signal that would leave no doubt they were stranded on a deserted island and needed to be rescued. The prizes, in addition to pil-lows and hammocks, were a spice rack (including soy sauce) and a hunt-ing knife. The latter two were added when the tribes insisted those were the things they most wanted, and filling a need creates better reality. The prizes would be dropped by parachute onto the winning team's beach.

Tagi, the family unit, carved a large "SOS" into the beach. An arrow made of driftwood and sea shells bobbed offshore, pointing to their loca-tion. They also planned to light a signal fire, use a piece of metal to reflect sunlight onto the plane, make a large arrow on the sand, and even don their yellow rain jackets and lie on the ground in a circle. Their heads would be in the middle of the circle, with their bodies extending outward like rays of the sun. To enhance the effect, they would move their arms and legs in unison, creating the sand equivalent of snow angels.

Pagong built a happy face.

DAY ELEVEN

"Tagi is Groggy" read the message Tagi carved into the sand next to their SOS. If that was truly the case, the grogginess came from hours of hard work rather than lack of food. In addition to their meticulously and ingeniously constructed latrine, communal dining area, cooking area, lean-to, and clothes drying area, they were building a bowling alley. They raked the sand clean of excess coral and driftwood. Like the Swiss Family Robinson, Tagi were determined to bend their island world into some-place civilized. They never stopped planning that next big construction project. They had come together. The beach was their home and they were proud of what they'd done with it.

Only Dirk, with his nervous metabolism, was getting painfully thin. The rest of Tagi had a healthy glow. For vitamins, they ate coconuts. Cutting a hole in the brightest and greenest ones, they sucked out the sweet milk. For food, in addition to rice, Tagi was eating a steady diet of fresh fish. Richard had begun swimming offshore to spear fish. At first it was just stingrays, which made easy prey as they lay flattened on the ocean bottom. Sean wasn't impressed, telling Richard he wanted fish—real fish. So Richard swam out again the next day and brought back lobster and floun-der. The hard work was slimming him down, which helped him with the Challenges. Even without his physical ability, he'd become indispensable to Tagi because of that fishing prowess, and he knew it. Richard, who'd looked so vulnerable for so long, would definitely be on Pulau Tiga awhile.

Surprisingly, the same was true for Rudy. His impassioned speech against ageism at the Tribal Council had been heard. While still largely stoic—he was turning out to be the island's only introvert—and prone to staring for hours into the cooking fire, Rudy was visibly happier and more talkative. His physical ability was astounding for a man his age, and he was an enormous asset during Challenges. Though Rudy still didn't frequent Richard's group discussions, he would occasionally show up and listen, then leave when things got too in-depth. "I stick around until they start talking about that gay stuff or that Jesus stuff, then I just walk away," he explained with his gruff accent.

Rudy and Richard enjoyed a platonic relationship dynamically similar to Greg and Colleen's alliance over at Pagong. Rudy and Colleen were both weaker players, relying on the strength of a stronger partner to give them clout. Richard and Greg needed their weaker partner to buy further time on the island through alliance. It was win-win for all involved.

Rudy and Richard actually made a cute pair. Rudy was the tribal cook. So Richard would catch the fish and bring them to Rudy, who would clean and prepare them. The arrangement gave them both a chance to shine, but it wouldn't have worked if Rudy had been a poor cook. Forty-five years in the Navy, though, including two tours of duty in the Mekong Delta, had taught him a thing or two about making a fine meal under abnormal conditions. In his more expansive moments he told Tagi about the time he'd taken a bath in a vat of soup he was preparing and the time when he needed a little moisture to help him knead flour for making bread, so he used the sweat dripping off his forehead. Rudy was earthy like that, and proud of his resourcefulness. The tribe members were duly impressed, but also made a mental note not to let Rudy prepare bread or soup under any circumstances.

Rudy's parents were Austrian immigrants, and he was a first-generation American. Hard on the heels of World War II, he joined the Navy in 1945 at the age of seventeen. Five years later he joined the UDT (Underwater Demolition Team), or frogmen. When that unit was turned into the specialty commando SEAL group, Rudy was among the first SEALs. As the years passed and he stayed with the special force, Rudy became the walking embodiment of the SEAL ethic. He worked hard every day, didn't complain about tough duty, and followed orders unflinchingly. He rose to become the most senior enlisted man in the Navy. Since his retirement at age sixty-two, he'd stayed close to the East Coast SEAL headquarters in Virginia Beach, Virginia (the West Coast headquarters is on Coronado Island, near San Diego). A typical day meant a morning of physical training (PT), driving to the base to do some shopping or chat with friends, then home for dinner, a beer, a night of sitcoms, then bed. His body was still rock solid, with clearly-defined abdominal muscles and sinewy arms. But Rudy complained that he'd lost fitness since leaving the SEALs, as his life was no longer consumed by push-ups and beach runs. His body was one of his few conceits, and in addition to muscle tone he took great care of his teeth. His lone luxury item was a toothbrush.

Because of his stoicism, Rudy was hard to judge in the early days on Pulau Tiga. He seemed resigned to being voted off early. There was no evidence he had a strategy, other than being himself and expecting others to take or leave him. He didn't learn other castaways' names unless absolutely necessary. "What do you think of Kelly?" a producer asked him one day.

"Kelly? Who's Kelly?"

"The one with the pierced tongue."

"Don't like her. If we were back on the mainland I wouldn't talk to her."

"What do you think of Susan?"

"Susan? Who's Susan?"

"Susan Hawk. The woman from Wisconsin."

"Don't like her."

"Do you know the names of any of the women in your tribe?"

"I don't know their names, and I don't wanna know their names."

But as Rudy lasted through one three-day cycle after another, and he actually believed he would be included in the final group of ten when the tribes merged, that stoicism was replaced with strategy. The friendship with Richard was based on the exigencies of the game, but showed the slightest shading of actual friendship, though Rudy often denied it. Words smacking of outright diplomacy began creeping into Rudy's more frequent speeches. When asked if he thought Dirk and Sean—standing to either side of Rudy at the time—were tough enough to become Navy SEALs, Rudy hesitated for an instant. The Rudy of the first six days on Pulau Tiga would have laughed or said simply "no." The Rudy now interested in being part of the final ten searched for the exact words that would express his doubts without hurting their feelings. "They'd have to get through the training first. I've seen some really tough guys drop out. Only one-third of all those who start ever make it all the way through, you know."

Not exactly a ringing endorsement, but neither was it a sneer. Both Dirk and Sean were actually empowered by Rudy's words, believing they would definitely be part of the elite one-third who survived all three brutal phases of SEAL training. Their friendship was important to Rudy, and he knew they admired his years of service for his country. Rudy the strategist wasn't afraid to use that admiration for leverage to avoid getting voted off. And in this simple, subtle way, Rudy built a majority voting bloc among the Tagi. He was getting safer every day.

If Rudy had one cause for concern it was that Susan had suddenly begun telling him he wouldn't get voted off because he was such a good cook. The last two people Susan had said that to left the island shortly after. Susan's comments signaled that Rudy was a growing threat.

Sean, however, since his display of weakness at the Tribal Council, was losing status with every passing day. His aim was to remind everyone that

Immunity Challenges required athletic teammates, and he was definitely athletic. Without his athleticism, in fact, Tagi would go back to the Tribal Council every three days. Or at least that's what he was continually reminding them of.

But Tagi's beach, though splendid, was still a very small corner of the world. And Tagi's members had little room to roam away from each other. They saw and heard everything everyone said. A person's true self was clearly visible. Sean's bravado was fooling no one. With Richard the fisherman and Rudy the cook—both valuable skills—being a shirtless Jerry Seinfeld wasn't going to keep him on the island forever. For that, Sean would need an alliance of his own.

Shortly after Tagi's distress signal won them the spice rack and pillows and hammocks and a shiny new stainless steel hunting knife that Richard immediately strapped onto his left calf (Dirk: "You gay guys sure know how to accessorize"), Sean and Dirk gathered the tribe's canteens and took a hike to Far Water.

The canteens were plastic, with olive-drab army covers and slings for easy carrying. Trekking through the jungle, following the trail of fabric the tribe had tied to tree branches to guide them to Far Water, Dirk and Sean talked of their immediate future. "I think I'm gonna be the next one to go," Sean began.

An alliance was born with that small comment. Dirk and Sean promised not to vote one another off. Theirs was the most fragile alliance on the island, for neither operated from a position of power. It was like a pair of Central American countries aligning themselves against the United States. Or, more appropriate to island life, a pair of Malaysian field rats trying to stand up to a yellow-banded krait. The krait, of course, was Susan. Until she was taken out of the picture, all alliances were nebulous at best. She had a gift for collusion.

Back on the beach, a crab in one of the fish traps bit Susan's finger. She threw it to the ground and smashed it to bits with her Reeboks.

DAY TWELVE

At every Reward Challenge and Immunity Challenge a flagpole flew three guidons. The top flag was green, and read "Outwit." The middle flag was yellow and said "Outplay." The bottom flag was orange. It said in black letters, "Outlast."

Put together, the three comprised "Survivor"'s motto. Separately, they eerily resembled the three factions living on Pulau Tiga. The green would stand for the production crew, desperately trying to stay one mental step ahead of the increasingly-brilliant castaways. The middle flag would go for the playful Pagong. Fittingly, their tribal banner was also yellow. The bottom flag would be the long-haul Tagi. Again, their banner matched their tribal color, orange.

After six castaways had been voted off, the remaining ten would become one tribe, and such distinctions would be superfluous. The more secure castaways—Susan, Greg, and, amazingly, Jenna—were already talking about the merger. This made for a precarious dynamic among the secure: Being competitive while still a tribal member to avoid losing Immunity Challenges, but forging casual friendships with the other tribe in anticipation of their future vote. Competitive but not cutthroat, warm even if insincere.

But on the twelfth day of "Survivor," all that was still over a week off. And as Tagi and Pagong gathered at a windless corner of the island for an Immunity Challenge, both tribes had become almost desperate for vic-

tory. No matter what the physical cost, winning the challenge was easier than the Tribal Council. Chief Jeff had become an expert on the tribe's strengths and weaknesses, spending his spare hours studying tapes of their beach life. When a tribe marched onto the Tribal Council set and gathered around the fire, Chief Jeff asked detailed questions about their relationships. He wanted to know who was vulnerable, who was strong, who was clueless about their fate. Of course, he already knew the answer. And each tribe member already knew the answer, for they'd debated all those questions mentally, privately. But to hear Chief Jeff draw them out on camera, knowing that their strengths and weaknesses were being filmed and would eventually be shown to all America...that was frightening. "Survivor" was all about keeping secrets. Chief Jeff's job was to focus a laser beam on those secrets, bringing them into the light.

So the Immunity Challenge was pivotal to island life. The fourth Immunity Challenge asked each tribe to select one person skilled in swimming, one in running, one in balance, one in paddling, and two in digging. On the surface it was just a relay race where the winning team found a buried treasure before the other. But the individual challenges meant a chance to show strength or weakness. Strength meant island life. Weakness or mistake, as already shown in each of the challenges, meant being voted off.

The race began with a 150-meter swim to a buoy. Anchored at the base of the buoy was a corked bottle with a treasure map inside. The swimmer dove down, retrieved the buoy, then swam to a nearby bamboo raft, where the bottle was handed off to another tribe member. That tribe member navigated a precarious floating bridge, then hopped in a waiting rowboat with another team member. They rowed to shore. The bottle was broken open. The map was removed. While one tribe member sprinted into the jungle for a trail run, two others took the map to find buried treasure. They would unearth the treasure, then carry it to the finish line. Once the runner returned, and all team members were present, the chest could be opened. The winning team would be the first one to have all members present for the opening.

What was glorious about the relay was not the way Sean and Colleen swam so hard, or how Greg and Kelly raced across the floating bridge, and so on. None of those things or anything else that occurred during the race could match the finale. All were wonderful physical acts, imbued with desperation and drive. But they all paled next to the shining moment right after Tagi's diggers found their treasure chest first. Richard and Rudy were the diggers, of course. They worked as a tireless pair, using a conch shell to scrape away five feet of sand in less than ten minutes. But when Richard extricated the heavy blue wooden chest, he chose not to lug it to the finish line alongside Rudy. Instead, Richard lifted the chest into Rudy's strong arms. Knowing an opportunity to strut when he saw one, Rudy didn't just waddle through the fine soft sand in that hundred-degree heat, straining to hold onto the chest. No, that seventy-two-year-old sprinted. Sprinted like it was the first day of SEAL training and a drill instructor was screaming into his ear. Sprinted because his tribe needed to see that he was virile, no matter what his birth certificate said.

Sprinted because he could.

If Rudy did nothing else in his time on Pulau Tiga, he would always have that moment of glory.

So thanks to Rudy and Richard, who'd pulled their treasure from the sand mere seconds before Pagong's digging crew of Colleen and Jenna, Tagi enjoyed a relaxing evening on the beach while Pagong once again burrowed into their separate egos and prepared to cast their vote.

But as Tagi sat before their fire, basking in the glow of victory, each mind went back to that morning. Pagong had once been so dominant that Tagi half expected them to win the day's Immunity Challenge. Richard, Rudy, Susan, Kelly, Dirk, Sean—all spent the hours between sunrise and the Immunity Challenge casting a mental vote.

Kelly began the morning with yoga, then sat in a tree and dissed Dirk. He made odd comments, things like, "If I were to marry you I would take your name." That bugged her. He was so immature, so lost, even. Not at all like Susan. Kelly adored Susan. In fact, she'd had a dream that she and Susan were the last two left on the island. The dream turned into a nightmare when Kelly realized her worst fear had come true: she had to vote Susan off.

When Susan and Kelly took a jungle hike to search for tapioca root an hour later, Dirk's name wasn't mentioned. Instead, they talked about Sean. They didn't like his bowling alley because it was a stupid idea. They didn't like that he worked out all the time and didn't bother fishing. He didn't, they both noted, work hard enough around the camp. They were downright offended that his luxury item was a razor—but he used it to shave his chest, in addition to his face. Susan, in a subtle display of power, had borrowed Sean's razor to shave her bathing suits lines.

Sean had to go, they both agreed.

Then they got back to the beach, a section of tapioca in hand, and were approached by Richard. The big man was slowly working his way into their alliance. Or so they thought. In actuality, Richard was slowly enfolding them into his. Who to trust was becoming hard to decipher, and no one knew that better than Sue.

Richard looked both ways before whispering that if he had to vote at that very moment, Dirk would be to the one to go. All that religion was getting old. Plus, Dirk didn't do much around the camp.

Dirk had to go, they all agreed.

A half-hour later Kelly and Dirk were swinging in a hammock together, as carefree as children. While the beach had made Dirk thin, Kelly looked just fine. She had a tan, her hair was pulled back neatly, and she always made a point to clean her clothes so she looked her best. For a rebel from Las Vegas, she was proving a remarkably mainstream individual. And either remarkably willing to be swayed, or plotting enough to curry favor with everyone.

Noon came right about then. Tagi could tell by the sun dial system they'd set up in their eating area. Facing southwest, they were able to chart the sun's progress from dawn until almost dusk. They packed their emotional baggage and hidden animosities and petty manipulations into a neat little bag. Like a family, with Richard and Susan as patriarch and matriarch; Kelly, Dirk, and Sean as the easily-manipulated children; and Rudy as the grandfather living in the spare room, they marched over to the Immunity Challenge to do battle.

They returned, a quick glance at the sun dial told them—why time was important in a calendar-less society, they didn't know; it just was—at close to five. Rudy cooked a little rice, threw in seasonings, and served his hungry, contented family a fine meal. They laughed about how Dirk teased Pagong's Jenna at the Immunity Challenge, thanking her openly for the spice rack. They praised Sean's swimming and Dirk's running. They repeated the story of Rudy running with the chest until they were tired of telling it. The glory. Oh, the glory. It was good to be a castaway, at least for another three days.

The sun was long gone by the time they shuffled off to sleep. At just about that time, at the Tribal Council, Greg was admitting to Chief Jeff that he cared about the competition. Gervase confessed to being confident, then immediately added that mentioning confidence aloud made him feel vulnerable. Jenna hugged Ramona, rubbing her back as they sat together at the fire, comforting her as she would a distressed sister. Alpha male Joel, refusing to drop the mantle for even a moment, bragged about Pagong being the better tribe.

"You weren't today," Chief Jeff shot back.

"Oh . . . kick us while we're down."

"Just stating a fact."

Joel grew quiet, but a line had been drawn. He would deal with Chief Jeff another day. He was physically strong. For tonight, Joel felt safe. He wasn't farsighted enough to see that those with physical strength would be brutally cast off when the tribes were joined. Only the mentally strong would survive then. But for tonight . . . . For tonight Joel felt safe.

Less than five minutes later, Jenna stared into a camera after writing Ramona's name in black ink. Her face was hard and mean. "Too little, too late," was the reason she gave. Then she walked back to the fire and gave Ramona a hug.

Variations on the theme echoed. Ramona was voted off.

EVOLUTION FIVE

Flying below the Radar

DAY THIRTEEN

Dawn on Tagi Beach found Kelly and Susan at the waterline, washing clothes by hand. Instead of detergent they used the silica-fine Pulau Tiga sand that was otherwise no good for anything but finding its way into dinners and bodily crevices.

"I think the clothes get even cleaner with the sand. Don't you?" Susan asked. They were relaxed, talkative, looking for all the world like a pair of washerwomen from some Renaissance painting. No sooner had the sun peeped over the horizon than they were at water's edge, working.

"Yeah," Kelly answered quickly. It felt good to be domestic. Reassuring. After washing clothes she planned to do some sewing. Her luxury item had been a small beaded bag for doing crafts. She was cross-stitching a sign for Rudy on a scrap of burlap. "Rowdy Rudy's Diner," it read. She would frame the sign with twigs when she was done, then present it to the old man. Kelly thought it would hang well in the kitchen.

Meanwhile, the tribe's bamboo raft floated lazily offshore. There was no wind. Sean and Dirk were on board, fishing. Or at least trying to fish. Neither had ever caught one, but fishing resembled work, so at least Susan thought they were doing something constructive and couldn't criticize them. "You ever wonder," Dirk was saying to the ocean, "who you would hang out with if you could go back in time?"

Sean didn't know. He was afraid to ask Dirk the same question because

Dirk was bound to bring up Jesus. That made Sean nervous. Dirk was a nice guy and all, but if he planned on convincing Sean to become a Born Again he had another thing coming. Sean was a playboy.

Sean distracted himself by ruminating about his favorite subject—not being voted off. Both he and Dirk were outside Tagi's core alliance. One of them would be gone next time Tagi went to the Tribal Council. It was inevitable. That certainty made for a constant nagging, and that nagging gave each day a terrible weight. Not getting voted off was the first thing Sean and Dirk thought of in the morning and the last thing on their minds at night. Dirk had an outlet for his worry, placing all his cares in God's very large hands. But Sean shouldered the burden alone. The weight had crushed his carefree spirit. His wit had become forced. The not knowing was incredibly painful.

Back in the "living room," Susan and Kelly fixed the sitting benches and rearranged stray pieces of driftwood and palm fronds. "Who do you think got voted off last night?" Kelly asked carelessly.

"Oh, I'm sure it was that Ramona. It's because of her attitude. Attitude is everything."

"Yeah. I think you're right." Kelly put the finishing touches on the job. She stood back a step and admired their work.

"I'm gonna make another spear," Susan said, standing up straight. She wandered off without looking at the finished job in the living room. That was her way. From one task straight into another. Working, she said, helped her think. "What're you gonna do?"

"I'm gonna exercise. Then I think I'll sew."

"Sure. Let's go into the jungle and find some tapioca roots in a bit." The women exchanged knowing smiles. No one else could find the precious tapioca root but them. Last time Sean and Dirk had volunteered to find tapioca they'd failed miserably. Instead of a handful of robust roots they'd come back with a few shriveled, inedible, maggot-infested plants.

"OK."

On the raft, Sean and Dirk hadn't had a nibble. But as Kelly did calf raises on the hard sand at water's edge, Richard lumbered from the surf carrying two rays and a fish. A tattoo of three humpback whales was on the left side of his chest. He had once played college water polo and rowed crew, so Richard had both an affinity for the water and enormous upper body strength. He'd gained a fair amount of weight in the fifteen years since, but was as comfortable bare-chested as ever.

Richard had become a worker in a way that played to his passion for water, spending five to six long hours every day in the ocean spearing fish. Back on land, he wove into the fabric of tribal life through inclusive conversation and a lively spirit. His friendship with Rudy was the most visible reminder. "We've become real good friends," Rudy said fondly of Richard. It was his most ringing endorsement yet. As a disclaimer for his old Navy buddies, Rudy added, "but not in no homosexual way."

Still, they were friends, and Rudy wasn't afraid to say so. For Richard to break down Rudy's homophobia and become a confidante was a sign Richard's popularity and place on the island transcended mere political correctness. Rudy and Richard, in fact, had become so close that members of the crew were comparing them to Darth Vader and Luke Skywalker, wondering aloud if Rudy weren't actually Richard's father. In a metaphorical, psychological sense, that notion may not have been far off the mark. More germane to Richard and his icon status was the fact that Rudy's attitude towards homosexuals was a brusque representation of mankind's historic take on gay life. Gays were weak, they were effeminate, they pranced.

Richard was showing the lie to those myths. Once "Survivor" aired, all of America, just like Rudy, would see Richard for being much more than a stereotype. The man was a flat-out, true blue, made-for-TV survivor. At thirty-eight, the product of West Point with an adopted nine-year old son seemed like he'd prepared his whole life for the experience. Indeed, he had. "Survivor" was more social survival than physical survival (despite the withering waistlines). It was an arena where hiding your true self, sharing secrets with only trusted friends, and existing under constant scrutiny in a tribal environment would determine the winner. No one on the island had lived that life before but Richard.

Those skills had translated into building the Tagi alliance—Richard, Rudy, Susan, Kelly—and planning his upcoming intertribal alliance. Entering the fifth three-day cycle on the island, the two tribes were just six days from merging. Richard already had his partners from Pagong selected. The point of Richard's alliances were not to band together and vote someone else off. That was too negative. Richard wandered through life constantly in search of positives.

The smarter goal—the one practiced only by Richard of Tagi and Gervase of Pagong—was finding people who would never, ever, not under any circumstances, vote against you. Get a majority of these people, and the Tribal Council was a happy ritual—a chance to hobnob with Chief Jeff on national television—instead of an ordeal. When the island was populated with sixteen people, that sort of alliance building was almost impossible. But with each tribe down to six, a majority alliance meant finding just three friends. So Rich got Rudy. Then he struck up a connection with that power block of Susan and Kelly and he had his four. Easy as pie. Let Sean and Dirk twist in the wind. They were too weak—too susceptible to the whims of emotion—to make good partners.

Richard's politicking sealed Sean and Dirk's fate. There were two more Tribal Councils before the merging of the tribes. Even if Tagi never won another Immunity Challenge, Richard and his allies were guaranteed to make that crucial final ten. They would never vote against each other, which meant all four would either vote for Sean or Dirk. Simple math said one of those two would go. In his more base moments, Richard even sidled up to his playmates to pick whether it should be Sean or Dirk. In this manner Tagi, though still a hardworking family, fragmented. Like a nation moving beyond subsistence, Tagi was able to shift its focus from getting by to getting ahead.

The beauty of Richard's manipulation was that Susan thought she was in charge. This made Richard unthreatening to the Wisconsin truck driver. That was important because Sue was quick to get rid of threats. Where Richard survived through social adeptness, lifelong hunter Susan had a special eye for clues and cues. Both looked like they were settling in for a long stay on Pulau Tiga.

Just as Richard's gayness didn't define him, neither did Susan's self-professed redneck qualities. Sure, she drove a truck, loved "The Drew Carey Show," and had an amazingly large black panther tattoo climbing up her back. She preferred *Penthouse* to the *National Review*. And back home she hunted often with her husband. Susan was a woman who possessed a stellar work ethic. Her hero was her father, because he taught her she could do anything she wanted in life—even something as crazy as electing to be stranded on a deserted island to win a million dollars.

When Susan was asked before the trip what qualities she valued in others for island life, her answer was brisk: "Hard work." At home she got up at 2:45 A.M. to begin her twelve-hour work day. As a trucker, she got paid by the load. The more she hauled, the larger her income. There was no difference in island life. Susan abhorred laziness and slacking in everyone. The more the tribe worked, the richer their lives would be.

What bothered Susan most about Dirk was the Bible reading and what she perceived as a lazy work ethic. With Sean it was the long workouts and endless pontifications designed to show mental superiority ("Kenniff's Intelligence Pyramid" was a favorite), but she felt that he did very little actual work. Sean and Dirk ignored Susan at their folly, figuring the tribe needed their strength and speed for challenges. But the day when their physical talents made or broke Tagi's fortunes was passing and they weren't savvy enough to see it. Sean and Dirk were doomed. Susan would see to it.

Susan liked Kelly, though. The river guide with the pierced tongue was like a daughter. The two worked side by side, gossiping and bonding. The process grew more pronounced once they became the only two women left in the tribe. "Do you realize," Susan said to Kelly as they searched for tapioca roots the afternoon of Day Thirteen, "that we are stranded on a deserted island with a neurotic doctor, a confused virgin, a masculine gay guy, and an old grump?"

Kelly had come to rely on Susan for insights like that. It seemed as though Kelly suspended her own thought processes in Susan's company. Susan was so worldly and had such insight. Plus, it felt like home to have a dynamic maternal figure so close. Kelly was the product of a single-parent household. Her mother raised four girls while attending college, then graduate school—and finishing at the top of her class. When Kelly considered applying for "Survivor" it was her mother who told her she was "bad-ass" enough to win.

The dilemma for Kelly on the island would be the same one Kelly faced in daily life: Stepping out from under that maternal shadow. She was trying, but the process felt too daunting. It was much easier to channel that energy into rage and self-destruction. The massive tattoo on her lower back and the pierced tongue were signs of that.

The old saying that "A man isn't a man until his father tells him so," could have applied, maternally, to Kelly. She wanted to do great things with her life, wanted to realize her potential. She was funny and smart and calm under pressure, but none of that translated into the heady independence of matriarchal authority. And though she had accomplished marvelous things in her life already, including guiding her own boat through the Grand Canyon on a three-week trip, Kelly would never be a grown woman until someone told her so. Or until she empowered herself by voting her symbolic mother off the island.

"I think," Kelly said to no one in particular late that afternoon, "the final five will be myself, Susan, Richard, Greg, and Gretchen. I would vote Richard off."

She waded out to where Sean was shaving his chest. He and Dirk had failed to catch any fish. "Boys who shave their chests," she said to him, sounding just like Susan, "are sissy boys. They're conceited, city slickers, and fancy pants."

Sean tried to make a joke, but he had nothing to say. What could he say? The alliance was strong. The last thing he wanted to do was offend one of its members. There was a slim chance they might change their mind about him.

Susan and Kelly supplanted Rudy as cooks that night, throwing tapioca and wild garlic into the rice. Then Richard led a group discussion on homosexuality that lasted long after the sun set.

As Sean and Dirk faced another long night of worry, the alliance relaxed. After all, they had plenty of good food, a nice climate, and thought-provoking conversation. What was there to worry about?

DAY FOURTEEN

The Malaysian field rat is not one the world's larger species of rat. The dreaded New York sewer rat, for instance, grows as big as a small cat. The Malaysian field rat is little more than a big mouse, and has about as much meat on it as a chicken wing. A banded krait coughs down a Malaysian field rat as easily as a baseball fan scarfs peanuts during the seventh-inning stretch.

They're not big rats.

But on the morning of Day Fourteen, a single Malaysian field rat roasting over a beach campfire was Pagong's breakfast. Joel did the cooking, extending a long skewer over the flames. The others looked on ravenously, waiting for their single half-swallow of rat meat. They would eat fish if they could, but Pagong was convinced the ocean off their beach was fishless. They'd given up trying. If Tagi were the island's "haves," Pagong were definitely the "have-nots." Instead of empowering themselves by working harder, like Tagi, the Pagongs victimized themselves. They wandered about and sat about and lay about and complained. All their problems were someone else's doing, especially their lack of food.

And food was their money. So they savored each grain of rice, because Gretchen made sure it was rationed carefully. And they sipped water from the canteens instead of guzzling, because it wasn't like turning on a faucet back home—the sooner the canteens were empty, the sooner someone would have to walk to the well and fill them again. And when Greg or one of the other guys caught a rat—a freaking *rat*—it was a great, great day.

That's what life had become for Pagong by Day Fourteen, and it all revolved around food. Without food Pagong's youthful enthusiasm had been replaced by crankiness and listlesssness. Their beach, for lack of a better word, was a slum. Compared with Tagi's smart, raked stretch of sand, where a foot never chanced upon a stray scrag of coral, Pagong's beach was a no man's land. Colleen had progressed beyond thin into bony, with her hair snarled and straggly all day, as if she'd just risen from bed.

Either Pagong did something quickly to save their tribe or they would all soon be too weak to be competitive at Immunity Challenges. They would get their chance that afternoon. A Reward Challenge named "The Battle of Borneo" would ask each tribe to select their best marksman in the blow dart, slingshot, and spear toss. The winning team would receive a basket of fresh fruit—watermelon, lemon, mango, apple, and even the odiferous durian. (Though the durian's fruit is soft and tropical in flavor, its aroma is Swiss cheese meets beached fish rotting in the sun.)

Pagong desperately needed to win that fruit, even the smelly durian. If ever the time had come to empower themselves, that was it.

Jenna practiced all day, as if their survival depended on it, honing newly-discovered blow dart skills. Joel and Gervase practiced spear throwing, trying to decide which one would throw at the competition, though everyone knew alpha male Joel wouldn't dream of letting Gervase steal potential glory. And on slingshot, Gretchen plunked away with bits of small rock and coral. She was a natural, hitting almost everything she shot at. While Pagong wasn't sure if Jenna was up to the blow dart thing, or whether Joel had the right stuff to knock off Tagi's spear thrower, not a single tribe member doubted Gretchen would win the slingshot competition. That's just the way it was with Gretchen—she was good at everything.

Testimony to her ability was her continued existence as a member of the Beach House (or, in their latest moniker from the production crew, "Party of Five"). Though Pagong's oldest tribal member—at thirty-eight, she was the same age as Susan Hawk and Richard Hatch—Gretchen Cordy was considered non-expendable. When Pagong's members talked privately about people who should be voted off, names like Jenna and Colleen came up frequently; after that came Joel and Gervase and an increasingly moody Greg. But Gretchen had a cold practicality and a maternal affection to her that, combined with her athleticism, made her great to have around.

And her appeal wasn't limited to Pagong. Richard was eyeing Gretchen for his alliance when the tribes merged. The initial merger would form a ten-member tribe. With Gretchen's fifth vote, his bloc would always control at least 50 percent of the Tribal Council vote.

But no one knew if Gretchen would join that alliance. For all her pragmatism, she could be an emotional and maternal woman. The boys and girls of Pagong were her children. Though she sometimes tired of their antics and might turn away from them while eating, Gretchen made it her business to ration the food supply and keep the compound as clean as possible. When the yellow Pagong banner dropped to the ground, it was Gretchen who picked it up and planted it firmly in the sand again. Noticing the lethargy of her fellow tribe members, she worried about their limited diet and tried to imagine creative ways to increase their daily caloric intake. She even stated candidly that she would rather vote herself off than vote off someone she liked. Coming from anyone else on the island, that statement would have sounded like a fib for the cameras. Coming from Gretchen, a compassionate woman whose heroes were Mother Teresa and Jimmy Carter, there was no doubt she grappled with that fear. "I wouldn't feel right about myself winning the million dollars if I had to change my behavior to do it," she stated flatly when asked about alliances. "I'm not going to vote someone off just because other people tell me to."

In a perfect world, if anyone deserved to win the million dollars, it was Gretchen, and not just because she was a good person. She was very smart, for one thing, with an IQ of 142. And her survival skills were so highly thought of when she first attended the U.S. Air Force's survival school that her classmates voted her the Cadre Award as the person most exemplifying "the spirit of survival." Amazingly, she was the only woman in her class. Her instructors thought so highly of her ability and work ethic that she was invited to become one of them. She eventually spent six years training fighter pilots to survive in all sorts of hostile environments. She gave that up to become a part-time preschool teacher. The shirt she chose to bring to the island—a lightweight survival shirt of a non-cotton material—had the names and stick figure representations of kids from her preschool class sewn on the back. Just looking at the shirt gave her inspiration.

Problem was, Gretchen was getting tired of life on Pulau Tiga and it wasn't just the food. Unlike the rest of Pagong, she had an actual life back in America. She missed her husband and two kids. She worried that her nine-year-old daughter was lonely, because the two always hung out together. Gretchen was too tough to quit, but getting voted off wasn't going to break her heart. So she wasn't likely to join Richard's alliance if it didn't feel right to her.

To "Survivor"'s crew, a group that never ceased to be amazed at the growing duplicity of castaway life (answering another abstract question:

how far would you bend your morals for a million dollars?), Gretchen's integrity was like a breath of fresh air. Mention of Gretchen's name in the production compound brought forth responses like "Don't you just love her?" and, "She must be going crazy over there at Pagong." The desire to see her win was almost unanimous. She was wholesome, she was a survivalist, she looked great in a bathing suit. She was worthy.

And while Gretchen didn't see eye to eye with her tribe members on everything—she'd butted heads with Joel so often that she had stopped listening to him—their island survival meant everything to her. She approached every challenge as if it were mortal combat. So although she gabbed happily with Tagi upon arriving at the "Battle of Borneo" Reward Challenge that afternoon, almost collapsing with relief to be enjoying adult conversation, there was blood in her eye when it came time for the slingshot competition. Jenna had already split with Sean in the blow dart competition. Each had successfully embedded darts into a half-dozen fruit targets. The rules stated that tribes got to keep whatever fruit they hit. That meant Pagong had enough fruit to last one day, maybe two if they rationed properly.

That wasn't good enough for Gretchen. She wanted to return to their beach with enough fruit to feed them for at least a week. With that goal in mind, she stepped to the line against Richard. Gretchen looked small and hard next to his fleshy immenseness. Ten yards from them was an array of fresh fruit and clay pots. Hit the fruit or break a pot, it was all the same—that fruit belonged to your team. Both shooters would fire at their own pace for two minutes.

On Chief Jeff's order, they commenced firing.

If the world of slingshot marksmanship ever gets around to selecting their version of Annie Oakley, it should select Gretchen Cordy. Wrist-rocket strapped in place, right eye squinched shut for proper aim, she shot rapidly and accurately. As soon as one shot hit its mark she immediately reloaded. Fruit juice bled all over the ground after being perforated with one small pellet after another. And while Richard was hitting his share of fruit, he was no match for Gretchen. When two minutes were up, the disparity between the fruit she'd won and the fruit he'd won was enormous. Thanks to Gretchen, Pagong was going home with a full shopping cart.

Then Chief Jeff announced a rule change—a twist, just for the sake of drama. "The spear-throwing contest will be winner-take-all. Losing team

goes back to their beach with nothing. Winning team goes back with *all* the fruit from both team's baskets and a special mystery prize."

Gretchen was crestfallen. All that hard work . . . that marksmanship . . . why, she could almost feel the red ripeness of watermelon dribbling down her chin. And now Pagong's fate rested in the hands of alpha male Joel. Of all the people . . . . Sometimes island living could be so unfair.

But winning the Big One was an alpha male specialty. It was fitting that Joel had the tribe's fate in his hands. He was the sort of individual, whether in football, basketball, or spear throwing, that wanted control with the Big Game on the line. Not only out of some dominance issue, but because—and that was the crux of being a true alpha male—they believed nobody could do the job better. And they were right. This was just such a moment.

Gretchen realized that. She knew Joel would come through. She set aside her disappointment and cheered her teammate on.

Joel, of course, couldn't have been happier. He was primed. Island living had made him lean and well-defined. His tan was almost bronze. Spear in hand, he strutted around the target area in just shorts. The man whose pet rottweiler, Zeus, waited back home in Sherwood, Arkansas, looked island-like and primal. But the island had brought out a greater compassion in Joel, as well. He had become less sarcastic and more willing to listen to others. For all their troubles, he cared deeply for his tribe mates. He felt responsible for their ultimate fate.

Facing off against Joel was Susan, the alpha female. She wore her eyeglasses for the occasion. Her shoulders were as broad as Joel's. She meant to kick his ass on national television and had stated as much to all of Tagi. Joel was the sort of man whose ego might never recover from losing to a woman. (Well, at least not for an hour or so.)

"Five throws each," Chief Jeff informed them calmly. "The throw closest to the center of the target wins. Remember, this is winner-take-all. No win, no fruit."

Susan was very good. She and her husband once managed a hunting lodge in the woods of Ontario, and hunting was still her favorite hobby. Anything having to do with targets was a natural extension of her thought process. But Joel sealed the victory with his fourth throw. He missed the bull's eye by just six inches. On a circular target taller than a man, that was a pretty great throw.

The cheer of relief and euphoria from Pagong was probably the most genuine display of emotion they'd shown on the island. They screamed and leapt about like a baseball team that had just won the World Series. Pagong wins!! Pagong wins!! Food!! Food!!

"And here's that mystery food item I told you about . . ." Chief Jeff gestured to a crate, then walked over and pulled out a live white pullet. ". . . three egg-laying chickens." He paused as Pagong looked on incredulously. "What are you going to name them?"

"Breakfast, lunch, and dinner," Jenna piped up.

Back at their beach, Pagong chose to let the chickens live a couple days longer. First they wanted eggs for breakfast.

The tribe sat around eating their fruit happily. Greg gave a lengthy, sincere speech thanking everyone for the good time he was having.

Of course, all that was too much seriousness for one day. Much to Gretchen's horror, her fellow tribe members began a food fight with their new winnings. They threw everything but the chickens before she screamed at them to come to their senses. "Don't waste food!!" It was like talking to children.

The food fight stopped. An hour later, thanks to the sudden infusion of fruit into his diet, Gervase had his first bowel movement since arriving on the island. "It felt," he screamed to his teammates, "like trying to pass New Jersey though the Holland Tunnel!"

Gretchen laughed along with everyone else. Sometimes island life was, well, not so bad.

DAY FIFTEEN

Dirk Been had no idea Day Fifteen would be his last on Pulau Tiga. The previous night had ended lightly enough, with Sean and Dirk discussing the question, "What's the most gay thing you've ever done for a girl?" This segued into Dirk asking Sean another toughie: "Would you break up with a girl if she told you to give up pizza?"

That philosophical vein continued first thing in the morning, with an hour of Bible study and prayer. Taking to heart Christ's admonition to pray alone, Dirk removed himself from the tribe. He opened his heart, hoping to hear the words of inspiration that would help him make it through another long day of island living. Without Christ, Dirk doubted if he would be able to last much longer. Physically and mentally, he was suffering greatly. He was hungry all the time, and aware that he and Sean were outcasts.

The Book of Romans reminded Dirk to embrace, not run away from, his suffering. "For suffering produces perseverance; perseverance, character; and character, hope. And hope does not disappoint us." The Book of James also told him to go the distance. "Consider it pure joy, my brothers, whenever you face trials of many kinds, because you know that the testing of your faith develops perseverance. Perseverance must finish its work so that you may be mature and complete."

And, of course, the four Gospels told of Jesus fasting forty days and nights in the desert. He was tempted by a serpent, and encouraged to sin, but did not.

The parallel between forty days in the desert and thirty-nine days on a deserted island wasn't lost on Dirk. He had come to Pulau Tiga adamant that he would ignore temptation, and not compromise himself for television or fame or fortune. Most of all, he would not turn his back on Christ during that time. Just because it wasn't politically correct to crack a Bible on national television didn't mean Dirk wasn't going to do it. The rebel in

him even delighted in being contrary like that. The evangelist in him—
Jesus called on all his followers to evangelize—hoped that his example
might lead others to Christ. "By their deeds you will know them," Christ
said. If just one soul was saved through Dirk's time on Pulau Tiga, that
would be a very great thing.

Dirk read by the amber light of dawn. The air was relatively cool and
smelled new, thanks to a torrential rain of two hours the night before.
Driftwood and tiny bits of tree bark coated the beach, as it always did
after a storm. The sun was friendly. Within an hour the heat would be too
intense to read for very long. Beads of sweat would roll down Dirk's long,
aquiline nose onto the thin pages of his Bible. Sand fleas and mosquitoes
would start feasting on his ankles. Jungle humidity would wrap around
him like a blanket, sabotaging his attempts to focus.

Thoughts of the tribe kept interrupting Dirk's prayers. Except for
Sean, they all thought he was a slacker. Dirk knew that as he prayed they
were making breakfast back at camp. And he also realized that if he set
aside his prayer time to run back to the cooking fire and help them, his
time on the island might be extended. But he wouldn't do it. God's plan
for Dirk Been had brought him to Pulau Tiga. It was God's plan that
would send him home. Whether that would be after fifteen days or thirty-
nine, Dirk didn't know. All he could do was pray and wait for God's will
to be done. Compromising time of prayer with something as earthly as
making breakfast wouldn't help matters a bit—and might just hurt.

Dirk sang a quiet hymn. He prayed for his tribe members. His prayer
was that Tagi get along with each other, and that they worked well as a
team during the afternoon's Immunity Challenge. He prayed for the tribe
even though he knew they were bonding against him and saying mean
things about his faith. The tribe didn't understand why he walked away
when they talked about subjects such as "Does size really matter to a
woman?" and "What does it feel like to get molested as a child?" They
thought he was being aloof or judgmental. He wasn't. Dirk walked away
so he wouldn't be seen on national television yielding to those thoughts.
Those temptations. Because those thoughts led to other thoughts—sinful
thoughts. And Dirk didn't think he was strong enough to do battle with
those thoughts. Better to avoid them altogether.

During "Survivor"'s application process, psychologist Ondrusek char-
acterized Dirk as a complex personality—someone who adopts an outside

structure system to bind up negative impulses. Rather than incorporate negative impulses into their lives, they shun them out of great fear.

Dirk often felt confused inside—about island life and women and temptation and what his future back home would be like. He'd done some work with handicapped children, but was unemployed when he left for Pulau Tiga. What he would do for a living, or even a career, was something he was still trying to figure out. A coach at Baylor University had offered him the chance to work with their basketball team and go to grad school. Dirk had turned him down politely. He was done with school.

Besides, who wanted to waste time in school when life was so short?

Dirk prayed and prayed. His time was running out. The sun was making its presence known. Behind him, the jungle was coming to life. The geckos were making their peculiar barking noise—it sounded like someone had smuggled a small dog onto the island. The car-alarm screech of cicadas bounced around the treetops. In fifteen days Dirk's body had adapted to the island heat, so hundred-degree days felt more like seventy back home. He had a coating on his face resembling a beard. His face was sharp from hunger, accentuating his receding hairline.

A bead of sweat trickled down Dirk's right sideburn. He wiped it away, then wiped the hand on his shirt before reading his Bible again. The thin pages tore too easily to risk turning them with a wet finger.

Dirk promised himself he wouldn't join an alliance. He didn't like the way the "Survivor" game was played, not when it became duplicitous and mean-spirited. If not joining an alliance got him voted off, that was God's will.

Dirk squirmed uncomfortably atop his log. Ants crawled across his shorts and down his bare legs. He swished them away, then quickly reached the back of one hand to his forehead and wiped away more sweat. A glance at the sky showed nothing but bright blue. The day would be a scorcher. He closed his Bible. He prayed again for his tribe, and stood to walk back to them. At that moment he decided that if he was voted off that night, he would leave his Bible behind for Tagi to read. Maybe it would give them comfort.

And so Dirk Been's missionary outreach to Pulau Tiga came to an end that night. He left his Bible at Tagi Beach, then walked to the Tribal Council, where he pleaded his case about being hard-working and misunderstood. He was still voted off.

After the Tribal Council, Dirk ate a dozen pieces of chicken and a tub of rice. After that, he ate shrimp for the first time in his life. Then the farm boy spent his last night on Pulau Tiga sitting on a small bench at the edge of the production compound. Under a sky shot through with stars, he stared out to sea until dawn. It was time to go back to Wisconsin.

Evolution Six

Fear and Loathing on Pulau Tiga

Day Sixteen

Pulau Tiga was being invaded, starting with the pair of Green Berets who waded ashore and promptly adopted the Sand Spit as their domain. Until their arrival the outside world was merely an image on the horizon after a cleansing storm, when the hills of Borneo seemed close enough to touch. The *Sabah Daily* arrived every three days by boat from the Magellan Sutera, along with Gene Ondrusek (who learned to weather Kevorkian jokes early on, as he only came to Pulau Tiga for a castaway's good-bye). But the news was only local and the sports, primarily Spanish League soccer. No one but the Malaysian sherpas who humped gear day in and day out bothered reading it, and then only after watching hours and hours of Filipino MTV.

The reason: real world reality was a dull substitute for island reality. And island reality was the all-encompassing passion—to know the elaborate interactions and politicking between tribes. As if watching a soap opera unfold, the crew speculated openly about the fate of despised and beloved castaways. And as with all good soap operas, the despised and the beloved traded places on a daily basis. Nothing else really mattered.

Lost in the reality of "Survivor" life, and the day-to-day routine of camera crews living in that reality, was the fact that "Survivor" was a TV show. Beginning on Day Sixteen, the press would reinforce that awareness by invading the island to write about the production (life imitating

99

art imitating life) and even to film the crews as the crews filmed the cast-aways. This onslaught of the production compound would last two weeks. Like the end of *Swiss Family Robinson*, when the family so desper-ate to return to civilization are saddened when that moment finally ar-rives, "Survivor"'s crew grew protective of their way of life when their island was invaded.

But it had to be done. "Survivor" was in the unusual predicament of needing publicity to build an audience, and stifling publicity so vital de-tails about castaway life wouldn't be leaked before the show began airing in late May. A huge part of the show's allure would be the viewing audi-ence not knowing, episode by episode, who was about to get voted off. Se-crecy was paramount. The production crew had all signed gag orders. Signs posted about the production compound—above the water cooler, next to the telephone, next to the "Big White Board" where production schedules were posted daily in blue and red dry-erase marker—stated in large bold letters: "Remember.... You have signed a confidentiality agreement for this show. There should be no discussion of the results of Tribal Councils or the Tribe's stories with anyone at any time."

Spouses back home, children, best friends, email buddies—discussion with anyone was forbidden. The crew was strict in keeping the vow of se-crecy. If the show hadn't felt important to the crew—if at some level these industry professionals didn't believe they were doing something ground-breaking and important—those details would have sifted into the western world by phone and email like water through a sieve. But the show mat-tered. That's what made six weeks on the island bearable. And so the news embargo held.

The press, of course, made it their business to try to crack that em-bargo. A low-grade curiosity about "Survivor" was spreading through America. CBS had only released the names and hometowns of the cast-aways, but newspapers and websites had taken to speculating on the fate of each. Of all the castaways voted off in the show's first eighteen days, only B.B. went straight home (Ramona and Stacey went traveling in Thai-land, Sonja and Dirk hung out at the Magellan Sutera in Kota Kinabalu). "B.B. sightings" were soon reported all over Kansas City, and websites quickly spread the word that he wasn't the million-dollar castaway.

Before coming to the island, all invited members of the press had signed confidentiality agreements similar to the crew's. They were forbidden to write about who had been voted off or who still remained. But each journalist made it his business to find loopholes in the agreement— some precious nugget of information about castaways and crew hating each other, or about physical deprivation leading to mental breakdown. They were just doing their jobs.

The press itinerary included a preview of the rough edit of the first show, a meal on the compound deck, a night on the beaches with the tribes (mostly spent in a dome tent, listening to rats fight outside), then another morning back in the compound, and a boat ride back to the Magellan Sutera Five-Star Air-Conditioned-Spa-Bar-Dining-Room-Lap-of-Luxury-Completely-Different-from-Pulau-Tiga Hotel. Somewhere between the moment their chartered boat arrived on the island and the time it left they morphed from being frightened of Pulau Tiga to feeling mildly comfortable. Once that moment arrived, they would slip away from their CBS handler, and cull a lone crew member from the flock, like a wolf spotting the weakest lamb to slaughter. Then the tape recorder would be clicked on—sometimes surreptitiously—and they would con-spiratorially whisper absurd questions like "So what's the real scoop?" or "Has anyone snapped yet?"

Then it was back to Los Angeles and Sydney and New York to write and run stories about the crazy goings-on over there on that little tiny blip

of land fifty miles off the Land of Headhunters. Some came to the island with the preconceived notion that "Survivor" was the most original show in the history of television. Some thought it was an abomination. None, however, seemed to notice that merely by setting foot on Pulau Tiga they had become cast members in the "production." With every passing day, life on Pulau Tiga was becoming more surreal.

The press' presence was the greatest reminder to the production crew that Pulau Tiga had changed them. The new visitors seemed milky-pale and bloated, like they needed a good sweat. Their clothing was too heavy and clean, and their manner walking the island trails entirely too cautious. By Day Sixteen, even the most urbane crew members were tripping along jungle paths as easily as walking through Central Park. Many even made the walk barefoot, except at night when the snakes came out in force. Or they hiked to the mud volcano for "treatments," coating their bodies in the grey mud, then letting it dry on the way back.

But no one ventured alone through the swampy southwest corner of the island where the reticulated pythons lived. Though the pythons ate a large meal just once a month, when they finally felt a powerful hunger coming on they had an annoying habit of positioning themselves in tree branches directly above trails. Lunch would invariably wander along and the snake would fall—literally, all twenty-five feet and three hundred pounds—onto their prey. The weight and force would stun, then the python would wrap lunch in a stranglehold and squeeze the life out of it. Unlike their smaller cousin, the Burmese python, reticulated pythons ate people. Their circumference approached that of a small ice chest. Crew members were warned by Borneo locals to travel in pairs through that section of jungle. If they smelled rotting flesh they were to stop and look up quickly into the trees—then turn around and run the other way. The smell of rotting flesh was synonymous with python. No one had bothered to give Pulau Tiga's wild pigs that advice; hence, they were no more.

The Green Berets knew a great recipe for python steak, so they weren't much worried about ranging through that southwest corridor. Sent to the island by the United States Army (a "Survivor" sponsor), Chief Warrant Officer James Lofton and First Sergeant William Wright did a daily jungle run right through python country. Training, of course, wasn't why they'd flown all the way to Pulau Tiga from Fort Lewis, Washington. The final inter-tribal Immunity Challenge would be a military-style, half-mile obstacle course atop the Sand Spit—wall climb, rope swing, low crawl, and much more. It would be the ultimate physical contest of "Survivor," a last great opportunity for tribes to work as teams before the merger. Lofton and Wright were to design and help build the course, then put the tribes through their paces.

Lofton was square and taciturn, a former policeman who'd joined the Green Berets to pad his resume sixteen years before and stayed. Wright had an angular face and an incredible ability to make and hold eye contact. Both spoke in the clipped, jargon-riddled language of the professional soldier. Their appearance and demeanor were markedly different from the production crew's, and they preferred to camp instead of sleep indoors, but Lofton and Wright insinuated themselves into the fabric of island living. Quickly grasping that they were now part of "Survivor"'s revolving cast of characters, they enjoyed a cold beer with the crew at the end of the working day. Promptly to bed at ten, then up again at dawn, the Green Berets worked twelve-hour shifts building an authentic military obstacle course (albeit of bamboo and ironwood). Their presence brought a certain hardcore mentality to the proceedings. I had faith that the end result would push the castaways to their mental, physical, and emotional limits.

Though Tagi desperately needed the win, it was Pagong that was almost assured of victory. Athleticism and youth were their hallmarks. Joel's clutch toss that won the chicken and fruit had restored their energy. Winning the Immunity Challenge a day later had given them momentum. Pagong were cocky for the first time in a week and had every reason to believe all six of them would remain when the tribes merged. That would give them a majority over Tagi's four. With the exception of Gretchen, all of Pagong favored—though only in the abstract—a voting bloc that would vote Tagi off, one by one. Only then would Pagong cannibalize their ranks.

Along with youth, however, came insecurity. That made alliance-building difficult, for Pagong's members were all more concerned with asserting personal independence than succumbing to the will of a leader. Greg, for instance, was beginning to display signs of disturbing behavior. He had taken to walking the beaches speaking into an empty coconut shell. The coconut was his "nature phone," he said. A voice in the phone spoke to him. Greg was hard at work on a satellite dish to increase reception. He was increasingly agitated that producer John Feist was asking the other members of Pagong specific questions about Greg's passive leadership. It was like Feist was giving the other tribe members a road map into Greg's brain.

Gervase, on the other hand, had begun objectifying women. The statement that "nothing is dumber than a woman, except maybe a cow" enraged Jenna, Colleen, and Gretchen. When Joel laughed a bit too hard at Gervase's comment, he was painted with the same brush. Gervase, the Teflon castaway, was only too happy to let Joel take some of the heat. Gretchen, especially, thought Joel overtly sexist. Meanwhile, Gervase gloated that he had contributed absolutely nothing to the group. Having done the bare minimum to avoid his tribe members' wrath, Gervase was sure his charm would be enough to allow him to win.

Another, more empowering, sign of independence came from Colleen and Jenna. Colleen had begun to bridle at being known as Greg's kitten. She still reveled in being smart-ass and sarcastic, like him, but was moving away from Greg. Having received two votes at Pagong's previous Tribal Council visit, Colleen was suddenly aware that Greg wasn't providing protection. He was, instead, a liability, ready to "snap the kitten's neck" and bent on twisting the game to his own means. She was aware that Greg thought himself smarter than the other "tiny little brains" on the island—including her. Slowly, the Miami college student began to plot her move out from Greg's shadow.

Jenna, on the other hand, had lost her manic edge and was showing an amazing sweetness. The happy-go-lucky cheerleader from Day One was now a competitive, slightly subdued member of Pagong. Island life had scrubbed away her defenses, revealing that she was deeply insecure and had deep feelings of anger towards men. She longed for independence from their betrayals. Just like Gretchen, she was enraged at Joel and Gervase's disparaging comments about women. But Jenna was too tired to be confrontational with her rage, and was content to let Gretchen stew.

Jennifer Leigh Lewis was, in many ways, a remarkable woman. The Franklin, New Hampshire, native had gotten pregnant at nineteen. She was unmarried, but ignored advice that she have an abortion. Twin girls, Sabrina and Sadie, were the result. Though Jenna married, she was soon separated and raising the girls alone. The independence made her stronger, and when the call for "Survivor" applicants went out, Jenna had just fulfilled her dream of pursuing a higher education by attending a local technical school. On the island, this woman whose hero was Joan of Arc and whose favorite topics of conversation centered around injustice toward women (sexual politics in Afghanistan, birth control in China) finally saw her life slow down. For the first time ever, she had long periods to think without distraction. The surplus of energy she used to hide her sadness and fears subsided, and she was able to look into her heart to prioritize the things that really mattered in life. Her love for her girls grew deeper with each passing day. What bothered Jenna most was that people back home insinuated that she was a bad mother for leaving Sadie and Sabrina for almost two months. Jenna's competitive side came forth on the same tide of emotion, feral and raw. Like Scarlett O'Hara swearing "As God is my witness I'll never go hungry again," Jenna stood on the sands of Pulau Tiga and swore she would win for herself and her girls.

A million dollars could buy a whole lot of independence.

Day Seventeen

Richard had a dream. He was on the Sand Spit with a man. Things were white hot, with lots of wrestling on the powdery earth. The tide lapped against their tawny bodies. The dream was vivid, with dialogue and in Technicolor. Sweat. Friction.

But it was pitch black when Richard woke up in the Tagi hooch, staring up at the nipa leaves lining the ceiling's interior. His four tribe members breathed silently. Their bodies were pressed close on the Philippine mahogany floorboards. With a sigh, he realized the fantasy wasn't real.

He willed himself back to sleep, but couldn't wait for morning. In the morning he would share the dream with Sean. For Sean had been the other man in the dream.

This new crush posed a dilemma for Richard. His artfully crafted alliance did not include the bright young neurosurgeon with the shaved chest, nipple ring, and careful stubble. Since it was almost certain Tagi would succumb to the Pagong juggernaut at the coming Immunity Challenge, Tagi would have to vote someone off. With Richard, Sue, Kelly, and Rudy all firmly ensconced in the alliance, that someone could only be Sean.

But he was so cute.

Richard never knew he could become so emotionally involved with his fellow tribe members. When camera crews questioned Richard directly about Sean he blushed. That wasn't the right way to wage war. And "Survivor" was most definitely war. Richard wondered how he might reconfigure the alliance to protect his little friend. Sue might be the answer. She had lately been threatened by Rudy. He was a lot smarter than she'd given him credit for. He was playing the game brilliantly, keeping his thoughts private, and saying provocative things for the camera about disdaining homosexuals and his fellow tribe members. "I wouldn't allow Richard in my home; wouldn't allow him to meet my family." But then Rudy, who could become downright gabby when it was in his best interests, would confide to Richard or Kelly that Richard's talks on homosexuality were enlightening. And Rudy was watching, watching, always watching, probing his fellow tribe members for weakness. Unbeknownst to Sue, before coming to Pulau Tiga Rudy had told a member of the production crew that if he had two weeks he "would figure everything out." After a shaky start, he seemed to be doing just that.

Susan had noticed Rudy's growing genius for this abstract new game called "Survivor." This made her nervous. She suggested to Richard that Rudy should go. Maybe the alliance could be just Richard, Kelly, and Susan. There was more loyalty in small numbers. Or maybe, Sean could take Rudy's place. That way Richard would have his alliance and a man to look at, as well.

But Richard, whom "Survivor" psychologist Ondrusek labeled as a consumate strategist, someone who had the game all figured out in his head, was incredibly disciplined about playing "Survivor." He knew Rudy was a solid partner. And certain sacrifices were necessary to gain a million dollars. So if someone had to go, it must be Sean.

For it was clear that young and immature Sean was itching to betray the Tagi alliance. He identified with Pagong members, especially Jenna, whom he flirted with at challenges. This meant Sean was likely to turn on his former Tagi comrades once the tribes merged.

On top of that, Sean had another agenda that made him a poor alliance partner. He nourished the rather smug belief that his great intelligence made him best suited to decide who was "worthy" of winning the million. As with all outrageousness during the tribal phase, that sort of boasting made him a target. But once the tribal phase ended, the "Survivor" game would change. It would be every man for himself. All Reward and Immunity Challenges would be individual. Instead of an entire tribe winning immunity, for instance, only the individual victor would be exempt from being voted off.

At that point things would really get strange.

The final nine castaways would be reunited (in addition to the two finalists, the other seven, after being kicked off Pulau Tiga, would be sequestered at the Magellan until the final vote). The winner would be the result of this vote.

A guy like Sean, who was physically fit and outwardly likeable, actually stood a chance of winning "Survivor"—*if he got past the tribal phase*. Once free of tribal alliances he could determine his own fate.

So while Richard pondered whether to let his sexual drive dictate his fate on "Survivor," Sean prayed with all his heart and soul that Tagi would win the final Immunity Challenge. He didn't know what that challenge would be yet, but from Tagi Beach he could look across the horizon and see something weird and monstrous being constructed on the Sand Spit. That something was obviously connected with the final Tribal Immunity Challenge. Sean wondered, worried, waited for the moment when the nature of that challenge would be revealed.

On the afternoon of Day Seventeen he got his answer.

Green Berets Lofton and Wright arrived unannounced on Tagi Beach, motoring to the beach in a dive boat. Producer Maria Baltazzi deliberately hadn't told Tagi of the landing, preferring the Green Beret "enter Tagi's reality" normally.

Lofton and Wright leapt from the boat when the chop was knee high. They waded ashore, a pair of latter-day Macarthur's. Dressed in boots and full camouflage outfits, their green berets angled just so, Lofton and Wright marched crisply to the Tagi fire pit. In curt but polite fashion they ordered Tagi to report to the Sand Spit the next day for the obstacle course Immunity Challenge.

Tagi, thrilled to see new faces, treated the Green Berets with deference. Richard and Rudy chatted them up about their military days. After ten minutes the Green Berets marched back down the beach to their waiting boat. The boat driver carefully navigated out through the reef fronting Tagi Beach and began motoring the mile north to Pagong.

In addition to the Green Berets and driver, I and a half dozen other production personnel were aboard. The fifteen-foot dive boat rode low in the water as a result of the weight. The South China Sea had been calm

when the dive boat left the production compound. But that was the leeward side of the island. Rounding the coast to the windward side to greet
the tribes, the skies turned dark. The approaching storm whipped up the
waves, tossing spray into the boat that drenched all aboard. Then the sea
calmed once the boat slipped into Tagi reef. The driver had had no problem coming into the beach.

Now, just as the most dangerous part of flying an airplane are the take-
offs and landings, the most dangerous part of piloting a boat is entering
and exiting the surf zone. Even in high seas, waves on the open ocean
don't curl and break as they do in the surf zone. When the sea is calm the
process of guiding a boat through waves is always troubling. When the sea
is roiled and angry, the maneuver is never less than perilous. A boat can
get turned sideways by a wave in a split second, then flipped over as casually as a rag doll in a spin cycle.

Entering Pagong Beach, the sea was an irate mess.

Without a reef to thwart breakers, surf rolled onto the beach in powerful sets. The storm was getting closer and the sea was so big that it
swamped over the boat's gunwales. As the driver moved in close to shore
a sudden wave spun the boat sideways. Three consecutive waves broke
over the boat until a foot of water filled the bottom and the boat lay lower
than ever in the water. With horror, everyone in the boat looked out to
sea and saw a monstrous wave bearing down. Rather than find out what it
was like to remain inside a boat during what sailors call a "rollover,"
everyone jumped overboard into the shoulder-high water and shoved on
the sides of the boat, trying to spin the nose out to sea. Somehow it
worked. The driver gunned the engines before the killer wave could crush
over his bow. His sinking boat wallowed out to sea, where it was safe for
the driver to begin bailing.

Soaking wet and rapidly losing their sense of humor, the Green Berets
approached the Pagong Tribe. Out of deference to Gretchen's military
background, the majority of Pagong chose to treat the Green Berets with
respect. Greg, however, immediately changed from his bathing suit into a
pair of shorts that were torn and exposed his genitals. He got out his nature phone. He began moaning that "Survivor" was becoming paramili-
tary, and began referring bitterly to Pagong as a "militia" instead of a tribe.

And while Greg eventually shut his mouth until the Green Berets left
(hiking back across the island with the production personnel) his barely

suppressed rage was becoming an issue. Though not physically violent, he was proving a master of mental manipulation. His goal was to control the pace of the island. To that end, he took to stalking camera crews when they trekked through the jungle. He delighted in leaping from bushes and scaring people. He recited rambling monologues into the camera, talking of the inner voices that guided him, and alluding to his genius compared with that of his tribe members and the production crew.

When Pagong went to the Tribal Council, Greg delighted in spewing odd sayings that made him look intelligent and insightful, or that skewered "Survivor" as absurd—like he was a part of the game, but removed from the game. As if he was better than the game.

But the harder he fought to act as though he were above it all, the more Greg became mired in the game. If he was going to screw with the production crew's reality, they were going to screw right back with his. John Feist became an expert at calling Greg's bluff on camera, holding him accountable for his antics and sayings. Greg was finding that he had little control over the game. All his life, Greg had been able to control social situations by entering and exiting on whim. And he had been able to do the same thing in the early days of "Survivor." But over an extended time, interacting with a limited group of people every minute of every day, his ability to manipulate dwindled. The happy otter look he feigned to disarm the world was being replaced by a hard stare. As his impotence grew, he began to allude to performing an act of violence against the island before he left.

While the rules of "Survivor" were proving pliable, Greg Buis' cold stare and Sean Kenniff's desperation and Richard Hatch's dreams were proving one fact irrefutable as the game grew longer: No matter how hard players tried to hide it, their truest selves eventually surfaced. On an island of multiple realities, the winner would be the person who dealt best with *that* reality.

Amid all this deception and scheming, a moment of community found its way to the men of Tagi. Richard came across the Bible Dirk had left. He opened it and began to read aloud. Rudy and Sean sat down to listen. For the next hour Richard continued to read. Rudy and Sean relaxed nearby with their eyes closed, savoring every word. Dirk had his prayers answered.

DAY EIGHTEEN

Sean Kenniff began what was sure to be his last day on Pulau Tiga scared stiff. The tribal merger was foremost on everyone's mind and his odds of making it that far in the game were thin. Wafer thin. He wore his fear and insecurity like a brightly decorated Malaysian sarong—wrapped tightly about him, one misstep away from revealing himself publicly.

Sean rose before dawn and sat alone before the fire while the rest of Tagi slept. The weight of his coming exit had prevented him from sleeping well. There were bags under his eyes and a resignation to his body language. In white sweatshirt and long green pants he sat, knees drawn tightly to his chest, arms folded. He ruminated aloud about the morning's Sand Spit Obstacle Course, saying Tagi shouldn't have voted Dirk off. Dirk was athletic and would have helped them win. Now Pagong had the upper hand. Sean rambled on, saying he knew he would go. There was no fight to him, no levity. The days of being Tagi's Seinfeld were past. Now he was just Sean Kenniff, hoping against hope that Tagi could produce a miracle on the obstacle course.

From his seat at the fire, Sean stared out toward the Sand Spit. The obstacle course poked into the air, backlit by the first pink glow of morning. Sean had volunteered to be one of Tagi's two competitors. The other was Kelly. Sean had rested the previous afternoon, making sure his legs were strong for what promised to be a half-mile of soft-sand running punctuated by whatever deviousness the Green Berets threw at him. In fact, all of Tagi lay in the sun and slept. Susan called it having a "Pagong Day."

"I've never even done an obstacle course," Sean said softly to himself, reaching into the fire to adjust a burning stick. "The closest I've come is high school gym class, and that was ten years ago." It had been a good eighteen days, Sean thought. He'd challenged himself, met some new friends, survived longer than five others.

Susan got out of the shelter and strolled down to the water. "'Morning, Susie!" Sean yelled cheerfully. He was back home, sitting on his porch, waving to the neighbor lady who was walking out to get her newspaper in her robe. All he needed was a mug of coffee to make the scene complete.

Susan waved back, but didn't answer. She wasn't awake yet.

"'Morning, Kelly."

Kelly didn't speak immediately either. She stopped at the fire before continuing to the beach for morning yoga. She wore a black bikini. Like a cat, she stretched before Sean. It wasn't a sensuous act, merely an absentminded morning sway to work out the kinks. Sean was like a brother to her, nothing more. She told him about a dream as he continued staring into the fire, and how she'd woken up halfway through the dream, then forced herself to fall back to sleep to let the dream finish. "You know how sometimes when you fall back to sleep you lose the dream?" Kelly said. It was just morning talk, meaningless patter that could have been directed at anyone. The steel ball of her pierced tongue interfered with making the letter S and the letter B, but the day when Sean paid attention to that was long past. Eighteen days, in fact.

"Oh, yeah. I hate when that happens." Sean thought about Richard's dream. It felt weird to be the subject of gay fantasy.

"Well, I was able to remember the dream and keep it going."

"Oh, that's great. I love that."

"Yeah."

Kelly swayed some more. She looked at the fire, then at the beach, trying to decide if the time was right for yoga. A camera crew had filmed

Sean and Kelly the entire time, but it was as though they didn't exist. Castaways' words and actions had become unfiltered, unaffected.

Sean stared out to the obstacle course once again. The sun was lighting up the Sand Spit. The day was cloudless. It would be hot out there, Sean knew. And heat led to dehydration, which led to reduced athletic performance. Maybe Pagong didn't know that. Sean made a mental note to drink plenty of water before heading out there. Every little bit helped.

Soon enough it was noon and time to race. Sean and Kelly stood at the starting line. Standing next to them, racing for Pagong, were Jenna and Joel. The Green Berets had walked them through the course moments before. As Sean feared, it was a half mile of soft-sand running. The obstacles ranged from a fifteen-foot wall to a low crawl to a rope swing. He was running for his island existence. The notion scared and energized simultaneously. If Tagi could somehow win, Sean would sidestep the alliance's shadow and have more control over his own future. Then maybe his optimism would return. Maybe, in the new tribe, he could go back to being Seinfeld again. Sean liked being Seinfeld.

What eventually bothered Pagong most about Sean dragging Kelly and Tagi to victory wasn't that he was a bad winner, because he wasn't. As a future member of the joint tribe he couldn't afford to ruffle any feathers.

And it wasn't that Sean and Kelly and Tagi had somehow cheated or done something slippery to win. They hadn't.

Or even that Tagi—old, fat, worker bee Tagi—had won a huge moral victory by trouncing Pagong in the most physical of Immunity Challenges.

No, what really torqued Pagong was that, upon returning to their beach all dejected and drained, a six-foot monitor lizard had eaten half of their last chicken. The tribe salvaged the remainder, cooked it, and voraciously devoured it. Though glad to have half a chicken, the knowledge that the teeth marks on their dinner belonged to a lizard tainted the dining experience somewhat.

So Day Eighteen wasn't Sean's last day after all. Like a death row inmate receiving a last-minute pardon from the governor, Sean breathed a deep sigh of relief and prepared to make a new life for himself.

Not so for Joel. The alpha male fell victim to a female voting bloc in Pagong. Gretchen had tired of his antics, even if it was Gervase who compared women with bovines. So the man who felt leadership was his greatest strength ("Being able to calm down a hot situation, and thinking clearly under huge amounts of pressure that personally affects many people is very common in my job") hadn't been able to rally the troops. Stunned, he left the Tribal Council. I felt bad for him.

Greg "awwrred" his trademark pirate scowl as Joel left. Ironically, Greg was the one male the Pagong women still loved and admired. "I know he's just playing the game," Gretchen noted, as though she was talking about her son, for Greg reminded her of the thirteen-year-old waiting back home. "That island phone doesn't come out until the cameras are rolling. His only problem is that he's too smart for his maturity level. Just watch: as the game changes, he'll change with it."

Even as she led the women against Joel, Gretchen was still wary of joining alliances. Morally and ethically, she wanted to set an example for her kids—at home in Tennessee and among Pagong. "I don't want to do anything I'll be ashamed of," she reiterated when pressed about joining alliances. "I'm voting my conscience."

On that note, the first phase of "Survivor" was done. The tribes would merge the next day, with the vaunted Tagi voting alliance and Party of Five just eighteen short days from deciding the million dollar Survivor. Who would win? Nobody knew. The rules of the game, so recently hoving into view, were proving as fluid and unpredictable as the sea lapping against the beaches.

All bets were off on Pulau Tiga. From Day Eighteen forward, nobody was safe. And everyone—*everyone*—was suspect.

Rattana Tribe

Richard Hatch
Rudy Boesch
Sean Kenniff
Kelly Wiglesworth
Gretchen Cordy
Susan Hawk
Jenna Lewis
Greg Buis
Colleen Haskell
Gervase Peterson

EVOLUTION SEVEN

Only the Good
Die Young

DAY NINETEEN

And then there were ten.

All were types.

The Gay Man (Richard), the Wild Woman (Kelly), the African American Male (Gervase), Fargo (Susan), the Rebel Without a Cause (Greg), the Coquette (Colleen), the Soccer Mom (Gretchen), the Old Man (Rudy), the Yuppie (Sean), and the Single Mom (Jenna).

One of them would win a million dollars.

One of them would go home in three days.

As I stared into an editing monitor, transporting myself creatively back to the island's first three days, trying to get the perfect tone and mixture of images for yet another rough cut of "Survivor"'s first episode, Tagi and Pagong woke up on their separate beaches fuzzy about the merger details. All they knew was that a message in their mailbox—tree-mail—bade each tribe send two representatives to Rocky Beach for a summit meeting that noon. Rocky Beach was the peninsula dividing Tagi and Pagong. Falling almost exactly halfway between the two tribes, it was an appropriately neutral meeting point.

If the tribes needed a reminder that Pulau Tiga was becoming more treacherous than ever, a yellow-lipped krait lunged at Richard while he was checking the tree-mail. Cocky as ever, Richard chose to taunt the snake until, horrified, he leapt back as the massive snake slithered away.

This meeting was a fitting beginning to "Survivor"'s final days. From Day One, Richard had stayed low to the ground, winding his way from individual to individual, building his alliance. Ondrusek was right—Richard did have the game figured out. And not just through the now-completed teamwork phase; he had it figured out right down to the awarding of the million-dollar check. His alliance would vote off Pagong, starting with the strong. Then Sean. When it was just the Tagi Four, Rudy would go first. Then Kelly. Then Susan. Richard would win on the popular vote, because he would spend his remaining eighteen days on Pulau Tiga building friendships. While some castaways saw the game the other way around—make friends first, then build an alliance—Richard knew from Day One that friendships were a luxury. Richard may have looked and acted like Baloo the Bear, but if "Survivor" were a grown-up version of the *Jungle Book*, he was definitely Ka, the scheming python.

Richard's closest counterpart, in terms of stealth and strategizing, among Pagong was Gervase. But rather than build alliances, the African-American whose luxury item was a deck of cards chose to focus on making friends. "For one million dollars," he boasted before coming to Pulau

Tiga, "there's no way I'm gonna be denied." Unemployed, unmarried, the father of three children, Gervase was a strange cast selection. At first glance, he was a poor representation of the African-American male, but Gervase was likeable. Really likeable. And smart. He knew that if he could just get on the island and make a few friends, he wouldn't get voted off for a long time—if at all. For as lazy as he could be—and Gervase took a perverse pride in contributing nothing to tribal welfare—and as pointed his comments could be—the "women as cows" remark was as hurtful a remark as anyone had made on Pulau Tiga—there was an enigmatic lovability to Gervase. He was loyal. He was goofy in a charming way ("admiring Salma Hayek" was a hobby). And he had a sunny outlook on life, learned from his mother, who raised four kids alone after Gervase's father died. Gervase was given to grinning and saying things like, "Someone else's life is always worse than your own." His fellow castaways couldn't help but like a guy with an attitude like that, especially when island life was getting tougher and tougher.

Gervase lost his wingman when Joel was voted off, but he still had the friendship of Jenna and Gretchen. All were parents. It was the thinnest of alliances, but Gervase clung to it, knowing it was far better than nothing. He went into the merger vowing to maintain his low profile, build new friends (the deck of cards was a big help), and slowly expand that support base.

The meeting at Rocky Point saw Sean from Tagi and Jenna from Pagong huddle with Chief Jeff to determine their tribal fate. The first order of business was to determine where they would live. "Sean, Jenna, you're the ambassadors," Chief Jeff instructed, and gave the new ambassadors a series of tasks, beginning with taking a tour of each other's camps. That night, a Tribal Summit would be held on the Sand Spit. Only Sean and Jenna would attend. They would agree on the living place, select a new name and color for the tribe, and design a new tribal flag.

The jungle path from Rocky Beach to Pagong paralleled the ocean, but a hundred yards inland. Unlike some of the lesser-used paths toward the hilly center of Pulau Tiga, the trail was clearly defined and flat. Sean ambled along it while Jenna marched to Tagi. Sean thought about Dirk getting voted off. Sean was still upset that his buddy was gone, and didn't know that Pagong had taken delight in mocking Dirk and his religion. Even if Sean had known, however, it wouldn't have mattered. Sean was free. The further from Tagi they walked, the more Sean's euphoria became apparent. He entered Pagong's camp like a long lost Gen X relative. Immediately, he moved to bond with them, choosing mankind's easiest ingratiation tool: gossip. He mocked his former tribe members, saying Richard was "a horny gay man" and Rudy "a crotchety old man who doesn't even know our names."

Pagong had no food to offer Sean other than a little leftover chicken feed. Sean didn't care. Thrilled to be with people more his age, he couldn't stop talking. "You guys have all the fun—everyone there thinks I'm so immature," he enthused. Then, just in case anyone thought him unworthy of winning the million, his gushing was followed by an explanation that, while he really was a neurosurgeon, his $50,000 medical school debt was debilitating. Sean was big on being worthy.

Sean, however, got very quiet when Pagong asked the most important questions of all: How strong was the Tagi Alliance, and did they plan on voting Pagong off one by one? "I don't know about that, guys," he backpedaled. His voice grew high and tight. "I really don't know. Really. I'm not really even a part of that alliance."

Sean looked around the group without making eye contact. His face took on the worried look it got when he experienced confrontation. Sean hated confrontation.

On Tagi Beach, meanwhile, Jenna arrived to find a group on their best behavior. It was a well-known fact that Sue and Richard and Rudy found Jenna obnoxious, but even those three were polite.

Lunch was waiting. Richard had speared fish and squid. Kelly reached into their stash and cut open a fresh green coconut. An amazed, starving Jenna couldn't eat fast enough. "We're moving over here," she kept saying. "We're moving over here. No way we're staying at Pagong."

Susan watched, ever the competitor. She couldn't resist a dig, just to let Jenna know who ran the show on Tagi Beach. "You're losing your tits," Sue suddenly blurted, figuratively slashing Jenna's Achilles' heel. Sue figured Jenna for one of those women who'd always traded on her looks. Women like that were always insecure about bust size. She didn't know Jenna was not just a tiny bit but *immensely* insecure about her looks. All through high school she'd been a gangly tomboy. Only in her late teens had she blossomed. Looks mattered to Jenna. Sexual appearance was part of her strategy to win. It's why she wore the hot pink (though now a little grubby from island wear and tear) bikini as often as possible.

So Sue's taunt hit home. Jenna tried not to wince too hard, but Sue still saw she'd scored a point. Jenna, however, didn't back down. "Now I really know we need to move over here," she chirped. "I need to eat to get them back."

The food situation got even better for Jenna on the Sand Spit. She and Sean paddled over in their tribal outriggers. They were amazed to find a feast—a romantic, gourmet, satiating, sleep-inducing feast. And the incredible atmosphere!! It looked like a credit card commercial: a sandy island in the middle of a calm turquoise sea, a balmy dusk. Two places were set at a table covered in a white tablecloth. A wine bucket chilled a light green bottle of Australian chardonnay. Chief-turned-butler Jeff emerged from a large white tent carrying two plates heaping with lobster and vegetables.

And as the sun set on the South China Sea, Sean and Jenna began their Tribal Summit. They sipped the chardonnay and wondered aloud how long it had been since they'd been drunk. They made small talk. Sean complimented Jenna on her eyes. Jenna told Sean how much she liked his bowling alley idea. The small town girl thought it a stroke of genius.

The flirtation grew more emboldened. Sean had always found Jenna attractive. And though she'd never actively returned the affection, she'd never discouraged it, either. The big white tent beckoned nearby, with its pair of downy beds with white sheets and soft pillows.

There was also, however, a camera crew and pair of producers recording their every move. Sean and Jenna knew secret cameras and microphones had been hidden throughout the tribal areas and around the watering holes. They suspected their Sand Spit boudoir was wired, too. Romantic notions died with that awareness. The drinking began in earnest.

Sean pressed too hard at first, playing Seinfeld again. By the end of the second bottle of wine he was drunk and relaxed, divulging Tagi's deepest of secrets. "They're conniving," he said with a nod of the head, straining to uncork the third bottle. He'd never known Australian wine was so good. Actually, he'd never known the Australians made wine.

"In what way?" Jenna asked. She was a good conversationalist, fond of talking about herself without prompting, but also good at drawing people out. Her survival instincts had been sharpened by three years as a single mom. She'd been betrayed too many times by people who feigned friendship, then spoke darkly behind her back. Rather than appear as guarded as she often felt, she feigned constant happiness, and learned to discern motives by reading eyes and body language. But drinking with Sean, she felt safe. Relaxed. The air was warm, and the breeze just brisk enough to shoo the mosquitoes. The world of "Survivor" was a finite place, where secrets and lies would end with the show. What did it matter if she spilled the beans to Sean about Pagong's true character? It wasn't like that would affect their relationship back home—if anything ever sparked.

But the years of betrayal had made Jenna too guarded. She could only trust herself and the twins. No one else in the world was safe. So she sipped her wine, keeping pace with Sean, but didn't divulge any real truths.

She smiled warmly as Sean continued. "They're conniving because they put together a voting bloc against Dirk. And Dirk was my friend. The least they could have done was told me what was going on. I mean, you should have seen the look on Dirk's face. He was stunned. It broke my heart."

"Maybe they didn't tell you because you were his friend."

"Yeah. Maybe."

"I think I'm going to have problems with Sue. She once said I looked like shit."

"You'll get along great with Sue. She's a sweetheart." Sean sipped more wine. "The one I'm thinking about is Greg."

"Oh, Greg's a loner and he's a little crazy, but he's really cool. Everyone likes him. Especially Gretchen. She's protective of all of us, but especially him."

"I don't know. I watched him blow up at a camera man one time. Tagi didn't think that was cool. If he shows the same kind of disrespect to any of Tagi they'll vote him off in a heartbeat."

From somewhere in that jumble of conversation and giddiness and surreal excess, the new tribal name emerged. It was a combination of the sturdy plant they'd all brushed against once or twice and some subconscious vestige of colonialism: Rattana. The tribes would begin sharing the same beach at noon the next day. Their color would be green (much to my relief, for I had only green Buff scarves on hand to replace the yellow and orange scarves from Tagi and Pagong).

Jenna and Sean talked until after midnight. They drank four bottles of wine. The million stars above twinkled fat and bright, not at all like the vague pinpricks back home. The constellations were clouded over by a storm racing toward the Bornean coast, then revealed again, but were spun into different positions by the earth's rotation. Someday—probably many somedays, for this was a night like no other, ever—Sean and Jenna would tell friends and children and parents about the perfect wonder of it all. But mostly they would hold the evening close to their hearts forever, counting it alongside wedding days and children's births and the time they lost their virginity as one of their top ten most wonderful experiences. For in all the world, no one was in a more romantic spot.

Only the camera crew rendered the romance imperfect, reminding Sean and Jenna that they were living inside a *Truman Show*-type dramality.

DAY TWENTY

Craig Piligian, the camera/sound team of Ninja and Fed, and senior producer Brady Connell had spent the night on the Spit outside Jenna and Sean's big white tent. Though nothing physically happened during the nocturnal hours of the Tribal Summit, Sean and Jenna woke up bonded and giggly. Chief Jeff arrived by boat to serve them a breakfast of eggs, coffee, and croissants atop the same ironwood table laid with a fine white tablecloth. The sunrise was as flawless as the previous night's sunset, a gentle umber watercolor smeared atop the inky forever of the South China Sea. Jenna doused her eggs with Tabasco while Sean ate his plain.

A boat arrived from the production compound when breakfast was done. A pair of sherpas loaded the ironwood table and chairs, white tablecloth, empty wine bottles, silverware, candles, beds, and spacious white tent atop the barge. Poof. The civilization bubble was burst. Castaways again, bare-chested Sean and pink-bikinied Jenna climbed into their separate outriggers—the orange one for Sean, the yellow one for Jenna—and began paddling back to Pagong Beach. Once they'd put ashore those colors would be retired in favor of the new green, and Pagong tribe would be given just five minutes to choose three items before vacating Pagong Beach forever.

Four hours later, Pagong paddled their raft onto Tagi Beach. They were greeted cordially, if warily. Like layabout relatives stepping into a world of prosperity, Pagong oohed and aahed about the fire pit, the clothesline, the eating area, the shelter. It was theirs now, just as much as it was Tagi's.

Sue and Richard and Kelly and Rudy had been busy in Sean's absence. They had been able to talk freely. To plot. The Tagi Alliance—the tribe was dead, but the name would live on—had become more unified than ever. They eyed the five newcomers and Sean, the man in the middle, and mentally ticked off which would go, when. In five more "Survivor" evolutions it would be just Tagi again, battling for the million. Greg, they knew, had to go first.

Greg had other plans. He knew his "rebel without a cause" strategy wouldn't work in Rattana. His mini-bloc with Colleen wasn't going to protect him either. To stay in the game he had to infiltrate the Tagi Alliance. The trick would be finding the alliance's weak link, then exploiting it. Greg had thought about that moment for a week, probing.

Kelly's youth was a possibility, and Greg considered dropping Colleen to flirt with her. But Kelly was too close to Susan. And Susan hated Greg.

So Kelly wasn't the answer.

Susan had a mind like dried cement—firmly set. It would take weeks of cajoling and flirting to spin her toward a compassionate embrace of Greg's World. She didn't like the nature phone. She didn't like his disrespect for authority. She certainly didn't marvel at Greg's intellect. Back home in Wisconsin, Greg would be the kind of cocky college boy she'd sneer at from across a crowded barroom, hoping someone would pick a fight and beat the living daylights out of him.

Greg crossed Susan off the list.

Rudy? Not in a million years.

That left Richard.

Greg was an ardent defender of fantasy and make-believe. His ability to slip from one reality into the other was either brilliant or spooky, depending upon an individual's point of view. For Greg to enter Richard's sphere of influence, a monstrous game of pretend would be required. As his island mental equal, Richard was predisposed to dislike Greg. Also, as the man who had the entire game wired already, Richard had his defenses up. But Richard was a needy intellectual, just like Greg. If Greg could exploit that connection he might be able to build a bridge.

Greg began his life in his new home by asking Rich if they might go

fishing together. At first, Rich was his usual hospitable self. But wary of having his provider role usurped, Richard got defensive when Greg waltzed back up the shore, a writhing resident of the South China Sea at the end of his spear. "That... uh... that kind of fish is inedible," Richard noted. "Better throw that one back."

"You're sure?" Greg did his best to appear humble. Actually, he kind of liked having a new friend, even if the friend was playing the game incredibly and would vote him from the wilds of Pulau Tiga back to the wilds of Plano, Texas, in a heartbeat.

"Oh, yeah."

Greg stayed close to Richard. Those long nights cuddling with Colleen were forgotten. Greg acted like he didn't know her. He didn't much care that the kitten wasn't bonding well with the other women. She'd grown used to being distant from the other castaways in her time with Greg. She'd been protected by that distance, but she'd also missed some very vital lessons in playing "Survivor." Unable to disappear into the jungle or Greg's protective shadow, Colleen looked frail, child-like. Her hair was frizzed from too many days in the sun. She had lost so much weight that her skintight shorts sagged.

All this combined to make Colleen obvious. Whether because her own ideals and beliefs were still forming ("I'll try anything and listen to any-one....I could be the yes girl") or because she felt new to the adult world ("I'm barely out of the just-a-kid phase"), the Maryland native trans-planted to Miami was reluctant to put any segment of her personality for-ward on Pulau Tiga. "I'd like there to be at least one good-looking guy on the island," she said before the journey. "And at least one complete idiot to make me feel like I'm not making the biggest fool of myself."

Colleen hadn't necessarily found both those people in Greg, but his antics did fulfill her desire to be entertained. "I still," she admitted, "like story time."

The greatest shame about Colleen was that the charming, cute, witty young woman revealed little of those qualities. She didn't tell anyone she was a fan of French films, or that she'd once worked as a firefighter in Ghana, or that she had spent six months interning with the London Film Festival. She quietly bided her time, breathing a deep sigh of relief after every Tribal Council because she expected to get voted off each time the names were revealed. But she kept dodging that bullet. Where Greg bri-dled at having his destiny controlled by others, Colleen accepted it as a foregone conclusion. She wasn't on Pulau Tiga to win. That would be im-possible. Colleen was just on Pulau Tiga for yet another intriguing expe-rience—and maybe a little money (second prize was $100,000). Sooner or later the collective Someone would decide the experience had ended. Colleen would be sitting on one of those stumps before the fire, staring down as always, when she would hear Jeff's "It's time for you to go." Colleen knew the odds—it would take a miracle for her to win.

That resignation made Colleen insecure. So she looked for behavior to copy—*adult* behavior, to help her leap from just-a-kid to full-fledged adult—that would delay the inevitable. She had a humanity about her every other contestant, save Gretchen, lacked. It was the insecure part of Colleen that begged to learn and grow, that allowed her to experience new things with little judgment. Someday—because she was not the sort to deny it—that insecurity would blossom into self-knowledge and inner con-fidence. Someday that insecurity would make her a wonderful grown-up.

Resignation also set Colleen free. During the tribal merger she felt no obligation to impress anyone. While everyone else acted like they were at a fraternity mixer; while Greg chased Richard, and Gervase talked Rudy and Sean into a nonstop game of cards; while all the other women formed the Pulau Tiga version of a sewing circle to build a new and improved shelter that would fit ten bodies; while camera crews stepped in and around the tempest, and that sun-humidity duo were once again conspiring to make midday unbearable, with all that frantic integration swirling around her, Colleen sat on the powdered sugar of Tagi Beach playing with a piece of rope. Maybe someone would come over and adopt her. That would be great. But if not, Colleen lived in a world without expectations, humming softly to herself.

Around the fire that first night of Rattana, Colleen glanced over at Greg shyly, hoping he would at least sit next to her and ease the transition. It was a sex-talk night. Colleen was too reserved to simply leap in and offer her experiences for mass consumption. Sean told a lengthy story about his first sexual experience. Rich told of the time he was molested as a child. Jenna described an experience inside a Volkswagon.

But Colleen followed Greg's lead and said nothing. He was always her cue, her guide to proper tribal behavior. Without him she felt totally lost.

She looked over at him again. Colleen had thought she knew Greg well, and could maybe even predict his actions. But as she looked over at the conflicted young man with the beautiful blond hair and spotty new beard, she was proven very wrong. For Greg was wooing Richard and the Alliance in the most obvious and unlikely way possible: Homosexuality. Greg sat on a log next to Richard. Their knees were almost touching. Their faces were close enough that Richard could smell Greg's breath. Greg hinted at experimenting with gay sex. Richard raised an eyebrow. "Someone," Richard said grandly to his new interest, "complimented me today on my DIC-tion."

"Oh really?" Greg answered, taking the bait. "What about *my* DIC-tion?"

"I don't know. Why don't you let me see your DIC-tion."

The fact that Greg was merely playing Richard like a bass fiddle was irrelevant. "He's cute," Richard noted.

That night, when Richard fell asleep on one of the log benches Tagi had positioned around the eating area, Greg didn't wander off to build a nest. Instead, he curled up on the sand at the big man's feet.

DAY TWENTY-ONE

The first days of life on a deserted island are disorienting. Life feels compressed. Weather wanders by but never settles. A mental claustrophobia sets in when the brain realizes that problems cannot be fled—instead they roost in the mind, waiting their turn to invoke anguish and fear. The body becomes primal, forgetting even that the world is round. Looking to the horizon day after day and seeing only water and what looks like a cliff beyond evokes sympathy for early man—damned if the edge of the world wasn't a waterfall, after all. Sail too far and you tumble into oblivion.

Things change after a few days. The island doesn't seem so small. The urge to flee lessens. The ocean becomes a cocoon, insulating you from the world and its problems. Political upheaval and sports scores and economic fluctuations in other lands mean absolutely nothing, and have no bearing on comfortable, sedate, tranquil island life. Thus, they are not—cannot possibly be—real.

The clothes go first, then the watch. Soon all life is fluid, revolving around sunrise and sunset, with lightning and wind as nightly entertainment. Images of freeways and fast-food drive-throughs; traumas like road rage and school kids shooting each other; trivialities like first weekend box office grosses and hair dryers—all seem otherworldly and absurd. Island life is simple, and simple is peaceful, and why would—how could—someone want to be anywhere else?

That's where the castaways were emotionally as their twenty-first day on Pulau Tiga began. Life was sociopolitically complex. But otherwise, the island was a pretty great place to be. They were settling into humanistic psychologist Abraham Maslow's famous hierarchy of needs: first basic amenities like food and oxygen, then on to security and safety, then on to love and belonging, competence and then prestige and self-fullfilment, then finally, curiosity and the need to understand. With simple physiological needs met in the first week, they had settled safety issues the second and third. Some castaways were stuck on the third level, seeking love. Others had even moved on to level four, quietly reveling in prestige and self-esteem.

But the formation of the new tribe of Rattana caused the balance to upset and set the hierarchy of needs back a couple weeks. Everyone was back to level two—security and safety. The proof would be in Day Twenty-One's Tribal Council, where the victim could be anyone.

As if some cataclysmic disturbance were taking place in the universe, the storm to end all storms struck Pula Tiga between midnight and dawn. Hundred-foot trees were entirely uprooted from the shallow, sandy soil. The enormous banyan in whose shade "Bugging Out" had been held two weeks before had its top half sheered off. Lightning struck the island repeatedly, followed by thunder booms like exploding bombs. Waves clawed the sand from Pulau's Tiga's beaches in jagged chunks. Tree trunks the size of surface-to-air missiles were lobbed onto the shore, washed there from deep in the heavily-logged Bornean coast.

In typical island fashion, the storm was long gone by sunrise. After skimming over the island it continued toward Vietnam, six-hundred-plus miles northwest. The only remnants were those logs and a still-choppy sea. Even the water inside the reefs, normally pastel green and smooth enough for water skiing, was roiled and dark.

But in those few hours, the damage had been done, and it appeared that the Tagi Alliance was already dying. The roof of Rattana's shelter had collapsed. In the strangest test of the alliance yet, the women bonded together to fix the damage. Gretchen, Sue, Kelly, and Jenna worked and gabbed. Colleen watched them, eating. She joined the detail after prompting from Gretchen, thus ensuring that the women were a solid core group.

Meanwhile, Gervase's card strategy was working beautifully. Shuffling and dealing like a Vegas croupier, he drew the Rattana men into card game after card game—gin, hearts, spades. The morning was passed in happy division, with the men playing cards and the women building the shelter. Rattana resembled a pride of lions, where the females do all the work while the male sleeps twenty hours a day.

At noon, though, life got noticeably more tense. The tribe was summoned to Snake Island, a mile off Pulau Tiga, for their first individual Immunity Challenge. The winner would go to the Tribal Council with the other nine, and even vote, but was safe from being voted off. With the Tagi Alliance theoretically weakening along gender lines, the Tribal Council vote looked to go either way. Winning immunity was the key to controlling individual destiny.

Snake Island's population of an estimated nine hundred sea kraits were nowhere to be seen as Rattana dropped into the water ten yards offshore. Immunity would be decided by an old-fashioned breath-

holding competition. On a signal from Chief Jeff, everyone dived underwater. One by one, they began popping back to the surface. Sue, a
smoker back home, was first. Then Jenna. Colleen. Kelly. Gretchen.
The five women looked at each other and laughed. The sisterhood was
strong and they knew that as long as they were all together, everything
would be OK at the Tribal Council.

Rudy came up next. At seventy-two years old, he was looking more
lean and fit with every passing day. His years of SEAL conditioning could
be seen in defined abdominal muscles and swimmer's long biceps and tri-
ceps. He grinned when he bobbed back to the surface, glad to have out-
lasted the women and seemingly unworried about the Tribal Council.

Richard came up after Rudy, openly disappointed by his poor performance. He'd been discouraged about being "old and fat," but expected
to excel in breath-holding. The former college water polo player with an
affinity for snorkel spear fishing took secret pride in being the most
aquatic man on the island. Would this display of weakness hurt him at the
Tribal Council? He tried not to look worried.

Gervase was next. For a man who'd only recently learned to swim, he
was proving remarkably comfortable in the water.

The only two left were Sean and Greg. As the other eight castaways
treaded water and waited, those last two stayed down longer and longer.
The day was turning dark again, with a massive wall of black sky sweeping in from the west. Whether or not it would produce weather to equal
the previous night's storm, no one knew. But the coming gale was a big
one. As if playing the part of opening act for the thunder and lightning
and wind and rain, the sea grew choppier with every passing second.

Sean popped up next. Greg was the guaranteed winner. Just to make
sure, Greg stayed down a few seconds longer. Two more rounds were
held, yielding first Sean and finally Gervase as other finalists. These
three—Greg, Sean, and Gervase—would compete in the final test, an
underwater distance race. Greg barely pipped Sean to the post. When
he popped to the surface he looked bashful for winning—as though he'd
been torn between guaranteed immunity and the awareness that victory
equated to physical strength, and physical strength equated to visibility
at future Tribal Councils. Nevertheless, he eagerly slipped the new Immunity Talisman—a beaded wooden necklace—over his shoulders. He
was safe.

That night, still wearing the Immunity Talisman, Greg entered the Tribal Council first. The wind had died but rain was imminent. Per his custom, Greg softly tapped the gong signifying his arrival. He was like a child who has been told to play quietly in the house or risk severe punishment. The others filed in somberly after him, the former members of Pagong first. If ever there was a night to be nervous at the Tribal Council, this was it. Kelly, Rudy, Sue, and Richard entered last. Taking their seats around the fire pit, they were visibly uncomfortable.

The Tribal Council set looked cluttered for the first time. Ten people were too many for the small area. If only to ease the seating arrangement, someone would have to leave the island. Chief Jeff took his traditional seat only after each member of Rattana had found a log. Within minutes of launching into the traditional pre-vote discussion of issues affecting tribal life, rain began splatting loudly against the uncovered fringes of the set. Chief Jeff had to lean closer and speak louder to ask his questions. Issue by issue, he dissected the problems facing the new tribe: men versus women, the too-small shelter (Rudy: "I had to go to the head all night long, but there was too many people in the shelter for me to get out without steppin' on someone"), whether or not Sean and Jenna felt any animosity from the other castaways after their great night on the Spit. Colleen was asked if she felt safe. So was Gervase.

The wind picked up as the voting began. As he had on Day Nine, Jeff returned from counting the votes soaked to the skin, his short brown hair plastered to his scalp. Unlike that calamitous night, however, Chief Jeff returned to announce the results wearing a look of thorough surprise. Before a Tribal Council it was his habit to prepare by polling producers about candidates likely to be voted off. As usual, he had done that. If anyone was in danger, the reply had come back, it was Colleen. So Chief Jeff had begun the night expecting Colleen to go. It made sense. She was the weakest.

But the game had changed.

Jeff began reading the votes, holding the white scraps of paper up one by one. The castaways could read their names in black block letters. Each time a castaway's name was read, they would experience that tightening of the throat that fear and betrayal brought on.

Chief Jeff read each vote loudly, so he might be heard above the storm. "Colleen."

A nervous, knowing giggle from shy Colleen. All eyes were on her. Then everyone looked back to Jeff to see and hear the next vote.

"Gretchen.

"Rudy.

"Susan.

"Colleen.

"Richard.

"Jenna.

"Gervase.

"Gretchen.

"Gretchen."

By the third vote against her, Gretchen knew. In one bold, glaring, awful vote, "Survivor" had changed. The show's moral compass was gone.

Whatever was good, whatever was honest, whatever was right about all the backbiting and duplicity and longing and fear and insecurity and outright deception in the game was gone.

Richard, Sue, Rudy, and Kelly hadn't looked uncomfortable entering the Tribal Council set that night because they were afraid. They had looked uncomfortable because they were preparing to vote off salt and light. Realpolitik made them feel guilty, but only for a while. Eventually, realpolitik would make them wealthy. Keeping Colleen—weak, pliable, expendable at any time—made perfect sense. She was a threat to no one. Gretchen was gone because she was stronger than any of them. She had to go. She might have won, otherwise.

"The Tagi Alliance," I said off-camera to another stunned observer, "is very strong. This changes the whole tenor of island life."

Chief Jeff looked at Gretchen with a sigh. He really liked her. Everyone really liked her. "It's time," he said, feeling sadness course through him, "for you to go."

She walked into the night. Before reaching the confessional taping area, Gretchen was enveloped in the arms of men and women she had never met before but who had watched her on tape dozens of times, marveling at her maternal determination. "I'm wrecked," a beefy sound engineer told her. "I am so incredibly bummed."

Maternal as ever, Gretchen hugged the big man right back. "It'll be OK. I'm sad now, but the good thing is I get to go home and be with my kids." Then she continued the long dark walk in the pouring rain. Not alone, though. Not alone.

Alone is how each member of the former Pagong tribe felt that night as they walked back across the island. Alone and naked and convinced their chances of winning were slim unless the "Survivor" rules could be changed immediately.

Among the Tagi Alliance, even Machiavellian Sue professed to be bothered by what had happened that night. "That's it," she whispered to Kelly. "No more women are getting voted off this island. For a while, at least." Only time would tell if Sue's word—not the most reliable in the past, though her new tribe members didn't know of her frequent betrayals—was good, or just more manipulation.

Evolution Eight

End of the Line

Day Twenty-Two

Gretchen dribbled a green coconut down the beach like a soccer ball. Her skin was clean. She'd taken a shower. Shaved her legs and under her arms. Used soap, shampoo—three times. Her hair was pulled back into a neat ponytail. She spoke in lamentations and optimisms. The words tumbled out stream-of-consciousness, in neat sentences mirroring her logical thought processes.

"I consider it a badge of honor to be voted off.

"At least now I get to see my kids.

"They don't understand Greg's humor. He's great.

"I'm gonna miss this place."

Whether happy or sad, Gretchen couched each sentence in a smile and spoke reassuringly, as though it were her job to keep discomfort as far from the conversation as possible.

Finally, *Sea Quest VIII*, the Magellan Sutera's private boat, thundered over the horizon. The bow twwopped up and down like a one-way seesaw on the six-foot swells. Its delicate white awning and pair of muscular Honda 200 outboard motors made for a neat juxtaposition between beauty and speed. On smooth seas, *Sea Quest VIII* could hold forty miles per hour all the way back to KK. The violent tantrum the ocean was displaying the morning of Day Twenty-Two, however, made forty mph a pipe dream. *Sea Quest* would be lucky to hold an uncomfortable twenty-five. Even then, those powerful engines would launch *Sea Quest* off wave after wave. Spray would soak everyone inside the open boat. Passengers would strap on life jackets without being reminded. Every time *Sea Quest*'s smooth bottom splatted into a trough the disks in their spines would compress, as gravity and violence shoved their weight hard into the boat's thin blue cushions. Their fists would curl tightly about the thin metal railing for fear of being bucked overboard.

Gretchen's ride back to civilization wouldn't be the smooth journey she deserved. She wouldn't step into the white Air Sabah helicopter with a million dollars cash spilling out of her carry-on, whisked back to the world ten feet off the deck, arriving at the Magellan in less than ten glorious minutes. But she didn't care. "This is going to be fun," Gretchen marveled, staring out to sea. Just enough of the twang the New York native acquired living in Tennessee poked through to make her sound like a genteel hillbilly. "At least I'll have another good memory to take home with me."

As she stepped on board *Sea Quest*, Gretchen was already rethinking her trip home. "I think," she began her last sentence on Pulau Tiga, "I'm going to delay my trip home until I see what happens to Greg."

With that, Gretchen Cordy bade farewell. She went back to the Magellan and called her family. She took another shower. She lay on a big, firm, king-sized mattress and couldn't believe how pure and wondrous clean cotton felt on freshly-scrubbed skin. Then she enjoyed a day without foraging, shelter building, campfire making, rat-eating, or picking sand fleas from her scalp. For dinner that night, she would have Thai food with a half-dozen members of the production crew in KK on R and R.

Back on the island, the former members of Pagong were numb with fear and disbelief. Colleen, Jenna, Gervase, and, especially, Greg, reeled now that their leader was gone. And it had been done in a most horrible way. Individually, they asked themselves the island's deepest moral question: Would they join an alliance to stay alive, knowing the moral consequences of that commitment?

As each searched his or her soul, each took the question a step further. Why was Gretchen's departure so unsettling? She was just another castaway, after all, someone whose time had come. Was it her goodness? Was that what made her ouster so shocking?

No. Every castaway was a good person. And it wasn't her motherhood. Jenna was a mother, too.

Her strong chance of winning? Closest to the mark. In addition to teaching survival, her military career included a stint training Air Force pilots to survive interrogation if downed during war. That took moxie and a huge ability to role play.

Subconsciously, all Pagong's former members knew why Gretchen's ouster was so shocking: It violated fair play, and the belief that the strong and fastest and smartest always came out on top. How to explain a game where the heavyset, slow, minimally educated, and wholly unethical stood the best chance of winning?

As the majority of Rattana recoiled from the game, Richard and Susan embraced it. Living their own version of *Macbeth*, they worked on building their alliances even as each plotted the other's demise. Richard told Sue he wanted it to come down to the two of them. Sue, despite assuring Richard she couldn't agree more, was already promising the same to Kelly. Each was thoroughly confident they would win. Rich, months before he'd been selected for "Survivor," informed his hometown newspaper of his imminent stardom. When producer Jay Bienstock showed up in Newport to film a small bit of background information, he was startled to see that newspaper framed over the bar in Richard's favorite restaurant. Once Jay began the interview, Richard corrected him each time the word "if" was used in conjunction with Richard's time on the island. "Not 'if,' Jay. When."

"Yeah, I know Richard. But let's say—hypothetically—you don't win."

"Not gonna happen. I will win the million dollars. I will."

As Ondrusek had said, this man had figured the game out before leaving home. To Richard, island living would not be some extension of physical might or even familial behavior. It would be an exact replica of corporate politics, where the eventual leader built convenient friendships and alliances without emotional attachment. Not only did Richard make his living analyzing and deconstructing corporate power, he knew that winning "Survivor" would be very, very good for business. He was already penciling himself in as a future spokesman for the Gay and Lesbian Alliance—once he won, of course.

Susan, preferring to go on gut instincts, figured out the game when she got to Pulau Tiga. She and her husband once managed a hunting lodge in the Canadian wilderness. Susan's awareness of primitive animal behavior was her guiding light on Pulau Tiga. Lying was perfectly acceptable. The ends, as Machiavelli said 468 years before, justified the means. He could have written the line specifically for Richard and Susan.

With the sullen, newly-mean Rattana down to the final nine contestants, those two were salivating at the prospect of taking the game to a new level—a level attainable by elite players only.

This core group of nine would decide the ultimate winner at the final Tribal Council on April 21, just eighteen days away. Every conversation between castaways from now on would be suspect. Not only was alliance-building necessary, but kindness mattered now too. Susan was weak in the kindness area, but determined to try harder. Richard had already set the tone. He wasn't being suckered by Greg's chickenhawk act. "He thinks he's outsmarting me so he can stay on the island, but it's the other way around. I'm just being his friend right now so when we get down to the final two he votes for me instead of someone else," Richard noted to a camera crew.

Play-acting was one thing. Being kind was okay, too. Greg was weird and hard to connect with, but he was ultimately a conflicted, brilliant young man. If he wanted to cozy up to Richard for strategic reasons, there was nothing at all wrong with that. In fact, it was rather touching to see Greg admit his neediness, if only indirectly.

No, the queasiness-inducing part was the lying. And some of the untruths and half-truths bordered on obscene. The morning after Gretchen's ouster, Susan and the remaining women of Rattana took the bamboo raft out for a float. Fishing wasn't on the agenda—Rich's skill in the water was untouchable. Susan only made the journey to soothe the sisterhood about Gretchen's demise. Kelly was with her.

Jenna was distraught over Gretchen's absence. "I know," Sue soothed her. "I feel the same way too. From now on, no women get voted off. We gotta make that happen."

The women hooted and high-fived, rocking their little raft. Jenna licked her lips and leaned in conspiratorially. "So," she said softly, carefully. The Alliance held her future in their hands. Like every former member of Pagong, Jenna woke up the morning of Day Twenty-two scared. She watched every single word she said to Sue. "Did you guys vote against Gretchen?"

"Me?" Sue said. "Are you kidding? I loved her. No way."

"What about you, Kelly?"

"No way. I voted for Rudy." Kelly hated lying. She was trying to lead a good life, free of bad karma. Going home and seeing herself screw people on national television wasn't going to feel good. It was the sort of action people regretted their entire lives.

As Kelly felt guilt nibble at her insides, Susan quickly changed the subject. Someday soon Sue would vote Kelly off. She certainly hadn't told the young river guide as much, but she would have no problem doing it. "So, Jenna," and then Sue winked at her fellow Rattana woman. "Did Sean try to hop in the sack with you out at the Sand Spit?"

"Yeah. But I told him no."

The women thought that was a great example of restraint and control. Begging for sex exposed men as weak. No, they all agreed as they bobbed out along the reef, tanning, it was time to pick the men off, one by one.

The women high-fived again. Together they were strong.

On shore, Sean was tormented. Scared again. He felt uncomfortable voting any of his new friends off, so he'd adopted an alphabetic voting pattern. The night before it had been Colleen. He warned her ahead of time the vote was coming. But seeing Gretchen go had shaken him on several levels. First, he had no friends. Second, the Tagi Alliance didn't want him. Third, he felt morally above alliances. But to win the game he would have to join one. All in all, his days were numbered.

He had one slim hope for survival: a change in tribal morality. If just one or two Alliance members could be convinced to regain their ethical senses, they might be able to vote off Richard and Sue. Not that Sean wanted to form a counter-alliance—well, maybe, though he wouldn't call it that—but Richard and Sue had to go. Quietly, he beckoned Gervase and Greg to hike to Far Water. Something, all three agreed, had to change quickly. And in that moment, Gretchen's moral compass was passed into three unlikely hands.

All they had to do was convince Rattana to do the right thing. They could do that, couldn't they?

DAY TWENTY-THREE

A tree-mail note announced the day's Reward Challenge. "It takes skill to carve the arc/May your aim be true and find its mark/Archery is the sport of kings/A reward from home is what victory brings."

Jenna craved a reward from home. She had been begging the producers

for a peek at the pictures of her twins she'd left at the Magellan. Maybe
that was the reward. Or maybe the reward was a letter. Or maybe just some
sort of keepsake. It didn't matter. Jenna was feeling more lonely with every
passing day on the island. Her morale was sagging. It took every bit of her
inner reserve to pick herself up each morning and face the day with a fake
smile plastered on her face. In the past four days, the desperation of trying
to claw into the Alliance had made her feel even more vulnerable and
needy. She desperately needed to empower herself. Winning a Reward
Challenge was the perfect way to make that happen. Well, winning an Immunity Challenge would be even more perfect. But Jenna was a competitive animal by nature. Any victory was great. Winning—and when Jenna
won it was never merely a victory, but an in-your-face celebration of her
greatness—was a release. If nothing else, victory would be empowering.

So when the producers dropped off the handmade bows, arrows, and
targets for the challenge, Jenna began practicing. She practiced and practiced and practiced, determined to win that reward from home.

There was one problem: She wasn't very good.

But it was heartening to see that none of her other tribe members were
archers either. Greg, so adept at acquiring new skills, was the best of the
bunch, and his talent was only middling. Richard was no good either.
Rudy practiced with a stiff, militaristic efficiency but was a poor marksman. Kelly took a few practice shots, then gave up, saying she was going
to "wing it" instead of practicing. Even Sue, the predator, was a poor shot.
Gervase, saving his strength for Immunity Challenges, napped.

So Jenna practiced and practiced and practiced. "This is one challenge
I am going to win," she said grimly, plunking arrow after arrow into the
target long after the others had given up and wandered off to swim or
stare into the fire. It felt good to practice, as if mere physical action less-
ened the Tagi Alliance's stranglehold on her future. Now that she was part
of the core nine she wanted more than ever to stay on the island and win
the "Survivor" game. She missed the girls. They'd inherited her competitive fire. What better way to set an example than by kicking butt on national television, starting with the Reward Challenge? Little victories,
that's what life was about. Little victories, because they added up.

Plunk. Plunk. Plunk.

Gervase lazed about the beach as Jenna fought to control her destiny.
He had no interest in winning the Reward Challenge. His strategy was to

win every Immunity Challenge from that day forth. For that, he needed strength. So he slept and thought for the millionth time that day how hungry he was.

A boat arrived from the production compound, nosing into the beach. The crew began unloading a curious group of items, handing them over the side with great care. A generator was first. Then, a large wooden crate. Jenna paused from her practicing to watch. "I'll bet it's a refrigerator," she said, eyeballing the crate's contours.

Colleen had gotten up to look. "Yeah."

Richard joined them. "I think you're right. They're bringing us a fridge with our favorite foods from home."

They stared at the crate's dimensions a little more. Even Gervase stirred. The size was right for a small refrigerator, but the crew weren't struggling with enough weight. The heft wasn't refrigerator-sized. "I think it's a TV," Jenna said, preparing to shoot again.

"I think you're right," Richard answered. "Wouldn't it be great if they showed us home movies."

The notion almost made Jenna sink to her knees. She would cry if she saw home movies of Sadie and Sabrina. Flat-out bawl. The tribe would see that the cheerleader who'd come ashore over three weeks before was capable of great emotion. They might think her weak. If so, she didn't care. She didn't care if they saw her cry, and she didn't care if they thought she was weak. Someone was going to betray her anyway, whether it was Sue or Greg or maybe even Gervase. The important thing was the girls. In them she would find strength and motivation. With their love as her touchstone, she could bear any betrayal.

The rest of the tribe knew about Jenna's longing to see a video of her daughters. None of them cared as much about seeing home movies. Once they figured out that that was the prize, they all rooted for her to win, if just to have her moment. Even Sue dropped her competitive veneer long enough to stroll over and encourage Jenna's practice, spinning motivational stories about bear hunting with bow and arrow.

Chief Jeff arrived and unveiled the television. He explained the Reward Challenge, then that he did, indeed, have videos from home. Jenna was crying with joy the minute she heard. Then Jeff continued. "Each of you will see a one-minute preview of your video from home. The winner will get to see their video in its entirety."

Jenna had imagined the twins looking into the camera and saying "I love you."

The videos began rolling. Richard's went first, with his son and then his friends wishing him luck. One by one the list of videos rolled past. Gervase went last, bookending Richard's video with a touching note from his daughter.

"How's that feel, Gervase?" Chief Jeff asked.

Gervase had trouble speaking. He tapped his heart. "That's my everything. I wish you hadn't shown it to me. It makes me wanna go home now."

Jenna was crying tears of joy for Gervase.

"And now," Jeff said slowly, "I have some very sad news..."

Jenna began shouting before he was done. "Don't, don't, don't, don't..."

"I'm sorry, Jenna. For whatever reason, we didn't receive the video. We tried several times, several different ways. It took a while to finally reach your family and as of now we didn't receive anything. I'm truly sorry." If she won the archery competition, Jeff went on to add, she could make a video to send home to her family.

Jenna was shattered. Her face sagged, then she broke down, betrayed again. At first she blamed her family. Then she realized that couldn't possibly be the case. Unless something had happened to her mom and little girls, there was no way they wouldn't have taped a video. Clearly, the production crew was conspiring against her. Somewhere on the island was a video with her name on it, filmed by her mom, featuring the twins. Whether it was me or Craig Piligian or even Jeff Probst, she was positive someone had made the executive decision to keep it from her. Jenna was enraged. Gathering herself again, scolding herself for trusting these people, Jenna decided it was time to win the archery competition.

She didn't. She was far too rattled to shoot straight.

Greg won. He'd thought about shooting his arrows into the air as protest against Jenna's bad luck, but decided it was fruitless. His five minutes of family video were either funny or deeply disturbing, depending on whether an individual understood the Buis family humor. His sister rambled through veiled incest jokes and a rage-filled rendition of "High Hopes." She was blond, like Greg, and their connection was obviously close. So there was no denying it was a slice of home for Greg. It just wasn't the warm and fuzzy moment a Jenna video would have engendered.

Greg's empathy for Jenna continued afterward. "I felt like it should have been Jenna who won. That victory meant nothing to me and everything to her. And I wish I'd shot my arrows into the air, but that would've changed the game and opened a big can of worms." He sighed. "I know this is only a game—not just the Reward Challenge, but all of "Survivor." I want to keep playing, and playing to win. I mean, I love this place and I'm having the best time of my life. But I don't want to play the dark side. I've acted honorably the whole time and have nothing to be ashamed of. But I'll tell you what, if I don't win Immunity tomorrow, I'm in trouble. They're going after the strong, one by one. And it'll be either me or Gervase next."

The honesty got too much for Greg then, and he retreated from Empathetic Greg into the Shocking Greg who had once polarized the island. "Did my sister's video bother me? No. And as for Colleen, if she goes, I'd like to be the one to vote her off. It's like your family: If you knew your family was going to get murdered, wouldn't you rather kill them yourself first?"

Down the beach, Jenna's rage and humiliation contrasted sharply with Greg's attempts at levity. As Chief Jeff prepared to board a boat back to the production compound, Jenna stamped over and angrily confronted him. "You set me up, didn't you? You did this to me on purpose."

"We would never, ever hurt you or anyone else," Chief Jeff replied.

"Then why do that challenge? Why do that when you knew I didn't have a video? There were so many other challenges to choose from."

"The truth is, that was the challenge that was already rescheduled because of this. We pushed it back as far as we could. There's no way we weren't going to do that challenge. The fact that there were two parts to the challenge, and that you would have the chance to make a video and send it home, allowed you to get something out of it if you won."

"Oh, yeah. Like my three-year-olds care about a video from Mommy. They could show them a video from five months ago and they wouldn't know the difference."

But no matter how much Chief Jeff explained that he empathized with her, and that he felt as bad as anyone that Jenna was denied, she wouldn't believe him. She couldn't. The alternative was either the disturbing thought that she'd suffered a betrayal at the hands of her family, or that some tragedy had befallen the twins. Either of those was too horrific to ponder, especially so far from home. Blaming Jeff and the production was much easier. She sagged back to the camp. Picking up the bow, she aimed an arrow at the target and fired.

Bull's eye.

Another arrow. Another shot. Bull's eye.

Later that night she would allow herself to be furious again, but this time at her family.

DAY TWENTY-FOUR

Just as gay sex was once famously described as "the love that dare not speak its name," so the Alliance had become a passionate, anonymous entity. Rudy was the only tribe member willing to talk about it openly. "Everything will be fine as long as they don't break ranks. Someone does that, and I start breaking kneecaps," he said, only half-kidding.

Former Tagi tribe members had built the Alliance. The former Pagong members lived in fear of it. And the only person not knowing which side of the line he stood was Sean. So Greg Buis' last day as a castaway began quite appropriately for Rattana, with Sean arguing against the Alliance and Richard coyly pretending it didn't exist—even as he defended it. "It's just bad karma to win that way," Sean protested. "I'm gonna vote my conscience. And that means voting the alphabet. Everyone here is worthy of winning."

"You're deluded if you think alliances are bad karma," Rich replied, rolling his eyes. His days of being infatuated with Sean were long past. "You need a reality check. This is nothing more than a game. The way to win the game is to vote people off."

"Yeah, but I don't want to win that way. I won't be able to live with myself."

"You won't be able to live with a million dollars? For playing a game intelligently?"

"Not if I have to vote against my conscience."

"Yeah. Then, like I said, you're deluding yourself."

Sean *was* deluding himself. Sometimes in life, doing nothing at all is the same as doing the right thing. Sometimes in life, only action constitutes the right thing. "Survivor" was a place for action. Since Sean had staked a self-appointed position as Rattana's moral arbiter, he had an obligation to that morality. He was honor-bound to do more than just talk too much and run from confrontation. Being moral arbiter meant taking a valid moral stand, then acting on that same passion to bring others around to his way of thinking. Otherwise Sean was just a voice droning for his own benefit.

For if the Dark Side of the Force was to be stopped, a Rebel Alliance was imperative. Sean pretending otherwise meant he was either incredibly naïve or incredibly selfish. The production crew sniffed the latter. They'd seen enough wanna-be actors to assume Sean was selling out the other castaways so he could look like the good guy on camera and thus build that television career he coveted.

Assuming the best about Sean, however—that he was not a schemer, but a good Irish-Catholic boy from Long Island who'd worked his way through medical school and wasn't cut out for leadership—the task of building that rebel, moral alliance was daunting. Sean's potential partners still had no clue about why they were on the island. They had no goals. They agreed on nothing.

On the other hand, Tagi's alliance partners knew exactly what they believed in (themselves, a million dollars). They knew where they were going and had a road map to get there. For twenty-three days they'd quietly debated, hashing out the fine points of their plan. In his first speech to Tagi, given just moments after landing on Pulau Tiga on Day One, Richard told his new teammates: "We need to communicate . . . to establish our goals. This is the correct way to maximize our success." And the Alliance had, even reaffirming those goals before the Tribal Merger. They were almost untouchable.

Almost.

The people on the bubble were Sean, Greg, Jenna, Gervase, and Colleen. If they could somehow band together, they would be able to vote off Richard or Sue, thus destroying the Alliance. Instead, they backed off from that challenge and chose to victimize themselves. Jenna couldn't say enough bad things about the people Sue instructed her to speak ill of (on Day Twenty-Four, Greg). When Sean, Gervase, and Colleen walked to Far Water, they didn't use the time alone as Tagi might have: to plot strategy. Instead, they bitched and moaned about how unfair the Alliance was. "I think Rudy is the real ringleader," Gervase grumbled.

"I don't care who it is. I just want you guys to know," Sean said, becoming a broken record, "I won't join any alliance. Just because I was in

Tagi before doesn't mean I'm part of their alliance now. I vote alphabetically. Last time it was Colleen, this time it's you, Gerv. Nothing personal."

"I know, Sean," Gervase nodded, as if he'd never heard Sean say such
a thing before. Gervase became more tuned to the game with every passing day. He may have played the slacker, but he burned with a passion for
winning. "I know. But I'll tell you one thing: voting for Gervase is a bad
idea. Gervase can help these people. And all they wanna do is vote me off.
That's what I'm talking about."

"That's the way it's gotta be, man. Alphabetical."

"Then I'll just have to win Immunity."

"That's the beauty of the system. You get skipped if you win Immunity.
I go straight to the next person on the list, which is Greg."

"So do you come back to me next time?"

"Nope. Like I said, that's the beauty. You decide your own fate. Once I
pass over you, I can't come back."

"It don't matter. I'm gonna keep myself on this island by winning every
Immunity Challenge until the end. No one's gonna vote me off because I
won't give them the chance." Gervase grew quiet. He hoped the afternoon's Immunity Challenge was physical. Not that he doubted his mental ability, but physical contests favored him over Tagi. His greatest fear
other than being voted off was that hunger would deprive him of strength
to compete. He was getting so skinny that his head actually looked like it
was shrinking.

"I just want to leave with my integrity intact," Colleen cooed. Sometimes she was so quiet people forgot she was there.

"Me too," Sean said. Then he repeated what he'd told Richard, hoping
for a more favorable response. "It's bad karma to join an alliance."

"It's not bad karma," Gervase shot back. He looked at Sean as though
the neurosurgeon were singularly dense. "It's just playing the game."

"So who you gonna vote for tonight?"

"Jenna, man. I'm voting her off. She's trying to join their alliance. I can
see it."

"I'm voting for Jenna, too," Colleen added. "She's cold."

And if Sean could have been persuaded to vote for Jenna, they might
have had the beginning of something. But Sean was adamant about voting for Gervase. The budding alliance was dead by the time they returned
to the beach with filled canteens.

To one side of the beach, Richard was briefing a producer on the Alliance's plans. He was like a general giving a press conference before the war was won. His words were chosen carefully, bereft of the word "alliance." "Greg will be the next out. After him, Gervase. I know Jenna thinks she's either worked her way into our group or is building a gender sub-voting bloc, but in reality she's just playing into our hands. We control her. She'll never vote against myself, Sue, Rudy, or Kelly. She'll be gone when we're done with her."

Gervase unwittingly expedited the Tagi plan by winning Immunity that afternoon. The challenge, "End of the Line," asked competitors to race through the jungle attached to rope by carabiners. Part mad dash, part mountaineering, the sprint over and around trees and stumps favored the young and fast. Gervase raced flat-out, finishing completely exhausted. Sean was right behind him. And while Kelly competed efficiently, her careful effort contrasted sharply with Gervase's desperation.

The older members of the Tagi Alliance were even less motivated, racing with the most minimal expenditure of energy. They weren't worried about immunity. When they'd caught their breaths, Sue and Richard leaned against a tree and gabbed casually about voting Greg off. They could have been ticking items off a grocery list.

They could see Greg from where they stood, quietly sitting on his haunches. He stared at the ground and panted. Sue and Richard hadn't known Greg well in the island's early days, or they would have been able to see how much he had changed since the merger. He was more polite, a better listener. Longing to be accepted, he'd been deferential to Richard, Rudy, and Sue. Greg no longer acted like he knew everything. The nature phone was cradled.

Aced out by Gervase, though, Greg was as good as voted off. If he could have won Immunity and lasted three or six more days, he might have had time to fully ingratiate himself. But Sue still loathed him and Richard still feared his potential. He hung his head and didn't say a word. His window of opportunity had just closed. He was six hours away from getting voted off and he knew it.

After the tribe returned to the beach, Greg took a long, slow walk alone. He absorbed the sights and sounds and smells of Pulau Tiga, as if seeing them for the first time. The sky was pink. The water was clear and unroiled. The jungle looked so innocuous and green, a benevolent forest. He would miss the place. Miss it a great deal. Someday, maybe when he was old, he would come back, just to walk the beaches again.

As he walked, Greg could see Richard casually wading off to go spear fishing, not a care in the world. Richard was an amazing sight in the water. Tall, wide, towing a three-foot wicker fish trap, he would swim a quarter-mile out to sea before starting his real work. Bobbing gently atop the reef, he would peer into the water searching for signs of movement. Then he would dive, sometimes twenty feet underwater. With his spear, he poked into every crevice the reef offered. Every toadstool coral bloom was a potential haven for dinner. No marine creature was safe. Lobster, flounder, eel—all felt the sharp barb of his spear. He shoved each in the trap and kicked back to the surface. After a short rest he would dive again. The process lasted until the wicker trap was filled or until Richard was exhausted. Sometime that took hours.

But on Day Twenty-Four he returned after just a half-hour with a three-foot shark. Greg had barely finished with his walk when the shark was gutted and dressed for broiling. A few feet off, Sue was pointing her nose toward Greg and whispering to Kelly, "This is judgment day for Greg. He's dead. He's out. I hate him and I can't wait to see him go."

Two hours later, during a gloves-off Tribal Council, Chief Jeff looked Sue in the eye. "Is there," he asked bluntly, "an alliance?"

Sue rocked back, then leveled him with a cold stare. "No," she lied.

"Richard," Jeff said, " is there an alliance?"

"Not that I know of, Jeff."

"Kelly?"

Lip jutting out slightly because of her pierced tongue's effect on dentition, Kelly looked Chief Jeff in the eye. Her heart went cold as she prepared to lie on national television. In a barely audible voice she said, "No. Uh-uh."

He was quiet a minute, giving her the chance to add a disclaimer. Chief Jeff's eyes held Kelly's. She didn't avert her gaze as her bottom wriggled involuntarily and her foot tapped. But Kelly held her tongue. Chief Jeff moved on.

The only honest answer of the night came from Colleen. "Why am I doing this?" she giggled, blossoming more every day outside Greg's shadow. "I'd be lying if I didn't say the million dollars."

Then Greg was voted off—enigmatic, lovable, despicable, chameleon Greg. The vote was six to three, with Sean's alphabetic ballot one of the six. Greg cried. No one could tell if it was real or he was just playing make-believe. Either way, ten minutes later he was rambling on about Star Wars and the Death Star and Rebel Alliances in the confessional booth, spinning one last tale of make-believe. Craig Piligian was waiting for Greg when the young man had finished. "How you doing?" he said, offering Greg a cigar. "I hear you've got a taste for tobacco."

Greg took the fat Cuban greedily. His body was skeletal. He stank badly. His hair bounced off his head in ten different directions. He looked less like Mowgli the Man Cub than Dennis the Menace on a drinking binge. But some sort of veneer had dropped. The days of make-believe were done. "This was the best time I ever had in my life," he told Craig enthusiastically.

It had been a game all along, Greg confided. The nature phone and the torn pants and the incredible body odor and the sleeping in the jungle had all been part of an elaborate character constructed just for "Survivor." Though he wasn't the final winner, in Greg's mind he had played "Survivor: better than anyone, and he was proud of it. Greg chose to look at the game as a wade into the netherworld between reality and drama. He'd planned his charades before coming to the island, grasping—even, I must admit, before I did—"Survivor"'s potential as a Peter Pan-like world where what was real and what was imagined were all in the eyes of the beholder. His skewering of reality on both sides of the island was the ultimate foray into dramality. Every day, in every one of his actions and words, Greg had both the production crew and fellow tribe members wondering who the real Greg was. He'd paid lip service to Kafka and *Star Wars*, then actively inserted himself an equally surreal world. His downfall lay in opting for those paradigms instead of Machiavelli's. Greg didn't have the stomach for Machiavelli. That was the realm of grown-ups. Greg was still a child.

Compared with Sean's passive disregard for the game, Greg's action's were genius. It wasn't an insult to "Survivor" that a lesser player such as Sean was allowed to keep playing, while Greg would board a boat to the Magellan. But it was definitely a sign that the weak were more necessary to the ultimate winners than the smart and strong.

Whale-sized cigar clenched between his teeth, Greg leaned close to Craig. He put one hand on the co-executive producer's shoulder, as if to hug him, but neither Greg nor Craig were the hugging type. "Tell Mark," Greg whispered softly, "that I loved the game."

The best part about the compliment that Greg was telling the truth.

EVOLUTION NINE

For the Love of the Game

DAY TWENTY-FIVE

Kelly woke up feeling haunted. In all her imaginings about castaway life, she'd never considered lying so publicly. A few months hence she would hunker down before a TV with family and friends to watch the eighth episode of "Survivor" and would see the moment replayed, just as she was replaying it in her head the morning after the eighth Tribal Council. Chief Jeff would ask Sue about the Alliance, then Richard. They would brush the suggestion off casually.

Then the boom camera would sweep low across the fire pit and aim directly at Kelly. Chief Jeff would ask her to truthfully answer about the existence of an alliance. All she had to do was say yes. What was so hard about that? Of course there was an alliance. Everybody knew there was an alliance. There was nothing illegal about one. Every office in the world, every family, every nation worth its salt as an international power engaged in some sort of alliance or another. That was human nature.

But Kelly hadn't had the courage to tell the truth. The lie had been almost a whisper, but it was out there. Her words had been digitally recorded for posterity. She could never take it back.

The time had come, Kelly decided, to start voting her conscience. She wasn't making a public break from the Alliance—not yet, she still needed them. Right after next-victim Jenna on Sean's alphabetical list was K for Kelly. So she wouldn't vote for Sue, Richard, or Rudy. But the lie had put her in a rebellious mood. It felt nicely mischievous to consider wandering away from the Alliance's parental sway. The world was suddenly filled with possibility. Maybe, probably, she would cast a vote for Sean or Gervase if they got on her nerves. For the time being, voting for Colleen or Jenna would have been unconscionable, as they were forming a loose friendship.

Kelly's defection was the first chink in the Alliance's armor, and signaled yet another potential twist in the "Survivor" game. Next came a pair of questions only Kelly could answer: How close was she emotionally wed to Sue? Was she finally ready to rid the island of Fargo? Whether Kelly would cast a single vote outside the Alliance as an act of contrition then leap back into the protective fold (shades of her "rebellious" nature at home, going her own way but never straying too far) or whether she would make the bold leap completely out of the Alliance remained to be seen.

As the morning passed, Kelly shared her grief with the producers, but kept it from Rich, Rudy, and Sue. She was deeply fearful that they would start gunning for her, leaving her to dangle, emotionally and physically exposed. So as she went about her morning routine, pretending to the Alliance that nothing was wrong, she carefully plotted her next move. First, she would have to make new friends. She couldn't stand Sean and she didn't find Gervase all that charming, and Kelly lacked Rich's ability to cozy up to the enemy. She either liked someone or she didn't. Her emotions were written on her face. She wandered the beach that morning, sorting out the meaning of life on Pulau Tiga, plumbing her morality for clues as to how far she would bend in the future.

Though Kelly was troubled, her actions didn't stand out much from the other castaways that morning. Since the tribal merger, ruminations like Kelly's had become standard the morning immediately following a Tribal Council. The shock of voting someone off had passed with the night. The grieving was underway. The next step would be the anxiety about personal future, the emotional state most common in castaway life. That sensation would kick in again towards nightfall. The castaways used these "reality" days—defined by the production crew as any day without a Reward Challenge, Immunity Challenge, or Tribal Council—for deep thought and regrouping. Each congratulated themselves on surviving one more Tribal Council, then questioned their resolve for the increasingly competitive push to the finish. Sometimes they struggled with their previous night's vote, for discarding friendships was never easy. Sometimes they rejoiced that a troubling face was no longer sharing the same beach. Wouldn't it be great, they all thought more than once, if you could get rid of problem relationships as easily in real life?

On the other side of the island, Chief Jeff was looking at a piece of his past. The final media group would be arriving that morning from KK, but instead of the usual hodgepodge of print journalists and camera crews, the last group was a single media outlet, the entertainment television show "Access Hollywood." In addition to the camera crew and segment producer, the on-air talent came too. "Access" would spend two complete days and nights on the island. Their report would show life in Pulau Tiga's dramality, from the production compound to castaway life and challenges.

Jeff Probst had once enjoyed a career as an on-air talent at "Access Hollywood." His job had been traveling to location shoots or on media boondoggles, interviewing the world's most famous movie stars. His time there ended amicably. The time had come to move on. As much as he had loved the job, some greater career desire nagged at him. Only by stepping away from "Access" could he get the emotional space to figure that out.

It was ironic. Tony Potts, the man who had replaced Jeff at "Access," was the talent stepping off the *Sea Quest VIII* in unwrinkled outdoor clothing and shiny new hiking boots. Potts wore three-days' stubble and Italian sunglasses with thin wire rims. In a sense, Jeff was looking at what he might have been himself had he not decided to leave "Access." More dramality. "Access"'s presence wasn't a dilemma for Jeff; it was a chance to effect closure as he moved from one stage of his career to another. In his quest for personal and career growth, he'd realized that being a celebrity reporter wasn't his niche. "Too many times I was the guy hanging around the set waiting to do an interview. I made a lot of money. I flew first class everywhere I went. I spent my time hanging around movie stars. The public saw me as a celebrity, but I was just the guy interviewing celebrities. I wanted to go in a different direction with my career. I wanted to use my God-given talents to their utmost, and I didn't feel like I was doing that at 'Access.'"

To that end, during his eighteen-month self-imposed hiatus between "Access" and "Survivor," Jeff had become a prolific writer. When "Survivor" wrapped, he was flying home to direct a script he'd written. His search for greater creative and emotional depth was coming full circle, with Pulau Tiga and "Survivor" the sanctuary bestowing blessed perspec-

tive. Whatever slivers of self-doubt he harbored about his career choices were dispelled by having "Access" come to "cover" him.

"It made me realize I was never comfortable in that job," he noted with an air of satisfaction. "That wasn't my gift. I mean, Tony is incredible in that job. He is a far better entertainment reporter than I could ever hope to be. Now I'm where I want to be. I'm totally at ease and comfortable in this job and in this island environment. It's bringing out a side of me I've always wanted."

Some of the crew were on the verge of marriage. Some were in the midst of divorce. Many of the crew—rootless because of their professions, unmarried, pleasantly surprised to be enjoying the close relationships of Pulau Tiga—pondered a lifestyle change that would allow more emphasis on family.

Life seemed simpler on the island. Mankind seemed so small in contrast to the sea and stars. Problems sorted themselves out. The isolation of Pulau Tiga made it the perfect place for emotional and spiritual rebirth.

The shiny, happy, impossibly well-scrubbed appearance of the "Access" team didn't just present a juxtaposition between Jeff's former and current lives, but contrasted with that of everyone on the island. Even more than the other invaders of the previous two weeks, "Access" represented the outside world. Not necessarily in a bad way; their crew was an outgoing, unfailingly pleasant and friendly group of people. But they scurried about frantically, driven by some self imposed deadline, never stopping long enough to enjoy a moment or ponder some hard truth. "Access"'s behavior was jolting because it represented how every member of the "Survivor" production team acted before finding their way to the island. As each inhabitant of Pulau Tiga burrowed into his own heart of darkness for answers and light, that outside world seemed a shallower, flashier place. Some production crew were even talking about staying on the island after everyone had left. Or, barring that, traveling through the back roads of Asia in search of a similar island—if only an emotional one.

As civilization became a distant memory and island friendships blossomed, conversations among the production crew had become eerily similar to those of the castaways. It was as though Richard Hatch were leading some sort of massive group discussion throughout Pulau Tiga. The inevitable discussions about sex and longing had given way to disclosures about pasts and love and philosophies and hopes and fears. The complex morality play evolving among Rattana embroiled the production crew. Questions about absolute right and absolute wrong were intertwined with discussions about the definition of good and evil. To an individual, the crew were repulsed that the game had reached a new moral low. Inherent in their initial attraction to the project was the chance to see greatness shine in humanity. A survivor, should be someone superlative for all the right reasons. Like the US Olympic hockey team beating the Russians in 1980, Kirk Gibson hitting the impossible home run in the 1988 World Series, and Dan Janssen finally winning his Olympic Gold after years of failure, the hope was that the winner of "Survivor" would touch that wondrous core essence of humanity. That the game was going in another direction was mildly distressing, like a mirror reflecting poorly on the crew's own humanity.

The castaways spent as much time thinking and healing and taking stock as the crew. The island demanded it. The absolute nature of island living stripped away hype and superficiality. The castaways were all good people. Even with a million dollars altering their perspective—and with just fifteen days left, that cool million seemed more and more attainable—the castaways would eventually do the right thing. Or would their behavior descend into the realm Freudians know as the Id? This force is bent on anarchy and amorality; its only function is guaranteeing the survival of its host. To this end the Id is laserlike in its focus and tenacity. Existentialists claim that denial of the Id leads to perversion of human nature. Moralists claim an unharnessed Id is a perversion unto itself, a preference for evil over man's singular ability to show reason and compassion.

The crew searched for the reemergence of good character in their castaways. So although Kelly's morning of anguish was painful for her, involving hours of soul searching, there was a quiet rejoicing throughout the production compound. Maybe, people said to each other over dinner, this marked the end of the Alliance. Maybe Kelly's dilemma marked the beginning of the end for the game's villains.

DAY TWENTY-SIX

Jenna's video arrived. Her mother had been traveling when the request came from "Survivor" that she make a personal video to overnight to Jenna. Belatedly, a darling movie featuring Jenna's twins appeared in the "Survivor" edit bay. A family man myself, I knew how hard it must have been for Jenna to go without the video. However, in fairness to the other castaways, I made the tough decision not to show it to her after the fact. When her time on the island was done she would see the video. To go through the complex process of hauling a television and generator back to Tagi Beach and running the video just for Jenna's satisfaction was not only hard physical labor, but might even hurt Jenna's place on the island. Her fellow castaways might think it preferential treatment, then vote her off. Some of the castaways had begun thinking like that, imagining the production favored one castaway over another. And while it was true that certain castaways were seen as villains and others good guys, that perception changed moment by moment, action by action. At no time did the production treat one castaway differently than any other.

Luckily, I didn't have to grapple with Jenna's video issue long. Day Twenty-Six offered Jenna another chance for a communiqué from home. The Reward Challenge would be held in the jungle a half-mile inland from

Pagong Beach. Known as "Out on a Limb," the challenge involved a web of ropes strung through and around thick grey-trunked banyans and ironwood trees. The ropes spidered outward in a series of configurations—a rope bridge, a hand-over-hand, a tightrope—like a military confidence course. There were eight sections in all. Starting from the center of the web, castaways would navigate each rope obstacle. They weren't allowed to touch the ground. It was a challenge designed for the fast, the agile, and the brave.

At the beginning and end of each section was a medallion. The castaways would grab the medallion and place it in a satchel. When they'd gathered sixteen medallions they would race back to the center. First to gather all sixteen and return to the center would win, with the grand prize a good, old-fashioned American barbecue dinner for one.

Several additional prizes would enhance the victory. The first was a cooler of Bud Light. The second was a letter from home. This time, if she won, a letter was waiting for Jenna. When Chief Jeff held up a sheaf of envelopes before t he challenge, hers was the thickest packet. The bulging collection of notes and children's drawings guaranteed to atone for the missing video.

In his pre-competition brief, Chief Jeff only mentioned the barbecue and letters to the castaways. Keeping with the Navy SEAL maxim that "It pays to be a winner," the Rewards Challenges were offering a progressively richer bounty as the "Survivor" game raced into the final stages. Immunity was everything, but rewards like food and comfort had their own enviable heft. The beer would be such a surprise, sprung after the competition was decided.

Jenna ached to win. The letter called to her. Jenna was one of those people who didn't like winning as much as she hated losing. She'd won Tribal Challenges as a part of Pagong, but hadn't won any of the individual challenges. Just once, because her mood was dimming further every day, Jenna wanted to win something. Pulau Tiga had replaced the façade of confidence that propped her up emotionally with a more honest front—moments of true happiness and the confidence to embrace deep sadness, if only tenuously. Changes likes that don't stick overnight. The confidence doesn't seem real. There were days and nights fraught with self-doubt. Hunger and the daily fear of getting voted off accentuated Jenna's self-doubt. So she needed to win something. The world, or at least all of America, needed to see that Jenna had the right stuff. Deep inside, she needed to see it too.

The castaways made their way to the "Out on a Limb" course. A hard rain had saturated Pulau Tiga the night before. As always after a rain, the mosquitoes were out in force. The trail was muck. The castaways stopped to gape at a 150-foot-tall banyan felled by the storm. The narrow tendrils of its shallow roots poked from the horizontal trunk. The patch of ground that had nurtured the banyan since its days as a seedling was a gaping hole. The banyan would rot where it fell. The sand and mud would eventually welcome a new flock of seedlings, and, someday, another banyan.

The trunk blocked the trail. The castaways detoured down its length and around the hole, through yet more swampy goo. In the first days of island life the castaways might have tiptoed around mud, looking for dry ground so their precious new Reebok sandals and running shoes wouldn't get dirty or wet. That time had long passed. Their shoes had seen ocean and rain, jungle mud, and three textures of sand. The castaways walked single-file through the muddy water, hardly noticing their footwear. Clean shoes would have seemed preposterous in comparison with their bug-bitten, sunburned, bony torsos.

"Welcome," Chief Jeff hailed from the center of the ropes course. The ropes were actually above him, ten feet off the ground. He stood next to a ladder. The castaways would climb the ladder into the hemp web, then begin their pseudo aviary experience on Chief Jeff's "Survivor's Ready… Go!" command.

The castaways looked at the course with awe. Their tree-mail messages rarely gave more than a hint about the nature of a challenge. Several times they'd shown up to find a game so utterly beyond their imaginations that the immensity and complexity stunned them. The castaways couldn't possibly know it, but art director Kelly van Patter, senior producer Brady Connell, and challenges producer John Kirhoffer labored twenty hours a day to give the challenges both a great sense of competition and an indigenous island look and feel. The games were either strenuous ("Quest for Fire") or entertaining ("Bugging Out"), but always true challenges, pushing the castaways in odd mental or physical ways and sometimes both. The challenges never descended into parody. At their worst, the challenges were merely stimulating. At their best, the challenges were the sort of once-in-a-lifetime experiences the castaways would remember long after leaving the island. "Out on a Limb" was just such a challenge.

Chief Jeff explained the rules. He instructed the castaways to poise for the start. They tensed, wondering if their tired and malnourished bodies were capable of racing.

"Survivor's ready..."

Jeff checked to make sure no one was bent over tying a shoe or tucking in their shirt or in any way unprepared to race.

"Go!"

The castaways clambered off in eight directions. Surprisingly, the most monkey-like was Rudy. Long years plying the Navy SEAL O- (for obstacle) Course in Virginia Beach gave him an ease on the thick hemp. Whether navigating the V-shaped bridge (a single strand of rope to walk on, with two waist-high ropes on either side as handrails) or the hand-over-hand single rope, he moved gracefully and easily. Sometimes it was hard to remember that Rudy was seventy-two years old. Men half his age moved with less coordination. To borrow a term from the espionage world, Rudy had become the consummate "gray man" on the island. He blended in wherever he went, coming and going without notice, just part of the scenery. But on the ropes some youthful instinct kicked in. Winning mattered. The barbecue had very little to do with it.

Gervase was on the other side of the course. In his whole life, the city boy from Philly had never done anything resembling "Out on a Limb." Ropes courses didn't abound in the inner city. But he was living with a hunger beyond gnawing pain, a catabolic jag almost done using his minimal body fat for an energy source. Next his body would feast on muscle and tissue, just to find calories.

Gervase wasn't racing for a moral victory. He raced for piles of red meat, bread, fruit, and vegetables—all of which he planned to smother in barbecue sauce and pack into his stomach. So he moved along the ropes with a fiendish intensity that made up for lack of experience. Flashing around the course, Gervase tottered on the edge of disaster. Sometimes he would slip and dangle by a fist, ten feet above the jungle floor. Sometimes the going was easier, and Gervase swung athletically from rope to rope, a born ropes man. What he lacked in experience he made up for in determination.

Of all the "Survivor" players remaining, Gervase was the one man who hadn't compromised his personality. He would be, he promised the producers before his selection, lazy on Pulau Tiga. Gervase wasn't going to some tropical island in the middle of nowhere to engage in manual labor. "Look, I'm not against work. I've had times in my life where I've worked three jobs, a hundred-twenty hours a week. So I know I can do it. But if I'm going to an island to compete with other people for a million dollars, I need my energy. I can't be wasting it by working all the time." Gerv promised to spend long hours reclining, coasting on his charm. People would keep him on the island because they liked him.

Amazingly, the strategy had worked. At no point had Gervase altered that behavior. And he wasn't deluded in his belief that he was charming, for Gervase was truly blessed with charm—a rare quality. He could be comical, speaking of himself in the third person. He was not a politically correct man; though he lived at home with his mother, he was the father of three children out of wedlock, with a fourth about to be born any day back in Philly. But Gervase Peterson was a man who believed that his natural charm would overcome all. With any luck he would fulfill his plan of winning immunity as often as possible to bust alliances, then go on to win the million. If only for having the moxie to be proud of being a charming layabout, Gervase Peterson was worthy of winning "Survivor."

But it was Colleen who bagged the medallions first. The little woman's behavior on the ropes matched her behavior on the island—quiet and careful. She was happiest when no one paid attention to her. Colleen had a rock climber's body, lithe and long-muscled. She shrieked with delight as Chief Jeff counted the medallions from her satchel. When he'd confirmed sixteen she thrust her fist into the air. "Barbecue!"

Jenna collapsed onto the rope canopy, dejected. Once again the most competitive individual on Pulau Tiga had failed to win a challenge. Once again, she would receive no news from home.

Gervase's stomach spasms called out to him angrily.

Rudy gasped for breath, suddenly exhausted.

Chief Jeff looked hard at Colleen. "I thought you might like to invite a friend to our little barbecue."

Colleen didn't think twice. "Jenna." Jenna shrieked and hugged Colleen. Beautiful, bony, and bikinied, they looked like a pair of runway models on a photo shoot gone horribly wrong.

All the other members of Rattana agreed. Jenna's lack of a video had bothered them. Despite their petty arguments and money lust, the tribe could be protective of each other. It was Rattana against the world, or at least, the other side of the island. "Yeah. That's fair," Sue nodded, "she's the only mom here. She deserves it."

So Jenna and Colleen had a little barbecue on the beach. Chief Jeff bade the women sit. He would cook the hot dogs, hamburgers, lamb, and shrimp; buns, mayonnaise, mustard, ketchup, lettuce, tomatoes, onions. There were also baked beans to be warmed and watermelon to be sliced. Jenna sobbed reading the letters from home. Colleen quickly skimmed through a card from a friend she'd known since first grade, then listened as Jenna read aloud. The women reclined in the shade of a mango tree, on the exact site of a long-decayed Japanese refueling dock from World War II. Only a rusted metal cleat fused by time to a tidepool remained of that history.

"Can I have something to drink, Jeff?" Jenna asked vacantly. "Is there a canteen around here?"

"You know," Jeff said. He'd been waiting for Jenna's request. "You've been in the jungle a while now…" Then he rambled a few seconds, telling Jenna and Colleen how they didn't smell so good and how they were look-ing skinny and filthy and bug-bitten and maybe a little hairy, and how it had

obviously been a long time since they'd enjoyed the comforts of home. That's when he spun around and reached for a hidden cooler. "So . . . despite all that"—and here he sold the moment—"there's no bad time for a Bud."

The women squealed as Jeff produced two iced Bud Lights. They struggled with the twist tops, then guzzled the pale lager greedily. They sat around that barbecue for hours, chugging beer and eating so much food that their skinny little bellies were distended in a noticeable pooch when they waddled back to camp.

But they had used their time away from the group wisely. Swearing Chief Jeff to secrecy, Jenna and Colleen declared they were sick and tired of being victims. The Tagi Alliance, they declared, must be defeated. Thus, the Barbecue Alliance was born.

DAY TWENTY-SEVEN

"April 8 is my birthday," Richard Hatch had been saying for weeks. "And I'm going to spend the whole day in my birthday suit." A man of his word, he rose at dawn and stripped. Nether regions blew in the wind as he strolled alone down the beach to enhance the sense of freedom. Breakfast was soon after, a bowl of Rudy's best rice eaten before the communal fire. Colleen was offended by the nudity, but Richard didn't care. It was his birthday, after all, and the Alliance had already decided when Colleen would be voted off. What did her opinion matter?

Besides, if Rich couldn't splurge on a huge dinner with family and friends or enjoy a rip-roaring night in Newport, a little Tagi Beach nudity was the next best thing. Spearfishing was on the agenda later in the morning—nothing like the happy sensation of daytime skinny-dipping. Then, in case we didn't get enough footage of Richard's maleness (strategically covered in an Austin Powers-like way, with tree leaves and coconut husks), the afternoon's Immunity Challenge would be held on the wide open spaces of Pagong Beach. Richard planned to avoid clothing for that moment in the sun, too. Let the censors deal with it.

The *coup de grâce* would be a night at the Tribal Council, Richard banging the gong and strolling across the log bridge to sit splay-legged before the fire. All of America would know that Richard was much more than just a smart "Survivor" player, but a free spirit as well.

All in all, a memorable way to celebrate his birth; a story for the ages.

When Richard waded off to go spearfishing, the cameramen opted to stay on the beach. They focused instead on Gervase, doing a one-on-one interview about the tribal vibe. "They keep talking about me joining an alliance," he told producer Jay Bienstock. "But I'm not gonna do that."

"Why not?"

"It's not the way you play the game."

Jay said nothing.

"It's not the way Gervase plays the game."

"Is your way working?"

"No," Gervase replied wearily. He paused. "Damn. You're right." A flash of inspiration played across Gervase's eyes.

And so Gervase altered the way he played "Survivor." Sidling up to Colleen and Jenna, he joined their fledgling Barbecue Alliance. Though he'd been one of their prime targets, Colleen agreed to take Gervase in if they could all vote Richard off. That nudity thing was really weighing on her.

"Happy Birthday, Richard," Jenna growled, anticipating the moment His Nakedness would walk sullenly into the jungle after being voted off. She hated any man controlling her destiny. But when an arrogant type like Richard controlled her destiny it was especially galling. Nothing would make her happier than crushing the big man and sending him home on his special day, hairy, naked body and all.

The Barbecue Alliance faced just one problem: With eight castaways left, their three didn't form a majority. To vote Richard off they needed one more vote for a tie and two for a majority. Kelly, Sue, Rudy, and Richard were spoken for, so they approached Sean. "I told you Jenna, no offense but I'm voting for *you* tonight. I'm voting the alphabet," he informed her. Sean could be very annoying when he was in a self-righteous mood. The tribe had begun to suspect the alphabet strategy was all about self-preservation. Was it only coincidence that all the former Pagong had names starting at the beginning of the alphabet, while Tagi's names came at the end? Despite the neurosurgeon's protestations of innocence, Jenna, Colleen, and Gervase doubted Sean's integrity. They thought he'd jump into the Tagi Alliance the first chance he got.

"I thought you were voting your conscience," Jenna said.

"My conscience is the alphabet."

"Yeah, yeah, yeah. You've told us that. But this is a chance to vote Richard off."

"I can't do it. I like everyone. I don't want to vote anyone off."

The coaxing went on awhile longer, but it was useless. Sean was stuck on voting his conscience or the alphabet, somehow making them one and the same. He was naively oblivious to the fact that the Alliance had spun his alphabet strategy in their favor. Since they knew his vote ahead of time, the Tagi Alliance could pile on and vote for that same person. For instance, when Sean was voting "G" for Greg, the Tagi Alliance simply swung all their votes behind Greg. The only question for the ninth Tribal Council was whether Sean was going alphabetically forward to Jenna or backward to Gervase. The Alliance were hoping Chief Jeff would ask Sean more about the voting strategy during the Council. If Sean specified whom he was voting for, they could confidently align behind that individual.

The best part for the Tagi Alliance was that they didn't even need Kelly's vote. Richard and Sue knew that she was remorseful over the last Tribal Council. As a pair of mature adults who'd known their share of re-bellion in younger days, they were aware that Kelly needed a Council now and then to spread her wings and vote on her own. The separation would make her feel mature, allowing her a sense of rebellion while, iron-ically, quelling her rebelliousness. Since she would never vote against one of them, Richard and Sue and Rudy were content to let Kelly go her own way. The three of them, plus the unwitting Sean, would make four votes.

Struck by a pang of worry that his nudity was offending more than just Colleen, Rich put his clothes on at noon before heading to the Immunity Challenge. Then, for a pleasant change of pace, Rudy won Immunity. The crusty old man with the homespun sound bites ("When them Green Berets were here, I made sure they knew Richard was queer. That's the sort of thing they need to know.") was proving himself the Matlock of Pulau Tiga, a master of the "Survivor" game. He was honest about life as a retired Navy SEAL ("After all those years in the ocean I don't even go in the water for fun anymore. It's like asking a mailman to take a walk."), and that playing "Survivor" meant double-dealing ("We're playing for a million dollars. Of course I'm gonna vote the competition off. This is cut-throat.") with new friends. He was a lifelong Navy man, defined by devo-tion to the mission. Sometimes that meant a certain amount of stealth. All the castaways, for instance, were respectful of Rudy, but might have been doubly so if they'd known that a book about his exploits, *The First SEAL*, was a classic in Special Forces circles. And not just in the U.S. Military, but worldwide. Rudy was a living legend. His fellow inhabitants of Pulau

Tiga, in his mind, were much better off not knowing that one of the greatest Special Forces men in history was in their midst.

Rudy proudly wore the Immunity Talisman walking into the Tribal Council. All along, Rudy had claimed the challenges favored the young and physical over the mature. More rock-hard than ever as the island burned away any retirement flab, accentuating traps and lats built through years of swimming and underwater demolition drills, Rudy could hardly have been considered frail. But he was over twice Gervase and Sean's age. Competing with them physically was almost impossible. With every challenge that he failed to win due to that physical disparity, Rudy soured on the system. So when he finally found a challenge suited to his strengths of strategizing and wile ("Squared Off" placed castaways on a human-sized chessboard and asked them to slowly edge one another into a corner, then off the board) Rudy exulted. He waltzed into the Tribal Council looking carefree for the first time in his Pulau Tiga existence, banging the gong with the zeal of a drum major. Still, when Chief Jeff asked whether age and guile helped Rudy win the challenge, the vet clammed up. He didn't want Rattana thinking he was smarter than them. Though protected by the Alliance, he'd learned long ago that nothing was a sure thing. Rattana might turn on him if they knew he had an advantage, gunning for Rudy the way he gunned for the physically gifted. "It wasn't nothing special," he told Chief Jeff after a few seconds of silence.

"Your experience, your intellect...none of that helped you today?" Jeff pressed.

"Nope. Just lucky, I guess."

"You're sure?"

"Oh, yeah."

That was all. Rudy would speak no more. Chief Jeff moved on to someone guaranteed to be more expansive. "Sean, tell me about your strategy."

It was left to Sean to ramble on and on and on about his alphabet and moral system and how the alphabet was conscience. He was very proud of himself. In his eagerness to offend no one he didn't realize he was offending everyone.

"Putz," someone whispered off-camera, listening to Sean. With every passing Tribal Council the suspense grew. The audience of production personnel grew with it. Standing behind the cameras, in the jungle, the audience received the final vote at the same time as the castaways. Cast-

aways' comments in the pre-vote discussion were listened to with fascina-
tion. Certain Tribal Council events, like Kelly's white lie and the time
Rudy found out there was a homosexual seated beside him, zinged into
the audience like a tracer round.

So it was with Sean's continual display of self-justification. Kelly referred to Sean as "the most arrogant man on the island," for just such dis-
plays as that. She'd confided to producer Jay Bienstock an hour before
hiking to the Tribal Council that Sean would get her vote that night.

"So," Chief Jeff said to Sean. "You're a doctor. Say you're in an emer-
gency room situation. Three patients come in, all equally injured. Would
you treat them alphabetically?"

"That's different."

"Really?"

"Sure. I get paid to make life and death decisions every day."

"So why can't you make a decision here? Sue, what do you think of that?"

"He doesn't have any balls," Sue blurted.

Sean held his tongue. His face wore the same fearful look he'd worn
the day he thought he'd be voted off. Sue held his future in his hands. She
was all-powerful. He was impotent. Lashing out was unthinkable.

"So . . ." Chief Jeff asked. "Who are you voting for tonight, Sean?"

"Jenna." He turned to Jenna, sitting on his left. "Nothing personal,
Jenna."

She giggled nervously.

"You don't go backwards in the alphabet to vote for Gervase?" Chief
Jeff pressed.

"No. He won immunity last time. He earned the right to get skipped."

The conversation went on twenty more minutes before Chief Jeff rose
slowly and cued them. "It's time," he barked, "to vote."

The final tally was one vote for Sean (Kelly), three votes for Richard
(Colleen, Jenna, and Gervase), and four votes for Jenna (Sean, Rudy,
Richard, and Sue). As Chief Jeff held up the final ballot, Jenna's name and
her fate writ large, he smiled grimly and looked into Sean's eyes.

"'J,'" Jeff said softly, "for Jenna."

EVOLUTION TEN

Full
Disclosure

DAY TWENTY-EIGHT

One medical relief for dysentery is a diet of rice and bananas. The two have a superlative binding effect.

Dysentery had never been a problem for the castaways. If anything, the converse reigned. While the castaway menu rarely featured bananas, rice was a staple of breakfast, lunch, and dinner. That, combined with dehydration, made constipation the quiet agony of castaway life. They hobbled, third trimester expectant, aching and bottled. The nagging throb left the castaways cranky.

Hunger added an additional pain. The producers had informed the castaways not to expect any more rice, so severe rationing was in force. The pain of an empty stomach doubled their misery. And the morning after getting three votes at the Tribal Council, on his birthday of all days, Rich was in no mood to fish. He ambled to the waterline, declared the water too cloudy, then sauntered back to the fire and plopped down on a log. His mood was surly. He felt like picking on someone. Halfheartedly, Rich poked fun at Sean and the alphabet voting, and was happy when a number of other castaways joined in. But Sean was too self-righteous for the insults to stick, so Rich quietly let it drop.

Just then, Gervase paddled the raft ashore. The city boy had fallen in love with Pulau Tiga and embraced her charms whenever possible. Whether it was midnight skinny-dipping, marveling at the green phos-

169

phorescence glow around his body, or just a simple paddle atop the reef to stare down into the jumble of coral and fish, Gervase tried everything, if only to say he'd done it. Gervase exuded wonder. "My Dad died when I was fifteen," he confided. "One day he just didn't come home from work. I realized then that life is soooo short. One minute you're here. Bam. The next minute you're gone. You gotta grab every experience you can, and live without regrets."

As Day Twenty-Eight marked four weeks on the island, Gervase was especially anxious to savor Pulau Tiga. He'd seen the writing on the wall. Competitive threats were getting voted off. Gretchen and Greg, the leaders, had gone first. Then it was Jenna because of the alphabet. Though "K" for Kelly was next, Gervase had a sneaking suspicion that the alphabet vote would be conveniently discarded. His athleticism made him a threat. Gervase had three days left on the island. No one knew it better than he.

The morning float was contemplative, Gervase strategizing about a last-ditch effort to save his place on the island. By the time he dragged the raft up the beach, then tied it off on a tree branch, he was OK with all that was about to occur. He would square off with his opponents. No begging. No regrets.

Gervase made his way to the fire. He was genuinely enthused, and knew nothing of Rich's anti-fishing pledge. "That reef is beautiful today. Damn, Rich. You're gonna catch some fish today. I've never seen that water more clear."

Rich harrumphed and fled the fire. He needed to be alone anyway. Spreading the folds of a hammock, he slowly lowered his heft into the red mesh, then felt it envelop him. The hammocks were small, almost mini-hammocks, so Rich wasn't entirely comfortable, but at least he was swaddled in his own little world. Rich forced himself to think strategy. Worry, however, kept interfering. He felt weak and vulnerable for the first time in the game. Three votes meant three people disliked him strongly enough to get rid of him. They hadn't selected Sue, or Kelly, or even Rudy. They'd ganged up on Richard. That they'd done it on his birthday imbued the act with malice.

Richard nudged his thoughts back to strategy. As he saw it, he had two options: solidify the Alliance by adding Sean, or forming an all-male alliance. Men were in the majority. Richard, Rudy, Gervase, Sean. Not a bad alliance.

But Gervase was too strong. His physical talents meant potential Immunity right down to the Final Two. Then Gervase would win the popular vote on his charm. The secret, Rich finally decided, was to solidify the Alliance by adding Sean. If nothing else, men would outnumber the women after Gervase and Colleen got voted off.

As Richard was thinking, Rudy found his way to the hammock area. He carefully plopped inside the unused hammock, then lay silent a minute. For all his zeal about the spoken word, Richard enjoyed the silent communication with Rudy. It was like an island shorthand. Richard liked to say that Rudy was like his father, only more open-minded. When they finally spoke, not a word was wasted. "I'm worried about Kelly," Rich stated.

"Yeah?"

"She's not being loyal to the Alliance."

"Loyalty is important. Same for honesty."

"I'm glad you're still in the Alliance, Rudy."

"I gave you my word. I'll stand by that. I expect the same from you." Rudy's voice was menacing.

"We'll stay together until the end, just the two of us."

"We're buddies. That's the way it's supposed to be."

Rudy heaved himself from the hammock and walked slowly back to stoke the fire. Richard felt reassured, knowing that Rudy was loyal. Not that he'd ever doubted the old man, but it was nice to hear the words. Richard's fear ebbed. He was able to focus again on winning the game. It was time to admit to Sean that there was an alliance, and to allow him to join.

"Richard." It was Sean, speaking conspiratorially. He might have used the same voice to pass state secrets or make a drug deal. "Can we talk?"

Richard's strength was returning. It flowed through him, energizing him, making him want to burst from the hammock and stir up a little controversy, just for kicks. But Rich remained calm, stoic. Silence was his ally. "What can I do for you, Sean?"

"I wanna join the Alliance."

"Alliance? I didn't know there was such a thing."

"Rich..." Sean looked both ways to make sure no one heard him. "Of course there's an Alliance."

Richard smiled. "In fact, Sean, there has been an Alliance since the day we got on the island. Sue and I and Kelly formalized it on Day Three."

"You guys should have let me know what was going on."

Rich ignored him. "You can join the Alliance now."

Sean's relief was palpable. "That's... that's great, Rich." Sean paused. "Look, how about we make a pact. We work together so it comes down to just me and you as the final two."

"We'll talk about that some other time, Sean." Richard looked his young charge in the eye. "No more alphabet. From now on, you vote the way I tell you."

"Sure, Rich. Of course."

"I mean, you have to admit that the alphabet thing was pretty stupid."

Intelligence was Sean's Achilles' heel. Telling him he was stupid was as devastating to Sean as telling him his jokes weren't funny. "It wasn't stupid," he argued, launching into one of his soliloquies. "It made me stronger. I was weak in the past. I'm totally OK with all my previous decisions at the Tribal Council. Plus, alphabet voting took care of Pagong, who all seemed to have names at the start of the alphabet."

"And alphabet voting allowed you to take the moral high road and stay likeable."

"Exactly. People like me here on the island because I'm open and honest and have no hidden agenda. You might think I'm an idiot—I know a lot of people do—but my strategy is actually sophisticated and well thought out. When you think about it, you'll see that the alphabet strategy was very intelligent."

Richard nodded, letting Sean have his moment. "But were you really voting your conscience?"

As Sean completed his Faustian bargain by admitting that his strategy had nothing to do with his conscience—had never had anything to do with his conscience—Sue and Kelly were having a private conversation of their own. Sue needed to bring her little friend back from rebellion before she strayed too far. With the end of the game drawing near, Sue wanted Kelly at her side. Just as Richard needed Rudy's reassurances, Sue needed Kelly's. It didn't take much prompting before Sue had Kelly talking about how much she hated Rich and barely tolerated him. Sue felt stronger for hearing those words. She was as sure as she could be that either she or Kelly would win the million. Sue controlled her own destiny and it felt great.

But she wasn't working as hard as Richard to influence the final vote. Both she and Richard planned on making the final two. The winner would then be decided by popular vote. Sue just assumed that people liked her and excused any of her obnoxious qualities. Sean, for instance, had said he didn't mind when Sue said he had no balls. "That's just the way Sue talks. It doesn't mean anything."

Of course, it did mean something. But Sue knew that Fargo accent made her sound dumber and less malicious than she really was. She was counting on that to sway votes her way.

Richard's accent, on the other hand, bordered on East Coast upper crust. While Sue's insults came out as folksy, Richard's compliments came out as arrogance. His every syllable bordered on the pompous, whether it was intended to be or not. So to make friends and influence the final vote, Richard had to charm his fellow castaways. "I'll do whatever it takes to endear myself to those getting voted off," he declared.

Once Richard brought Sean into the Alliance, and felt powerful enough to plot strategy again, he even set animosity aside to court Gervase. "I just want you to know, Gerv," Richard confided. "That I'm incredibly sympathetic to the plight of African-Americans."

Gervase just nodded his head, taking it in. He'd heard confessions of white guilt for years. No reason someone like Rich shouldn't pander as well.

Before Rich could enter the realm of the truly obsequious, a tree-mail was discovered. Tree-mail was always greeted with relish because it made life more interesting or brought news of another twist in the "Survivor" game. Rattana gathered around to read the mail. This piece of news was unparalleled: Gervase was a father again. The day before, in Philadelphia, Gunnar Peterson had been born.

Gervase covered his face with his hands and said a silent prayer of thanks.

Cigars had come with the tree-mail. And so the men and women of Rattana sat on their ramshackle beach in the middle of the South China Sea, smoking cigars in honor of a new child halfway around the world. Constipation, hunger, crankiness, and alliances were set aside to bask in a fellow castaway's happiness. "His middle name is gonna be," Gervase said, tilting his head back and blowing a smoke ring, "Tiga."

Someday, long after Gervase had forgotten the special glow of phosphorescence or the complex beauty of a reef seen through clear blue water, that vestige of his time on Pulau Tiga would live on. And when his young son was old enough to ask about his curious middle name, Gervase would tell a wonderful story about a beautiful, surreal island in the middle of nowhere.

DAY TWENTY-NINE

Not everyone thought that Gervase fathering four children out of wedlock was darling and romantic. As Gervase enjoyed a thirty-minute phone call home (not a gift, but won as part of a challenge known as "Bamboozled") to Carmela and baby Gunnar, the men and women of Rattana debated the morality of his actions. "I don't like it," Rudy grumbled. "Having four kids and no wife is not OK. It's not the right thing to do."

"I agree with Rudy," Sean said. Sean's relationship with his own father was extremely close. Though Sean considered himself the black sheep of his family, he also considered his father to be his best friend. Sean was like that when it came to relationships, alternately feeling very close to people and sensing some unspoken disapproval.

"A child needs a father," Rich said. He'd given the matter a great deal of thought. Richard's issues with his father made it impossible for him to maintain neutrality on Gervase's rootlessness. Children, in one of Richard's most fervent opinions, needed to be loved. Held. Hugged. He'd adopted his son at the age of six, rescuing the child from a life of sharing hotel rooms with a prostitute mother and her clients. "I can't imagine being halfway around the world for the birth of a child. That's one of life's all-time great moments."

The men all nodded knowingly. Richard and Rudy were the only other parents in the entire bunch, male or female. Their words seemed to carry greater heft.

"You can make a mistake once," Sue noted slyly. She had a way of sliding the quick one-liner into a conversation. "Four times, though? Come on . . ."

But Kelly and Colleen's youth made them see Gervase as some sort of hero. Their worldview leaned toward a "live and let live" philosophy. A person was only ethically incorrect, in their book, by committing an act of cruelty or by being terminally unhip. Every other action was fair game. "He's here to help pay for the kids," Colleen noted. "That's a good thing."

Kelly nodded without saying anything.

"I'll tell you what, though," Sue concluded. "Just because he has all those kids to pay for doesn't affect how I'm gonna vote. All of us have different needs. We all need the money just as badly. Except Sean, of course. He's a doctor."

"Hey," Sean said. "I have almost a quarter million dollars in student loans. I need the money as bad as anyone else. I'm definitely worthy."

Sue smiled. "I know, Sean. I was only joking."

If Susan Hawk had a pet phrase, "I was only joking" was it. She was fond of saying the mean or rude or shocking, then trying to make it all

OK by throwing those four words into the air. For the most part, she was succeeding. The other castaways were wary of her, but they liked her. The only person immune to Sue's zingers was Richard, because their alliance partnership depended upon mutual respect. When Richard did something ludicrous or pompous that Sue was dying to lampoon, she walked away before making a face. Or she'd wait until she and Kelly were alone, then speak her mind. To his face, Rich was Sue's partner. She'd promised him loyalty. Their alliance would go down to the Final Two. Their team was the only one that mattered.

But behind his back, Sue called Rich names. She mocked his intellect and homosexuality. She thought he was grumpy and hard to live with. His childish behavior, arrogant tirades, and recent refusal to fish had only reinforced that opinion. "Rich," Susan said, "thinks I'm just a dumb redneck. But that's just a game I'm playing. If I play the part of the dumb redneck no one's threatened by me, especially a city slicker and snake like Rich. Well, I may be a redneck, but I ain't so dumb. I can't wait to take him down. That's gonna feel so good."

Sue's partner in Rich's demise would be Kelly. The two would work as a team to vote Rich off. Their plan was a blindsiding of Rich, so he would be totally, absolutely surprised. Before a national television audience, Rich Hatch would be stripped of his arrogance. Sue and Kelly spent long hours talking about that inevitable night, and how they couldn't wait to see the look of shock and betrayal on his face when the votes were announced.

Sue didn't hate Rich because he was fat or gay but because he was arrogant. She hated him because he thought he was smarter than she was. Rich talked Sue up around camp, made her feel like co-leader. But she knew Richard thought himself capable of controlling her. All her life, people like Rich heard Sue open her mouth, then made fun of her. They treated her like an imbecile, mocked her Midwestern roots. The movie *Fargo* had given her accent a certain cachet, but people like Rich often forgot that the movie's heroine was a genius. They equated the Fargo voice with simple minded rednecks. Well, Sue was a genius—in her own way, of course, and with her own special charms. She'd known a tough life, but she'd survived, and even managed to find great happiness in the midst of it all. She and her husband Timmy were deeply in love.

Richard would be the sacrificial lamb atoning for the insults and aspersions cast by a thousand New Yorkers and Los Angelenos. Sue would get respect for the Midwest once and for all.

To make it work, however, vulnerability had to be avoided at all costs. Not even Kelly could know that Sue had a soft side. That was why Sue walked far away from the tribe to discuss her feelings toward Kelly the morning of Day Twenty-Nine. In a tear-filled interview with producer Maria Baltazzi, Sue revealed the story of a very special friend she once had. The two were inseparable, almost sisters. On Easter weekend twenty years ago, that friend was killed in a car crash. Sue had never let go of the memory, nor the void left by her dear friend's passing. "Every week," she cried, angrily wiping tears away, "I think of her and miss her." It was symbolic that the thirty-ninth and final day of "Survivor" was Good Thursday, the traditional start of the Easter observation. Sue wasn't religious; in fact she shied away from the tribe's lone Bible, and even agreed with Marx that religion was the opiate of the masses. But she embraced life, and had a deeply sentimental side. "Look, I won't lie to you: If it comes down to just me and Kelly in the finals, people are gonna vote for her over me. That part's just a popularity contest. I'd be much smarter to get rid of her early, so it's just me and Rich in the final. Everybody would vote for me and I'd win a million dollars."

She halted for a second again, about to cry again. "So, yeah, if I don't vote Kelly off, I'm making a nine-hundred-thousand-dollar mistake. But I don't mind. I'd sacrifice that money in the name of friendship." She dried her eyes, then screwed her face into a cold-eyed scowl. "There ain't no way I'd fuck Kelly over, no way."

Kelly, unfortunately, was having very specific thoughts about screwing over Sue. She was approaching Colleen and Gervase to form a voting group of younger tribe members. Then she took her machinations to a far more insidious level. Pulling Rich aside, Kelly proposed an alliance between the two of them. The final vote would just be Kelly and Rich. "What do you think?" she asked. "We could work together."

"Let me think about it," Rich answered sagely. He felt all happy inside. For all its pains, he loved the "Survivor" game very, very much. "I'll get back to you."

Rich left Kelly and walked straight down the beach to Sue. "I have something to tell you . . ." he began softly. "Something about Kelly . . ."

DAY THIRTY

Gervase wore a target emblem on his shirt for the Tenth Tribal Council. He'd made it from tape inside the medical supply kit. Colleen wore a sitting duck. Befitting their respective self-images, Gervase's target was very large, beginning at the base of his neck and extending far below his waist. Colleen's duck was a cute little thing, artfully taped, barely covering her sternum. "This evening, Jeff,' Gervase announced as Rattana arrayed themselves around the fire, "I would like to be known as Target."

Across the fire, sitting silently, Greg Buis and Jenna Lewis looked on. Because they would be involved in the final tribal vote, the two of them had been brought back to the island as a jury. On Tribal Council nights they would take *Sea Quest VIII* over from the Magellan, where they were living on room service and lying by the pool. The next five voted off would join their ranks. The jury wasn't allowed to participate in the proceedings in any way. Their job was to look on and form an opinion. Nothing more. But with just ten days left in the game, and popular vote the key to ultimate victory, the castaways were already courting the vote. Colleen made eyes at Greg across the fire. Richard brought Jenna a pair of beautiful shells to take home to her daughters.

Chief Jeff moved quickly to nip fraternization in the bud, stepping in and taking Richard's shells away before they could be passed to Jenna. It was clear that Richard was trying to use the Tribal Council as a means of engendering Jenna's good will, now that he'd voted her off—he needed her vote for the final. "Tribal Council is not a message center or gift exchange," he told Richard sternly. Chastized, Richard merely shrugged and pretended he'd been performing a humanitarian act.

The Council began on that awkward note and soon descended into a theater of madness and disclosure. Sean admitted publicly that alphabet voting was a mistake. But only, he insisted, because it was such a great idea that everyone "began jumping on the bandwagon."

Something Sean said made Sue want to clear the air. For the first time, the Alliance went public. "There's nothing wrong with alliances, you know," Sue said defensively. A lot had happened in the last few days. She looked confident as she finally stepped from the shadows and revealed her leadership position. "People make alliances all the time. It happens in businesses, it happens in churches. You've got people going to church just to sell more insurance, not because they're churchgoers. That's an alliance."

"So how long," Chief Jeff asked, "has the Alliance been in existence?"

"Oh, I'd say since the third day we were on the island," Sue answered. "Rich come to me and talked about it then."

Jeff didn't go to Rich for his thoughts on the irony of Sue comparing island life with the corporate world. Their first day on the island, Rich had made a similar comparison and Sue had scoffed. She said island living had nothing to do with the corporate world. Even though the Big Man had won Immunity the night before at "Fast Fire," a fire starting challenge, Chief Jeff knew he wouldn't be smug about Sue's admission. Something like that could crush the Alliance. Better to let Sue continue than digress with Rich. "The way I basically vote," Sue continued, "is to keep people I like on the island and to get rid of people who are threats. I'm older and more mature, and so are most of the former Tagi tribe. We get along because of that, but we're also vulnerable to physical challenges. I don't want people on the island who are going to win challenges and keep immunity."

All eyes turned to Gervase.

"Give me," Chief Jeff said, "three good reasons why you should stay on the island."

Gervase's moment commenced.

Someday, when Gunnar Tiga Peterson will be old enough to watch the videotape of his father's bold statements, he will see a model for manhood. He will see a power in his father's words. Decisiveness. Fearlessness. More than anything, Gunnar will see a refusal to kowtow to oppression. Rather than give Rattana power by submitting, Gervase displayed his strength. A sub-current of the "Survivor" game had been fear and submission. Gervase didn't change that, but at least he refused to pay homage.

"They'd *better* vote me off. Gervase learned long ago that the only person responsible for Gervase is Gervase. If they don't vote me off tonight I will win this game. I will win every Immunity Challenge, and get rid of them one by one. If they don't vote me off, I *will* win the million. I *will* make them pay for this mistake." He paused, shook his head while looking at the ground—a trademark Gervase move. Then he looked back up at Jeff. "That's all I got to say. Don't make the mistake of keeping me around because I—will—beat—your—ass."

Gervase was voted off.

It was fitting. Gervase never really belonged on Pulau Tiga. He'd always been a long shot. The million was an attraction, and Gervase would have loved to win. But "Survivor"'s greatest attribute was the way it peeled back layer after layer to expose a person's essence. That was part of the game's appeal for spectators, and was why villains could turn to heroes overnight and vice versa. Sue Hawk, for instance, was turning out to be softer and more maternal than she initially let on. Kelly Wiglesworth had acquiesced to authority for almost four weeks before rebelling, then lashing out vindictively at her maternal companion. Richard Hatch, it was becoming obvious, liked to pretend he had the world all figured out, and was the brains behind the voting alliance. Sean Kenniff was a nice, indecisive guy from Long Island who was proving to be as smart as he liked to proclaim, and though a slow learner was playing the game better and better with every passing day. Rudy was Rudy, and far smarter than anyone gave him credit for. Sean had begun to see that Rudy was "as wily as a fox."

What the game revealed about Gervase was sweetness. Not just charm, but a deeply felt love for life and a comfort in his own skin. In life's survival situations, such as the business world, sweetness will get you only so far. And so it was on Pulau Tiga. Gervase lacked that extra little character tic required to be truly cutthroat—and truly powerful. He got exactly as far as he knew he would. When he finally changed strategy slightly by joining an alliance, it was too little, too late.

After walking off the Tribal Council set and taping a five-minute confessional, Gervase went through the psychological debriefing with Gene Ondrusek. The party began after that, a celebration in a sequestered area of the jungle with his fellow Pulau Tiga expatriates, Greg and Jenna. They drank beer and wine, told bad jokes about the island, and eased each other's disappointment about being voted off. They could finally speak freely about who they liked and didn't like.

"I really liked it here. No. Gervase *loved* it here. I'm gonna remember this the rest of my life. So I didn't win the million dollars. So what. The important thing is I played the game Gervase's way. I can go home and hold my head up, knowing I didn't change one bit. This is going to be just one more great experience in my life. I don't have any regrets at all," Gervase said emphatically. His words were less a defense than a philosophy.

Gervase said a lot more that night. He got wound up, and was so glad to be able to speak freely after four weeks of guarded conversation, that he couldn't stop talking.

On the other side of the island, five castaways and one scared little duck completed their trek back through the jungle blackness. Trying to ignore the rats and snakes, they lay down to sleep.

EVOLUTION ELEVEN

Broken
Promises

DAY THIRTY-ONE

On the afternoon of Day Thirty, a few hours before the Tribal Council, I had stood on the compound deck, a bullhorn in one hand. The volume was turned all the way up. "Tomorrow's challenge will start and end on time. There will be no negotiation."

The announcement was an inside joke among production personnel, but not necessarily a humorous one. For some reason no one could explain, the challenges always began at least an hour after they were scheduled to. The difficulties were ever changing—a problem positioning cameras, or the tide approach or receding too quickly, or some last minute fine-tuning of the challenge. Forty individuals would stand around in the blazing heat or the pouring rain (Pulau Tiga was like that) waiting for the problem to be fixed. Only when every last detail was perfect would supervising producer Scott Messick ask for quiet on the set. Gabbing would stop instantly, and the only noises would be the screech of wild birds and the thunder and hiss of waves crashing onto the beach, straining up the sand only to die for lack of momentum. Only then would Scott slowly look around to make sure everything was in place. "And ... action," he would say calmly. Scott had determined early in the production that the best way to be heard in nature's chaos was to whisper. "It's your show, Jeff."

On Tribal Council nights, the late starts were especially irksome. An Immunity Challenge scheduled for afternoon might run so long that it would spill into Council set-up time, forcing a postponement of the Tribal Council. On two occasions, late evening thunderstorms hurled themselves down on the Tribal Council, storms that would have passed over an empty set if the Tribal Council had started and finished on time.

And while the "hurry up and wait" effect of the delays caused a small amount of bitching and moaning among both castaways and production, in the greater scheme of things late starts had a minimal effect on island life—dinner might be delayed an hour, or the sunset not observed so closely. But two issues drove me to try to insist on keeping to schedule: The obvious one was money. If we delayed to the point of needing extra shooting days, we might go over budget.

The other was respect for the castaways. Unlike a traditional television show, the stars of "Survivor" weren't lounging in air-conditioned trailers as the crew set up camera and sound. "Survivor"'s stars were standing in equatorial sun and rain. Making them wait not only angered them, it was rude. If they perceived us as such, they could band together, mutiny, and become the puppeteers.

The challenge of Day Thirty-One had an added need for punctuality, hence, the bullhorn. A complicated surprise was in the works. Even as I paced the deck, seven castaways' loved ones fidgeted on standby at a hotel near Los Angeles International Airport. Seven airline tickets to Kota Kinabalu had been purchased. Only one would ticket would be redeemed. The castaways knew nothing of that.

The advertised reward of Day Thirty-One's Reward Challenge, "Survival of the Wittest," was to spend the following night on a luxury yacht. What the castaways didn't know was that a very special loved one would join them.

The tight scheduling element lay in travel time. Eight A.M. Monday morning in Pulau Tiga was five P.M. Sunday night in Los Angeles. The flight from Los Angeles to KK left at nine P.M. In order for the winning castaway's relative to get to the airport, check in, and make the flight (and for the six unused tickets to be canceled), "Survival of the Wittest" had to start no later than seven A.M. and finish no later than eight. Had to. Otherwise, the relative wouldn't make the flight, and that great emotional moment of reuniting wouldn't occur. Anxiously, then, bags packed, Susan's husband, Richard's partner, Sean's father, Kelly's boyfriend, Rudy's wife, and Colleen's mother awaited word that they would either fly halfway around the world or fly home. The game had to go off on time, and their loved one had to win.

Pulau Tiga picked that morning to entice yet another major tropical storm. The horizon grew black almost as soon as dawn had wedged light into the castaway's world. The sea kicked up. The rain didn't even bother with a preliminary sprinkle, going straight from threatening to downpour.

The castaways hadn't even begun their post-Tribal Council soul-searching and alliance redefining (though, to be honest, Gervase's absence had no effect on anyone but Colleen, who suddenly found herself the only surviving Pagong member) when camera crews and Chief Jeff entered their reality. The game must go off on time, rain or no rain. The time was 6:15. The castaways were loaded into a boat and motored to Tagi Point, a promontory just north of the castaways' beach (newly renamed Rattana Beach). It was seven A.M. The game was already behind schedule.

"Survival of the Wittest" had once been titled "'Survivor' Jeopardy." The game favored the intellectual. The knowledge was arcane, uncommon to anything but jungle life. There were questions about snake bites, leeches, drinking fresh water from green bamboo stalks, ridding the body of stomach parasites, and the like. The first castaway to answer six questions correctly would win. In the instance of a tie, the game would advance to a Lightning Round. Chief Jeff, thanks to his time on VH1's "Rock and Roll Jeopardy," knew how to phrase and lob questions professionally, imbuing them with the perfect amount of suspense and heft. The castaways, already whispering to each other about how listless they felt that morning, were aching to win any game involving a meal. There would be no lack of drama. A torrential downpour crashing down on the game could only help.

Time passed. The rain was making preparation difficult. The castaways stood to one side in their yellow slickers, waiting for word of the start. Like the budding television personalities that they were, each castaway had become accustomed to the pre-taping ritual of a sound technician snaking a microphone into their clothing (miking only occurred at challenges and Tribal Councils; a boom mike was used for all other reality) and clipping a transmitter to the back of their pants. The women's microphones were generally nestled inside bikini tops. The men, however, posed a special problem. On the days that they chose to wear a shirts, Sean, Rudy, and Richard's microphones were clipped inside the crew

neck. On bare-chested days, Sean's microphone was placed inside his omnipresent light blue baseball cap. Richard, memorably, had his mike hidden in the Immunity Talisman necklace at the Tenth Tribal Council.
Otherwise, all men were boom-miked when shirtless.

The rain stopped at eight A.M. The game still hadn't begun. I paced
nervously. "Let's get this game going, people. We are behind schedule.
I've got a phone call to make."

The sun came out at 8:10, just as Chief Jeff lobbed the first question.
The castaways still wore their slickers, just to be safe. By 8:20 Colleen
had a commanding lead, and the rain was pouring down again. By 8:25
everyone was drenched, especially Chief Jeff, who wasn't wearing a
slicker. Getting soaked by torrential rain was becoming a key part of his
job description.

By 8:30, Sean had defeated Richard in the Lightning Round, correctly
answering a question about curing intestinal parasites. Drinking a tea-
spoon of kerosene, he deduced, was the remedy, instead of mango juice or
ginger ale.

The call to Los Angeles was made immediately. Sean's father would fly
to KK to surprise his son on the *Sipadan Princess*. To defer suspicion
about why Sean's reward on the boat would happen the following night

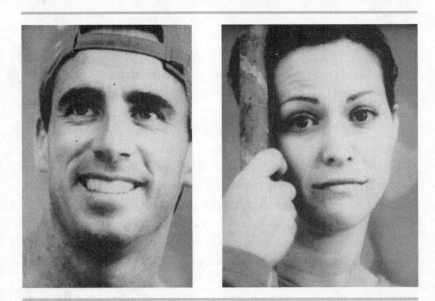

instead of immediately, Chief Jeff concocted a story about the *Princess* being unavailable until then. "Now all you've gotta do, Sean," Chief Jeff told the winner, knowing how Sean hated making decisions. "Is decide whom you want to invite onto the yacht. You'll be given one of three scenarios to choose from: Is it going to be you on the yacht with a friend, you on the yacht with everyone, or you on the yacht with everyone except one person?"

Rudy piped up immediately, ever the curmudgeon. "I don't wanna go. I'll stay here instead of sleeping on some yacht." Too many years on ships had cured him of any maritime romance.

Then, as the ocean grew progressively stormier, the castaways were motored back to Rattana Beach. The rain's thick curtain would continue for fifteen solid hours. The castaways would later call Day Thirty One their worst on the island. In that time, the "Survivor" production would know its first calamity.

The *Sea Quest VIII*, a water taxi which wasn't part of the "Survivor" production, lost hydraulic power in the heavy seas late that afternoon. She had dropped off crew on the island, then been invited to stay because of the weather and recurring steering problems. The captain, eager to return to KK, declined. Despite strong protests from the "Survivor" safety staff, he put to sea.

Sea Quest VIII lost steering shortly after beginning the trip home. Unable to steer to safety, she was pushed out to sea and lost with two crew on board. One was an experienced ocean man; the other was a young boy new to the sea. They had no water, no maps, no radio. *Sea Quest VIII*'s only saving grace was her canopy. Led by Pulau Tiga security chief Phil Kennington, an aerial search began immediately.

DAY THIRTY-TWO

Disgusted by Kelly's betrayal, Sue couldn't vote her off the island fast enough. "The one thing I learned on the island is that you can't trust anyone," Sue swore. She no longer spoke with Kelly or sat in her vicinity. The hurt was all the deeper for having trusted. When duplicitous castaways broke trusts it was expected. Rudy, for instance, was honest in saying that he acted strategically at all times. He might be polite to a fellow castaway walking into to the Tribal Council, then vote him or her off ten minutes later. Whenever he voted, he looked straight into the camera and said, "I'm eliminating the competition." That wasn't just a Rudy-ism; that was a mantra.

But when an ostensibly moral person cozied up to another, pretended friendship, then let greed and the game alter their behavior, the disappointment was crushing. For a woman like Sue, for whom trust came reluctantly, that disappointment rapidly turned to vengeance. She despised Kelly for betraying what Sue thought was genuine friendship. When people treated Sue poorly, they eventually paid the price. Just like hunting bear in Siberia, patience and stealth were the keys to bringing down enemies.

Rich seized on Sue's discomfort to firm their alliance. "Kelly goes next," the two agreed. The word was quickly passed to Rudy and Sean.

For Sean, this posed yet another dilemma. The producers had confirmed that he would spend the night alone on the *Sipadan Princess*, and was to select a single guest for breakfast. Sean didn't even have to think about it. "I owe you one, Kelly," he said immediately, New York in his voice, failing to really explain what he meant, but then again, he never did.

If Sean were merely interested in performing a humanitarian act, Colleen would have been the more obvious choice. But all her friends were gone and she had no strategic heft and was thus overlooked, which was too bad. Colleen's physical condition had progressed beyond mere island malnourishment to the point where she might eventually require serious medical care. She'd lost a tenth of her pre-island body weight. Rich's reluctance to fish depleted her energy further by depriving her of protein. Welts from horsefly, sand fly, and mosquito bites speckled her arms and legs. Worst of all, a fungal infection raged from ankles to hips on both legs. Deep lesions and scabs would scar her for life. "It's not fun anymore," she would lament listlessly. Or, "Game over." Colleen had lost all perspective and the will to fight. With just eight days left in the game she was closer to being a millionaire than she might ever be again. But she was beyond caring. All she wanted to do was go back to the Magellan and hang out with the former Pagong members. "Maybe," she said in an optimistic moment, picking at her scabs as she spoke. "If I can last to the final five, then win a few Immunity Challenges to stay alive. But that's just not going to happen. I'm next off this island, and I know it."

When the *Sipadan Princess* steamed into sight, lit up like a Christmas tree, Colleen looked on jealously. She longed to sleep on clean sheets, take a shower, wear clean clothes. The politicking and harsh behavior of Pulau Tiga's temporary residents had broken her spirit. Her only solace was that Kelly, her new best friend, would get to enjoy breakfast in luxury.

But Sean was having a change of heart. He'd received word that Kelly was on the Alliance's hit list. Better that the breakfast go to Sue or Rich. As Chief Jeff came ashore in the *Princess'* launch to pick up Sean, the young doctor fretted about the best way to dump his date. "So tell me, Sean," Chief Jeff asked in front of everyone. "Who have you selected to enjoy breakfast with you tomorrow morning?"

"Kelly," Sean said quickly. "But Kelly, Rich was really looking forward to scrambled eggs. If you want to give it to Rich . . ."

Kelly was livid. "It's your decision, Sean."

"OK, Rich, buddy. It's you and me tomorrow," Sean said a little too quickly.

As Sean motored to the yacht, a rainbow spreading from one end of the horizon to another, Kelly stomped back to the fire. Plopping down next to Colleen, she raged against Sean. "He has no balls. No balls whatsoever," Kelly said through gritted teeth. "He has no spine. He's wishy-washy. I'm definitely voting him off next time."

Sue and Rich looked on, each thrilled in their own way. The sight of Kelly in torment after a hard betrayal smacked of close to the perfect comeuppance in Sue's mind. Only seeing the little pierced-tongue manipulator voted off the island would make Sue happier.

Rich, of course, had the best of both worlds. Not only had he displayed political superiority to Kelly, but in the morning he would eat a hot breakfast on a yacht. When Rich had the island wired like that, making his own luck, life felt very sweet indeed.

Meanwhile, Sean was living yet another dream. His time on Pulau Tiga had been almost a highlight reel of once-in-a-lifetime moments. That night on the Sand Spit with Jenna had been superlative, beyond imagination. Sean had gotten a figurative second wind on Pulau Tiga by making it to the Tribal Merger. That summit reaffirmed Sean's waning faith in himself. He'd become a Survivor then, reluctantly learning how to play a game of brinkmanship and deception.

For at his core, Sean was a very, very nice man. In that way, he was like his idol Jerry Seinfeld, whose careful, distant delivery was designed to hold himself apart from the fray. But Sean had adapted to Pulau Tiga, and he was still in the game. Ten other players, some more masterful than he, had already boarded the boat back to the Magellan.

The wonder increased. Immediately after stepping aboard the *Sipadan Princess*, Sean was placed in the capable hands of masseuse Junko Takeya. For an hour, she kneaded away knots along his shoulders, spine, and legs. Hot oil, and Junko's unhurried massage, made the experience all the more pleasurable. In her non-dramality life, Junko was a tape logger in "Survivor" postproduction. She had volunteered to play along on Sean's big night. Junko chatted with him as she rubbed, careful to keep coming events secret.

All Sean knew was that he would shower after the massage, then enjoy dinner with Chief Jeff. He had no idea that his father had landed in KK two hours earlier, then been whisked through customs. Jim Kenniff, looking not at all jet-lagged, was boarding the *Sipadan Princess* as his son got the first massage of his life. The production crew hustled the tall New York fireman upstairs to the bridge, and fitted him with a captain's coat and hat. The plan was that before dinner, Chief Jeff would suddenly remember that the captain wanted to meet Sean. The father and son reunion would take place on the bridge of the *Sipadan Princess*. If there was any doubt the moment might be special for Sean, that had been allayed earlier in the day when he had said, without prompting, how much he missed his folks. "If my parents were here I'd be in heaven."

Junko spanked Sean hard on the bottom to announce the end of his massage. "Hey, do that again," he cried. It had been weeks since Sean had felt a woman's touch, and even a hint of pain was nurturing, albeit erotic. So she spanked the other cheek. Then Sean raised from the table, folded the fluffy white towel around himself, and sequestered himself in the shower for the next twenty minutes. "It was," Chief Jeff noted, "the longest shower I have ever heard in my life."

Sean came out squeaky clean, rambling on and on about how much dirt had rolled off his body. The weeks of island living had settled into his pores, filling him with a grit known only to explorers and the homeless. He looked refreshed, happy. "Well..." Jeff said with great anticipation. "Let's eat...oh, wait a second. I forgot. The captain wants to meet you. Let's head on up to the bridge before we eat dinner."

Sean entered the bridge from the rear companionway. The captain stood with his hands on the wheel, facing away from Sean, out to sea.

"Uh . . . hi," Sean said as he entered the captain's domain. His words bounced off the captain's immobile back.

Sean crept further into the bridge. Chief Jeff was a few steps behind. "Uh . . . hi."

The captain still didn't turn around. "Go in a little further," Chief Jeff nudged. "I don't think he can hear you."

Sean walked until he could almost view the captain in profile. "Uh . . ." Jim Kennif turned to face his son.

"Dad!!!" Sean threw his arms around his father. "I love you, Dad."

"I love you too, boy." Jim Kenniff's words were muffled, his son's arms were wrapped around his face so tightly.

Sean pulled away, threw his arms around Chief Jeff for good measure, then hugged his dad hard again.

After dinner with Chief Jeff, father and son retired to the afterdeck to get silly and drunk. If the ship had been a tavern they would have been drinking long after last call.

Once again Sean lived a paradise experience. A beer commercial. A moment framed, never to be forgotten. The greatest part on the *Sipadan Princess*, and what made it even better than the wondrous night on the Sand Spit, was that he got to share the moment with his best friend.

Meanwhile, a very different boating experience was being played out in the South China Sea. *Sea Quest VIII* was still missing. The aerial search for Suleiman, the captain, and David, his young assistant, had turned up nothing. I had two great concerns. First, that these men be returned home safely. Second, that the media not distort the circumstances or *Sea Quest's* relationship to the show, painting "Survivor" as a metaphorical sinking ship, beset by calamity.

I prepared to issue a formal statement. A pall had been cast over the production. Whether termed reality, dramality, or just TV, the social Darwinism of Pulau Tiga's residents suddenly seemed a pale imitation of true survival.

DAY THIRTY-THREE

Outwit, outplay, outlast. Names like B.B., Ramona, Sonja, and even Joel were reminders of some long ago time when the game was young and unknown. Going into the eleventh Tribal Council, the game was in the last, crucial phase. Endurance was the key component. All that mattered was winning the game. The allure of Reward and Immunity Challenges was waning, despite Sean's luxury night. With the end in sight, the castaways cared only about finding some hidden reserve to make it to the end. Even Richard was getting tired of the game on Day Thirty-three. "This isn't reality," he motioned about the island. Then, waving a sheaf of documents, he noted, "*This* is reality."

After breakfast with Sean and his father, Richard returned to the beach with the pair. Before a tour of the facilities, Sean's father played Santa Claus, passing out care packages from home for each castaway. Among the homemade cookies that the castaways shared freely with each other were more personal reminders of what they were missing. From Rudy's wife, Marjorie, a hat with a built-in solar-powered fan and a beer. From Richard's family and friends a thick stack of e-mails. Each man reacted differently. Rudy was strengthened emotionally by the gift, feeling confident enough to admit that his fellow castaways were all "full of shit."

Richard, on the other hand, went into a tailspin. He began talking of nothing but home and getting off the island. "The e-mails gave me perspective. There's a world outside of this game, just waiting for me. I've got friends, a son, loved ones. While a million dollars is still desirable, it's no big deal if I don't win."

Part of Rich's depression had to do with more than home. He was the least popular person on the island. Even if he made the Final Two, he was sure to get outvoted. Nobody liked him, and a few of the castaways even hated him. In fact, Rudy was the only person guaranteed to vote for Rich. The only solace he could find, amid the sugar rush and e-mails he read and reread, was that he wouldn't go that evening. Sue was adamant that Kelly would be voted off. Like a fly neatly spun into a spider's web then stuck in a corner for a rainy day, Colleen would be preserved for three more days. She might go then. Or it might even be Sean, for he was a physical threat during the final four challenges. But at least Rich was around for awhile, most likely another week. He struggled to find ways to raise his spirits.

The afternoon's Immunity Challenge did little to help. In a simple balancing contest, "Walk the Plank," the castaways balanced atop a thin piece of wood suspended above the ocean off Rattana Beach. It was a game of attrition. All the castaways had to do was stand there. And stand. And stand. And stand. Losing their balance and falling in the water meant disqualification. When the production crew practiced the game on the other side of an island, they estimated that the eventual winner would be able to stay up for three hours.

Almost to the minute, that's how long Colleen and Kelly had stayed on the plank when Colleen switched her foot position and fell into the water. She had looked so strong until then, balancing gracefully, almost balletically, as castaway after castaway toppled into the water. Rudy had fallen first. Glancing up at the sun he noted, "It's four o'clock. Time to fix the rice." A minute later he dropped into the water, waded ashore, and began cooking. Protected by the Alliance, challenges were superfluous to Rudy.

Richard fell most memorably. To annoy the others, he had launched into a loud, obnoxious version of "Ninety-Nine Bottles of Beer." Chief Jeff interrupted after the first chorus, warning that Richard was shifting his weight as he bellowed, and was likely to fall. Richard ignored him. "OK, then," Chief Jeff suggested, "as long as you're going to sing, we

might as well make this interesting. Sing 'Ninety-Nine Bottles of Beer' a la *Les Miserables.*"

For the next thirty seconds it was as though Jean Valjean himself were balancing atop the plank. Richard's sang mournfully, passionately.

"OK, now do it like *Oklahoma.*"

Three words into Richard's best Curly imitation—definitely not enough time to properly evoke wind sweeping down the plains—he toppled in with a mighty splash.

Kelly, meanwhile, wavered back and forth, on the brink of falling five times, but somehow managed to keep her balance.

When it came down to Kelly and Colleen, the two stood for a whole hour after the others had fallen. They made small talk, complimented each other on their balance. As they chatted, they compared balance techniques. Their banter was friendly, almost sisterly. But underscoring every minute of their drama was the knowledge that the loser would no longer be a member of the tribe. Kelly said as much out loud. "If I lose I'm going to get voted off tonight," Kelly said.

"Me too," Colleen replied.

Back on shore, Sue and Richard and Rudy sat together. They wanted Colleen to win. It was time, they had decided, for Kelly to go.

Then Colleen lost her balance. The girl who acted like the game didn't matter swam angrily to shore. Only when her time had come did she realize how badly she wanted to stay on the island. A million dollars was lost due to bad footing. Colleen would remember the misstep the rest of her life. Wading ashore, she walked to the shelter and slowly began gathering her belongings for the Tribal Council. It was time for her to go. "My people are at the Magellan," Colleen said of Pagong, trying to downplay her disappointment. "I belong there."

But she was secretly devastated. In some corner of her brain, a corner she'd only allowed herself to glimpse recently, Colleen had begun to think she could win "Survivor." She was close. It wasn't in her nature to be overly animated; that just wasn't cool. But she'd seen that she was the mental equivalent of anyone on the island, and she was certainly the physical better of Sue, Richard, Kelly, and Sean. With every insect bite and spread of her fungal infection, Colleen had gotten stronger. Her mind and body were in tune with the game, the jungle, and the island. When Greg left, and everyone thought she would crumble, she got stronger.

When she balanced atop the two-by-four for two hours, and it was just her sure sense of balance against Kelly's unsteadiness, Colleen was never more sure she could win. And while it was a statement far too bold for her to say out loud then, Colleen had crossed the line from child to adult. She was the coquette no longer. Colleen was one bad ass, tough, gnarled, wily, prove-it-all-night "Survivor" and she knew it. Getting voted off was not going to be the anticlimax she'd imagined. Getting voted off was going to hurt. A lot.

Quiet, demure, polite, sweet Colleen swore a blue streak as she packed her belongings. She felt just as betrayed by Kelly as Sue had felt just a day before. "Kelly," in Colleen's words, "is a liar. She's a member of the alliance. She caused me to lose my balance on the pole out there. It's her fault I'm going to get voted off and she knows it. She plays like she's this nice girl who's everybody's best friend. Well, she's nothing like that..." The rant continued, devolving into profanity and bitterness. Did Colleen care about the game? Oh, yeah.

The *Sea Quest VIII* was found at sunset, just as Colleen was dropping into the water. The South China Sea calmed after the storm. Waves weren't a problem but intense heat had scorched the open boat. Suleiman and David had lain down to conserve energy and expend as little bodily moisture through sweating as possible. Current had pushed the *Sea Quest VIII* eighty miles due north, almost to the Philippine Island of Palawan. Thirsty, but otherwise unharmed, Suleiman and David were lifted from the deck by an Air Sabah Jet Ranger and flown to the Magellan. The production breathed a collective sigh of relief.

Tribal Council was a strangely open affair that night. The mood was one of animosity and regret. Rich, for his part, was deeply disappointed that he wasn't voting against Kelly. "This is Kelly's fault, if only she didn't mess up our plan.... I was just starting to like you... unfortunately, Colleen you are the sacrifice..." he said that night at the voting booth, staring into a camera, holding up the white scrap of papyrus on which he'd just written Colleen's name. Rich wrote in a slapdash style, his tongue poking from one corner of his mouth. The seeming lack of deliberation gave lie to the long hours he spent plotting individual fates.

Rich's words had a special poignance, for Kelly had displayed her most rebellious moment to date just a few minutes earlier. Almost as soon as the Tribal Council began, emboldened by the Immunity Talisman dangling from her neck, she laid into Sean hard. Not only had he reneged on his promise of a great breakfast, but he'd thrown responsibility for the decision back to her. She was as scared of playing the bad guy as Sean. Her strategy was to fly low, and deflect bad vibes onto others. Sean had put her in a bad spot.

"Hey, Kelly. Rich is a great provider. It made sense for him to go. Also, he had just been talking that afternoon about how much he missed scrambled eggs."

"I'm not saying Rich didn't deserve it. I'm saying I don't like your indecisiveness." This was the most Kelly had ever said at a Tribal Council. Her rage was total.

"Hey, look. I made a decision. All the time, you guys are getting on me about being indecisive. I finally make a decision. And because you don't like it, you come after me and give me a hard time. You know, come to New York and I'll owe you two dinners, so come on already."

Kelly just rolled her eyes, as if she thought Sean would find a way to wriggle out of that promise, too.

Rich, Sue, and Rudy listened with a rage of their own. They all wished they didn't have to wait three days for the next Tribal Council. Given their druthers, they'd have voted Kelly off that minute. Only they couldn't, because she wore the Immunity Talisman. So Colleen had her torch snuffed by Chief Jeff, then heard the words.

"Be nice," Colleen said sweetly. The game was down to five serious players. Very soon, alliance would be forgotten and a cutthroat dash for a million dollars would begin. Like Gervase just three days before, it was fitting Colleen wouldn't be there for that descent. She wasn't hard like that. "Play fair."

Colleen was the last member of Pagong. Her departure made the final a sweep for Tagi.

EVOLUTION TWELVE

Sex, Lies, and Videotape

DAY THIRTY-FOUR

There were two mud volcanoes on Pulau Tiga, one in the swampy, spooky southwest quadrant, the other at the island's geographical center. When castaways and production talked of taking a trip to the mud volcano, however, they referred to the latter. The gray, smooth mud oozed from the ground cold. Methane gas pockets drove the muck upward and made it bubble ever so slightly. The methane could not be seen or smelled, but lighting a match over the escaping gas produced a nice visual: a spear of flame standing straight up and down, three feet off the ground. The apparition lasted a millisecond, then burned itself out.

The mud volcano was the recreational hub of castaway and crew life. The two forces never met there, merging their realities, but each visited the mud for its therapeutic effects: slathered on the torso, the face, even massaged into the scalp, the mud was a skin tonic. By the time castaways made their mile-long trek back to Rattana Beach, the mud was dried, the skin was taut and smoothed, and a dip in the ocean washed the muck away instantly. Likewise for the crew.

It was fitting then, that the ultimate convergence of castaway and crew reality took place via the mud volcano. Not that it was planned that way. What I had in mind was the silliest of Reward Challenges, something that wouldn't tax the tired castaways emotionally or physically. The Reward Challenge would be a mud game. The castaways would have two minutes to coat their bodies with as much mud as possible. After, they would squeegee the mud into individual buckets. The buckets would be weighed. Winning castaway would be the one with the most mud on their body, proven by having the heaviest bucket. The reward was one cold Bud Light.

But as I and Chief Jeff trekked to the mud volcano for the challenge, word came by walkie-talkie from the producers. The castaways, the message said, thought the reward was going to be spectacular, especially after Sean's night of fine dining. I'd underestimated the level of expectation we'd created among the castaways. By offering grandiose rewards like Sean's night on the *Sipadan Princess*, the bar had been raised very high. It had become impossible to lower it without severely damaging their morale. The word came back that the castaways genuinely believed that the winner would receive a brand new Pontiac Aztek.

That wouldn't do. There was no car. There was, on the island, just one bottle of Bud Light.

Trailing behind me on the narrow uphill trail were a dozen corporate sponsors of "Survivor," excited after watching twenty minutes of "Survivor"'s rough cut. Though only on the island for six hours, the advertisers were being given a condensed slice of Pulau Tiga life. They'd motored past the castaway beach, eaten lunch in the compound, viewed the rough cut, and were making an authentic jungle hike to the mud volcanoes. Everything had gone swimmingly. The sponsors couldn't have been more enraptured. I was seeing the "Survivor" concept's corporate success guaranteed. The day couldn't have been going more perfectly.

We were less than two minutes walk from the mud volcano when I got the walkie-talkie message. "What shall we do ?" I said aloud, rhetorically. I knew we had to think fast. My mouth was tightening into the hard half smile I tend to show under pressure. Chief Jeff was a step behind, sweating so hard his fingertips had wrinkled as though he'd been in a bath too long. He felt just as much responsibility for the show as I did. We had to come up with a prize the castaways would immediately crave My first thought was the sponsor's excitement. It proved the inspiration I needed. A flurry of sudden ideas blasted forth.

"Well, we could..."

By the time they'd reached the mud volcano, not only was mutiny forgotten, but the castaways were downright greedy to win the challenge. "The winner," Chief Jeff announced, "will receive dinner and a night in a local Malaysian bar on a nearby island . . . *and* the chance to watch a portion of the show."

Wow. The castaways were visibly thrilled. The one thing missing from island life had been a glimpse of how they looked on television. What a golden opportunity.

Chief Jeff and I had lobbed the show as reward confidently. For after, literally, weeks of editing to establish a "Survivor" look and feel and sound, nearly fifty minutes of crisp television had emerged. The proof had come from the crew themselves, perhaps the island's toughest critics. An early version of the first episode had been shown one evening, but elicited laughter in all the wrong places. The editing crew, the island's palest residents for their long hours indoors before the island's four AVID editing machines, had gone back to work.

When the crew gathered on the compound deck a second time one week later, the laughter came in all the right places. The applause over the final fade was heartfelt. Some whooped in appreciation. Some were too moved to make a noise. Coming from the most jaded island residents, that was high praise.

So that shored up half the reward. There was no doubt Kelly, who eventually won the "Mud Pack" challenge by slathering enough ooze over her torso to tighten her skin for a decade, would be thrilled after watching the show.

That Malaysian bar was an entirely different story.

Kelly wanted desperately to visit a cool bar. That played on island lore, Robert Louis Stevenson, pirate mythology, even *Stars Wars* and *Top Gun*. Standard to all these tales is the "rogue barroom scene." Basically, for every stripe and profession, a tavern exists. Only their language is spoken. Only their culture is valued. To enter is to be immersed in a whole other world. To sit at the bar and suck down a cold one quietly, furtively, straining not to draw attention in the company of these navigators, is to witness a brand of excellence not valued by traditional society. In *Star Wars'* famous tavern scene, it was Luke Skywalker entering the domain of Han Solo and Chewbacca. In *Top Gun*, Kelly McGillis's Charlie character enters the world of Ice Man, Maverick, and Goose. The list of famous barroom scenes that began long before *Casablanca* and will continue long after *Shakespeare in Love*'s Marlow and Shakespeare confrontation has conditioned the modern mind to the notion that there is nothing more prevalent, and no sanctuary with more mystique, than these elite barrooms.

While Kelly walked back to Rattana Beach to rinse off her mud and don her Sunday best, I raced back to the compound to strategize. The small war room where so many "Survivor" story beats were hashed out was soon filled as more and more people were informed that tonight—that very night, two hours away—the compound "Survivor bar" would be transformed into a really cool local bar.

Art director Kelly van Patter entered the room and heard what was going on. Something of an artsy genius, Kelly is a perfectionist. The success or failure of the barroom scene—defined by whether or not Kelly (the castaway) was fooled into thinking she was in an actual Malaysian cantina—rested on Kelly's (the art director's) shoulders. After a moment of understandable rage at the abbreviated time table had subsided into resolve, she went to work. Bamboo curtains were hung, tables were moved, all vestiges of "Survivor" production personnel were removed. Meanwhile, the small group of Malays who'd boated over to Pulau Tiga to assist the production were brought together and promised a night of free food and drink. All they had to do was act naturally.

By sunset, the compound deck resembled, well, the compound deck. Partitions had been hung. Bungalows were visible, the path to Tribal Council was visible, the compound generator loomed tall and yellow on the beach. However, when the sun set and bungalow lights were extinguished, what remained was darkness surrounding a very real Malaysian tavern. The generator hummed peacefully, anonymously.

"You think we're gonna pull it off?" Craig Piligian asked.

"We have to."

"Good answer."

Craig Piligian and John Kirhoffer left in a boat for the other side of the island to pick Kelly up. She was led on board, then blindfolded. For the next hour, the *Tiga 5* rambled aimlessly about the glassy South China Sea, turning left then right the left again, painting broad meaningless arcs on the water. When it finally docked at the production compound, Kelly Wiglesworth would have needed a built-in global positioning system to know where she was.

Chief Jeff hailed the boat and helped Kelly out, but didn't take her blindfold off. In the distance, Kelly heard music on a jukebox. Malaysian

voices were singing along. She smelled cigarette smoke wafting her direction in thick clouds. Meanwhile, Chief Jeff briefed her on what she was about to see. He told her of an island near Pulau Tiga where the crew escaped every seventh day for a night on the town. KK was too far off for the casual night out. The tavern was primarily a local hangout, though. And while the Malays knew of the production, and happily drank with the crews, they were only vaguely aware of the castaways existence. Other than the gazes inherent in being an attractive young woman, Kelly wouldn't get a second look.

Still, she felt grubby. Kelly had done her best to tie her hair back and clean her face and even find articles of clothing that weren't filthy. That had proven impossible, however, and she was quite aware that she wasn't especially well-dressed.

Chief Jeff took the blindfold off as they stepped into the tavern. Kelly didn't give the cameras and lighting a second glance. She was so used to have cameras pointed her way that their absence would have been cause for alarm. She and Chief Jeff took their seats. Kelly fidgeted and looked around while Chief Jeff walked to the bar and got a couple beers. All around, Kelly saw a thick swarm of locals. They were partying hard, deep into their beer, not giving her a second look. As soon as Chief Jeff returned, Kelly took a small sip of beer, then asked for food.

Before returning to Rattana Beach, Kelly consumed three serving bowls of pasta. She took it easy on the beer to save room in her stomach for food. She listened to new music, heard mostly deep male voices speak a strange language, and ironically—or dramatically—enjoyed the only "authentic" Malaysian night of her entire trip to Borneo. It was the only time of the adventure she wasn't surrounded by Americans. All in all, she told her fellow castaways on returning to the beach, it had been one incredible evening.

She never suspected a thing.

DAY THIRTY-FIVE

Five days left. Castaway morale was at rock bottom. Nobody trusted anyone. The castaways had become five people going in five furtive directions, building friendships and alliances on the fly and disregarding them just as quickly.

The day was fragmented, a series of snapshots of the castaways' souls.

Snapshot: Dawn. Kelly and Sue shouting at each other on the surf line. Kelly's last action before leaving for her night out with Chief Jeff had been to write a long, impassioned letter of explanation to Sue. Like a wayward daughter seeking to return to the fold, Kelly explained how much Sue meant to her, and why she had approached Richard. Sue didn't believe Kelly. In Sue's mind, Kelly had ceased being trustworthy. She was no longer a daughter or a sister but an enemy. The letter, Sue stated in hard, angry words, had just been written because Kelly was obviously the next to be voted off.

Snapshot: Kelly talking about how much she liked her reward, describing how much fun she had and how much food she ate, and using great detail to depict the Malaysian barroom. She mentions that the name of the establishment was the Survivor Bar, named by locals because the production had poured so much money into the area. But Rich and Sue shoot her down, trying to demoralize her. Sean, they noted, had gotten to see his father. Kelly just got a few bowls of pasta and a couple of cold ones, then came home smelling of beer and tobacco. They want to know if Kelly was disappointed that her boyfriend didn't come. They point out that Sean's reward was a lot cooler. Kelly's face gets hard, but she doesn't let them break her.

Snapshot: Sean warmly recalling his morning bowel movement, describing in great detail the wondrous sensation, urgency, and deep relief. Somehow he segues from defecation directly into food and gardening, then rambles on about those subjects like a college professor free-associating before a roomful of students. Then, not quite finished hearing himself talk, Sean holds forth on the great restaurants of New York City. He salivates listing all the food he would eat and restaurants he would visit immediately upon arriving home. With any luck, he would be greeted as a celebrity, even at the best places, and be given a celebrity's table.

Snapshot: Sue and Rich stealing away to talk about who they'll vote off next. Rich admits to Sue that he feels vulnerable. He's afraid that if the vote comes down to just two people, he will lose. There is a caginess to Rich's voice. He's begun looking over his shoulder to make sure he isn't heard doublecrossing Rudy. His paranoia, however, is well founded. During the night, Rich and Sean were picked up by a hidden microphone, plotting strategy. Rich was quoted as saying: "I am going to undermine Sue. I'm hoping that when it comes down to the final voting, people will have had a chance to think about all the hard work I've done here. I know I'm not favored. In fact, I know most people like me the least of anyone on the island. I think they think I'm too cocky."

"I think you're overconfident sometimes," Sean agreed. "But I'll do whatever you say. I know that you're in charge."

Snapshot: The castaways playing their favorite game, "Study the Production Crew." Like inmates in some primitive penal colony, the castaways know every detail about their island existence. They know that every third day an airliner flies overhead at exactly eight o'clock. They anticipate sunrise and sunset; full moons and new moons; high tides and low tides. But most of all, they study the crew. They know the crew changes shifts at dawn and dusk, sometimes as early as six and sometimes as late as eight. The castaways learn to tell time on cloudy days by pretending to ask a production member a question, then stealing a glance at their watch. They lean close for crew conversations, learning the names of husbands and wives and children. They know which crew members like baseball, and which don't care for sports at all. They know who is gay and who is straight. They know hometowns.

"We watch you all the time," Sue tells one of the sound engineers. "This is our world. Our ears are tuned to anything and everything that goes on here."

Snapshot: Sue being interviewed alone. She's become emotionally vulnerable since crying on camera a few days before. When she talks on camera now, it's with an honesty missing in her discussions with other castaways. She says she's competing for her and her husband Timmy. She misses her dogs, Elly and Stinky. "I'm doing what's best for my family. My family is my alliance. I can use a million bucks, ya know? That's why I'm voting Kelly off the island. I'm not here to make friends, though I did get pretty friendly with Kelly for a while there. I'm here to win." She smiles a lot during the interview, especially when the subject turns to home. She can't wait to get back. She talks about dinner with her husband. Sue also admits to carrying a heavy piece of carry-on on flights, in case someone offends her. "That way you can pretend to accidentally drop it, and whack them on the head."

The instant the camera shuts off, Sue's sweet smile disappears. Once again, she looks tired, feral, angry.

Snapshot: Sean, in another one-on-one interview, calling the other castaways "the most backstabbing, double-dealing group of people I have ever met. America will say this is a whiny, disastrous, underhanded, self-serving group of people."

In a case of the pot calling the kettle black, this is the same Sean caught by hidden microphone with Rich saying, "They fell for it . . . we're home free now," in reference to a strategy conversation where Rich, Rudy, and Sue pretended to want to vote off Sean. Strangely, Sean isn't referring to other castaways being fooled, but the production crew. The castaways have entered the production's reality in a big way, taking delight in keeping motivations and emotions secret. In effect, nothing the castaways say and do on camera any more is certifiably real. They have taken to contriving arguments and strategy discussions in front of the crew. Is Sue really mad at Kelly? Is Sean really in trouble? Is Rich really worried? After five weeks of having cameras stuck in their face, the castaways are changing the rules of dramality by intruding into the production crews, instead of the other way around. Sean, the man so offended with duplicity, is a leading culprit.

Two sound engineers, Alicia Alexander and Pat Sielski, get suspicious after one of the castaways' in-depth strategy sessions doesn't ring true. When the castaways leave Rattana Beach for one of the Reward Challenges, Alicia stays behind and plants the hidden microphones that later catch Sean.

Snapshot: More fact and fiction from Sean. No longer trying to play the good guy all the time, he becomes elusive when asked why he invited Rich to have breakfast on the yacht. First, jokingly, it was: "Rich just wanted to have gay sex with me." Then it became: "Rich just wanted to have breakfast." Finally, Sean admits that Rich is "the epicenter of power."

Snapshot: With home getting closer, the castaways keep pointing conversations to things they miss most.

Snapshot: Sean saying, "I know I talk too much. This girl I was just about to have sex with told me to shut up. But I kept talking anyway, because I wasn't done telling her what I had to tell her."

Snapshot: Kelly's quote, "We're not bad people. We just play them on TV."

Snapshot: Sue saying she'd had sex in an antique store, at Disneyworld, and in an igloo inside a museum. This follows up on a discussion of two days earlier, when Sue had noted that one of the highlights of truck driving was looking down from the cab and watching sexual acts, then vividly described an instance of particularly daring roadside sex she'd witnessed in Pennsylvania.

Snapshot: Rich and Sean talking about getting fan mail. Of the five remaining castaways, they're the two most obsessed with fame.

Snapshot: The castaways reading the tree-mail note announcing that afternoon's Immunity Challenge, a takeoff on the movie *The Blair Witch Project* called "Survivor Witch Hunt." Sue is excited, exclaiming how much fun it will be to run through the jungle with a camera, making their own shaky-cam video. Kelly's sensing that if she doesn't win the Immunity Challenge, she's as good as voted off.

Snapshot: Kelly winning yet another Immunity Challenge, edging Sean in a sprint finish. She squeals with glee, then collapses onto the sand in relief, immune.

Snapshot: Sean, worried again, realizing for the millionth time in his island existence that he needs to do some quick alliance building or he'll be voted off.

DAY THIRTY-SIX

An amazing coincidence had taken place since the castaways had merged tribes: At every Tribal Council, the torch of the person being voted off went out by itself. Way back at their first visit to Tribal Council, each castaway had lit their torch in the communal fire, reminded by Chief Jeff that "fire represents life on the island." Customarily, immediately upon being voted off, castaways brought their torch to Chief Jeff. In front of the entire tribe, that torch was extinguished. The doused torches of former castaways decorated stage left, behind the growing jury.

Strangely, though, the torch of each Tribal Council victim had begun extinguishing itself during the voting. It began with Gretchen and had continued through Greg, Jenna, Gervase, and Colleen.

The production crew was bemused, calling it a fine dramatic coincidence. The Malays, however, found nothing funny in the incidents. Torches going out, they said ominously, were the work of the island gods. These sometimes playful, sometimes sinister spirits were a formidable presence on Pulau Tiga. When Jude Weng, one of the writers, had gone to bed very late one night, falling asleep on her stomach, she woke to the sensation of a person sitting on her back and two cold hands pressing into her spine. Thinking it was her roommate, she called out, crankily saying the joke wasn't very funny. Her roommate, however, was sound asleep. When Jude related the story to Gideon, a jungle guide, he asked her a single question: "Were you the last person in the camp to go to bed that night?"

"Yes. It was almost 4 A.M. Nobody else was up."

"That was the island gods. They always follow the last person home. They're not mean, and you have nothing to be worried about. They just like to let you know they're there."

When Gideon, James, and Eric, the three Malay guides, walked through the jungle, they never called each other by name. Instead, they made bird noises or animal growls. The reason was that tree spirits would steal their names, then mimic their friends' voices and mislead them. Eric liked to tell the story of the day he left Rattana Beach on his way back across the island. Though he knew the jungle extremely well, he heard James calling to him up ahead, and followed the voice. After hiking an hour and a half, Eric found himself back at Rattana. Sensing that the tree spirits were responsible for his misdirection, he made a hoop from a length of rattan. Eric then stepped into the hoop, passed it up the length of his body, and said his name aloud. In so doing, he entered a portal separating life and death and reclaimed his name from the tree spirits. Then he entered the jungle anew, and walked without incident to the compound.

There were many other spirit incidents. Before production began, local ritual was honored through the sacrifice of a goat at the base of the island's largest banyan tree. Tradition was broken, however, because the blood was not sprinkled all the way around the tree. Though warned that this would bring bad luck, the production shrugged it off. Less than a week later, that same banyan (in whose shade the "Bugging Out" Reward Challenge was filmed) was sheared in two. The top fell onto several pieces of equipment, crushing them.

One night while filming at Rattana, camera man Jim Harrington saw a banded sea krait slithering towards him. Inexplicably, the krait coiled and then rose straight up off the ground until it was three feet in the air. Slowly lowering itself back to the ground, the krait slithered towards the fire. The snake rising off the ground had astonished Harrington, but to see a snake slither toward flame was unprecedented. Animals universally shy away from fire.

Harrington, who had filmed the entire sequence, showed the footage back at the compound the next morning. Gideon was very nonchalant at the occurrence, saying that when the krait lifted itself off the ground it was not really a snake, but a friendly spirit inside the snake's body. Such spirits exist to point out beauty. Hence, it moved toward the flame.

On the other hand, Gideon pointed out, killing or harassing a snake angers the spirits. Joel Klug chased away a pit viper that was minding its own business.

That night Joel was voted off.

On the night of the twelfth Tribal Council, not only did Sean's torch go out during the Council, but it went out on the walk over, as well. Chief Jeff had just informed the castaways of the coincidental torch extinguishing the day before at "Survivor Witch Challenge." At the time, the castaways hadn't believed Jeff, thinking he was trying to get inside their heads. So when Sean's torch went out, enveloping him in jungle blackness, the castaways joked playfully. However, they knew the omen would be proved real that night. For the twelfth Tribal Council was the last place where the

Alliance could strut its stuff. Kelly, their projected target, had Immunity. Sean would go in her place.

After the twelfth Tribal Council, "Survivor" would become a poker game. For seventy-two hours, four players would sit at a metaphorical table, playing for a million dollars. A castaway would be voted off every night for the next four nights. The Alliance had gotten them to the table, but the Alliance's time was past. The game was entirely individual. The "Survivor" winner would be the best poker player.

Sensing the end of their tenuous friendships, Sue, Sean, Kelly, Rich, and Rudy entered the Council set somberly. Chief Jeff usually centered his Council discussions around Alliance talk. But the time had come for personal focus. He needed to delineate the heroes and villains, the proud and regretful. "Would your mother," Chief Jeff asked Rich, "be proud of your behavior?"

And to Sean, "Would your father be proud of you?"

To Sue, "Have you done anything you'd regret?"

To Rudy, "Will you and Rich be friends when this is all over?"

While Rich and Sean thought everyone who ever lived would be proud of them, Sue admitted to regret over lying to Jenna about voting in favor of Gretchen's ouster. She publicly apologized, looking across the fire at mute juror Jenna as she spoke. And whether a shallow attempt to curry jury favor for the final popular vote or heartfelt, it didn't really matter. Sue had admitted a weakness, something she hadn't done until then. Her fears about being portrayed as weak were passed. Through honesty and confrontation she had become strong. The blowout with Kelly two days before had been cathartic. The words Sue chose to scream at Kelly were the same words she might have spoken to herself. She accused Kelly of being weak, and "acting like a girl." Rich, Sue told Kelly bluntly, wasn't a threat in the finals, so she was definitely voting Kelly off as soon as possible. When a tearful Kelly warned Sue that Rich would stab her in the back, Sue ignored her. But at least Sue had been honest, and had played the game with a new attitude, one that transcended duplicity. Sue was becoming more likeable with every passing day on the island.

Rudy, as usual, didn't care who liked him. His friendship with Rich was slowly dying. Rich being gay had little to do with it. But before the Tribal Council the two had had words. "If he goes back on his word about our partnership, I've got friends who'll come after him." In SEAL parlance, that was called pulling an "op" on someone.

"Yeah? Well, I'm not scared," Rich shot back. "I've got friends, too." An image of the Village People breaking into Rudy's Virginia Beach home came to mind.

The two patched things up before the Tribal Council, if only for the sake of one last Alliance vote. But that their friendship, the island's longest and deepest, was hitting the rocks was the greatest indicator of the cutthroat events to come. Sue and Kelly's attempts to patch things up were heartening, but equally indicative of their coming bloodshed.

Sean went slowly into the night, leaving behind his unlit torch. He was the perfect example of a good man distorted by the game. For all his indecisiveness he made the hard, even brilliant, decision to rid the island of Pagong in favor of Tagi. With Tagi he got Machiavellian ruthlessness, but with Pagong he got anarchy. A man like Sean, with his complex brain and inherent need for structure, could manipulate and outwit Machiavelli easier than anarchy. He'd succeeded, partly. And he would make his million in his lifetime. Neurologists do that. No amount of money could have paid for his night on the Sand Spit, or drinking with his Dad on the *Sipadan Princess*.

"Did you see that your torch went out?" Chief Jeff asked as Sean heard the final votes.

Sean laughed. Torch or no torch, he knew it was coming. He'd said goodbye to Rattana while he cast his vote. "No, it didn't. You had somebody sneak up and put it out."

"No, we didn't." Chief Jeff arched an eyebrow. "It's time for you to go."

Sean walked away and Chief Jeff turned to face his Final Four. The table was set, the chips were being issued: Sue, Rich, Rudy, Kelly. "Survivor" was anyone's game.

The Final Four

Rudy Boesch
Kelly Wiglesworth
Sue Hawk
Rich Hatch

FINAL EVOLUTION

Staring into the Sun

DAY THIRTY-SEVEN

Full moon over the equator.

In the midst of their island experience, Maslow's hierarchy of needs crept up on the four remaining castaways yet again as they pondered life with a million dollars. The first stage, basic physiological needs, had been met a month before. Security and safety followed soon after, when the island's dangers become bearable. Love and feelings of belonging were closely followed by competence, prestige, and esteem. And while level six, curiosity and the need to understand might happen upon any of them at another point in life (or, in Rudy's case, had been accomplished decades before coming to the island and stayed with him throughout), the question of level five, self-fulfillment, gave a philosophical tinge to castaway life.

Simply, a million dollars was just three days away. They could see it, smell it, taste it. They dreamed of spending it. Would it change them? Would it complete them? Would it make them happy? Or had the previous five-weeks-and-a-day of existence been a futile pursuit? Castaway thoughts wandered to the philosophical and mildly spiritual.

Sooner or later, if Maslow is to be believed, an individual arrives at self-fulfillment. Peace. "A musician must make music, an artist must paint, a poet must write, if he is ultimately to be at peace with himself. What a man *can* be, he *must* be," Maslow wrote. The trick is finding that source of peace.

213

So where did the four castaways stand philosophically, three days before winning a million? At four predictably distant metaphysical compass points.

Sue Hawk festered with rage toward Kelly. On moral and ethical grounds, she wanted to rise above the rage and keep her early pact not to vote Kelly off. "I want to show that I'm a better person than she is. That I don't stab my friends in the back," Sue noted. Vulnerability and rage were becoming synonymous with Sue's character. She spoke frankly, had ceased being guarded in word or action, and, with every day closer to going home, was more aware than ever that acts of duplicity would be replayed on national television. She didn't want to be seen that way. "I've got a life after this," she said bluntly. "I've got to go back to work and look people in the eye and have them know my word is good. Plus, I feel lucky. I've been with Timmy fifteen years. We've got something really special. That's where my life is. When all this is done I'm going back home and know that I'm with someone I love. That's a great feeling, and money can't buy that. I've done some hard things on this show, like vote Gretchen off. But I've also done the right thing, as far as the game goes. Like when I voted Sonja off. She didn't belong here. The night before that, after she'd gotten soaked in the water, she woke up shivering like you wouldn't believe. I threw my body over her to keep her warm. So it may have looked heartless for me to vote off that nice old lady, but I was just trying to do the right thing. That's also why I brought up the alliances at the Tribal Council that one time. I was sick of people pretending they didn't exist. That's what I'm about. I may be blunt, but I'm honest. And I think that scares people like Kelly, who plays the game by lying to other people all the time, pretending to be their friend then stabbing them in the back."

Rich and self-fulfillment weren't as easy to decipher. The façade of arrogance Rich used to bolster his self-worth was slipping. The Great and Powerful Oz was proving to be a kind man behind a large curtain. Aside from his sexuality, he stood for no set of values or ideals. If he won the million he would continue renovating his house, and enjoy a slightly higher standard of living. He planned to open a wilderness camp for problem children. Fame as the ultimate survivor would put his business into a new realm. He would become famous, the gay icon. As the committed father of a small boy, Rich would continue searching for happiness through relationship. The money, in other words, wouldn't fulfill him or complete him or really change him. It was the victory that would elevate Rich Hatch, showing the world and his disapproving father that Rich was one sharp character.

Kelly, on the other hand, would use the million for independence, but until she broke away from her maternal issues, she would find that even money couldn't bring peace of mind. She would be a millionaire, but an unhappy one, still looking for ways to flaunt her independence and tweak the world. If she won the game she would be a beautiful and bland guest on David Letterman and the morning shows. Her picture would grace the cover of *People*. She would marry, have kids, work hard to maintain her cutting-edge mentality before giving in and buying a minivan and enjoying suburban life. In ten years she would be the subject of a "Where Are They Now?" photo essay, discussing how it was only several years after winning that she found something resembling happiness. Even then, she wouldn't call it happiness or self-fulfillment or inner peace, but something hip, like "coming to terms with what I'm all about." She was Las Vegas, a pleasant boomtown craving substance, but not quite sure where to find it.

Rudy was giving the money to his kids. He and his wife enjoyed a great marriage, loved snow skiing together, and knew a contentment in their

life that a sudden influx of wealth or fame wouldn't change. He would continue going to SEAL reunions. He would continue cooking for his wife now and again, because even away from the island, Rudy found joy in preparing a fine dinner.

Regardless of the changes money would or would not make in their lives, one hard fact stared at the Final Four as they lay about the beach on Day Thirty-Seven, pondering what it would feel like to become a millionaire: For three of them, the end would be nasty, brutish, and short. One would be voted off that very night.

With that in mind, the castaways began the dusk trek to the Tribal Council. Their line of just four seemed too short. There was anonymity in numbers. When there had been ten or even six marching to the Tribal Council, a castaway had the luxury of being quiet or arrogant. With just four, quiet could be mistaken for rude; arrogant for annoying. Either one meant a vote.

The moon had risen by the time the castaways arrived at the Tribal Council. Husky and harvest, the moon forebode a weird juju on Pulau Tiga. The pull of an equatorial full moon is greater there than anywhere else on earth, and thus a greater potential for weirdness.

The four settled around the fire for their first on-set Immunity Challenge. The game would be "Fallen Comrades," a question-and-answer session about castaways already voted off. Questions like "Who received only one vote at the first Tribal Council?" (Stacey) and "What is the title on the cover of Dirk's Bible?" (The Quest) forced the castaways to think back on their island life. Kelly won, the fourth time in a row she had won a challenge. Rudy, to everyone's surprise, was a close second, only four correct answers behind. The old man who swore he didn't know anyone and didn't want to had been paying close attention all those hours sitting before the fire.

Then Rich's torch went out. It flickered, then went black, shortly after Kelly won Immunity. Rich tried not to let it bother him. After the string of snuffs, however, every castaway believed in the island's ability to predict the voting.

In a way, the island was right again. Rich and Sue split the votes. For the first time, there was a tie. Only Rudy and Kelly would vote a second time. They would determine the loser. With the two of them safe, they were only allowed to vote for either Rich or Sue. One of those two was gone.

With Rich's unlit torch before her, Kelly re-voted first. She deliberated almost a minute before writing her answer, then stuffing it in the box.

Rudy took just a second to write his answer. He carried the ballot box back to the campfire and sat down.

Licking his lips and speaking slowly, Chief Jeff held up the ballots one at a time, reading Rudy's first. "Sue," Chief Jeff said. That was to be expected. Rudy would never go back on his promise to Rich. Loyalty and honor were everything to the lifelong sailor.

Chief Jeff removed the next ballot and held it up. "Sue."

Kelly had betrayed Sue again. Sue turned hotly to Kelly, looked in her eyes. "Sorry," was all Kelly could say, refusing to return Sue's stare.

A fierce rain began falling then, punctuated by increasingly louder booms of thunder and flashes of lightning. An hour after the Tribal Council, thunder and lightning hit the Tribal Council set. It was empty. No one was hurt. Over in the production compound, the jungle guides nodded at each other knowingly. "The jungle gods said who they wanted voted off, and were ignored," James said. "This storm is them showing their anger."

On Rattana Beach, Rich and Kelly and Rudy huddled in their hooch. Chief Jeff had warned them that the next day would start very early. In vain, all three tried to sleep, silently thrilled to be just two more nights away from a million.

Day Thirty-Eight

Episode 37 of "Gilligan's Island," "Gilligan's Mother-in-Law," had Gilligan and the Skipper immersed in Pacific islander tribal culture. A family of natives arrive from another island. The daughter longs for Gilligan's hand. First, however, Gilligan must endure a rite of passage that includes a test of strength, a test of bravery, and a feast. Of secondary importance to the plot is yet another group of outrageous visitors mysteriously arriving on Gilligan's Island, then disappearing.

So it was with Pulau Tiga. To help answer another million-dollar question ("Would you walk across hot coals for a million dollars?") a most unlikely pair of visitors entered castaway reality and breathed a little tribal culture on the castaways. Bill Bastian ("My background is fifteen years in mind/body connection, hypnotherapy, breath work, and the belief that the mind can heal the body") and Mark Reynolds ("Ten years experience, starting in corporate management and employee development") arrived to lead a fire-walking session. Part rite of passage, part test of bravery and worthiness, the fire walk would see the castaways confront their greatest fears and close out the show on the same fire-oriented note that "Quest for Fire" began it. For fire, as all the castaways knew, symbolized life on the island. The jungle guides told the production early on that fire signified an individual as coming from the land of the living, for the jungle gods couldn't make fire. And while "Quest for Fire" was about lighting fire to begin the living process, fire-walking on dying embers was about putting it out.

Wiry and intense, a pair of true believers that could have passed for brothers, Bill and Mark strode around the production compound eager to explain fire-walking and spirituality to anyone willing to listen. Predictably, the two principals of Sparks World Development Foundation ("Sparks Development for short") gave self- and corporate-empowerment seminars for a living. Equally predictably, they were from San Francisco. They said without apology that no one knew how fire-walking worked, physiologically. It just did. "Kisses," the crew soon learned, were the little blisters the fire gave to those not in tune with its energy.

"The fire is energetic," Bill said. He was the leader, the shorter of the two. They always walked barefoot. "The fire's energy is a life-force energy. Some call cultures it 'chi,' some cultures call it 'prana,' one tribe in the Kalahari Desert calls it 'num.' Here in Malaysia it's called the 'sundovan.' When the energy in a being matches or surpasses the energy of the fire, you walk. You don't walk over the fire, you walk with the fire. At a level *with* the fire. The most important thing a fire-walker has to ask himself or herself is 'Why am I walking?' Is it a rite of passage? Is it healing? The strengthening of personal or career goals? You need to know that, so when you meet yourself on the other side of the fire, you meet the path you've chosen to be."

More relevant to "Survivor," Bill had a goal for the castaway fire-walkers: Find a sense of fulfillment. "San Francisco gets sixty-four new millionaires every day. Are they instantly fulfilled? No. They still have a lot of work to do, emotionally and spiritually."

It was 2 A.M. as Bill and Mark made their fire on the sand spit (using only cedar flown in for the occasion, due to the delicate "popcorn" sensation it produced when being walked over). Chief Jeff arrived two hours later. He left again to wake up the castaways and boat them over. It was 5:20 when he returned. Sunrise was an hour away. The sky was inky, but the moon shown so brightly that the ocean bottom was visible. Neither Rudy, Kelly, nor Rich looked like they had slept much. The storm had lasted until after midnight. Their hooch had stayed dry, but hunger, thunder, and the uncertain time of their wake-up call made sleep hard come by.

Once on the Spit, Chief Jeff stepped aside as Bill and Mark led the castaways through a thirty-minute workshop on fire-walking. Bill told them about the sundovan, and the spirit of the jungle and the ocean and the fish, then reminded them that the fire had the same energy. The fire was simmering to a bright orange and white as Bill spoke. The contrast of moon and fire, darkness and pre-dusk horizon, added a certain heft to Bill's words. The air smelled of wood smoke and salt spray. The air was heavy from the rain, but warm.

As a prewalk ritual, the contestants lathered up in mud brought specially from the Sand Spit. Rudy and Kelly coated their bodies. Rich, who had shown an aversion to dirt, lightly daubed finger streaks on his chest and face. Nervously, the castaways looked at each other and prepared to walk. Rudy would go first. Then Rich. Then Kelly.

"Before you begin," Chief Jeff said to them, "I've got something to say to you." The cameras were off. Only the crew and Bill and Mark were watching and listening. With the ocean as symphonic accompaniment, Chief Jeff told the castaways how impressed the crew had been with their behavior and fortitude. The speech was short and heartfelt, and when Chief Jeff finished, the crew applauded the castaways for over a minute. The castaways, visibly touched, applauded back. It was the lone moment in the show when the dramality was purposely ignored. The island's residents showed each other that the long days and nights of hard work, hunger, bug bites, and perseverance meant something beyond just television.

By the time that magic moment had ended, on top of nearly six weeks of hardcore confidence building, the castaways were emotionally sky-high. If there was any doubt that those three castaways could walk on fire—million dollars or no—that was long gone. Stepping boldly to the fire, they heard the words of Bill Bastian: "When you participate in fire-walking, you step into a lineage of fire-walkers before you, and a fire-walkers to come." Bastian then quoted a Native American saying that summed up the fire walk, but could have summed up the show just as easily. "Those of you who face your fears squarely and give up your patterns of belief will walk on the sun."

Rudy strolled. Rich took midsized steps. Kelly, who had long wanted to walk on fire, crossed in long strides. The fire pit was ten feet long. Not a single castaway was kissed. The sun's first rays touched the Sand Spit as the castaway's finished, shaking each other's hands in congratulation.

Their work, however, was not done. In fact, the hard part was just beginning. Chief Jeff led them to the Immunity Idol, perched on a six-foot-high pedestal at the end of the Spit. "For Immunity," his voice boomed, "keep your hands on the idol. Last one with a hand attached wins."

As the sun rose, Kelly and Rudy questioned the wisdom of coating their bodies in so much mud. The temperature quickly climbed to over a hundred degrees. Though it formed an effective sunblock, the gray ooze caked on their faces and torsos and arms like some hideous form of papier mâché. Standing atop stumps to keep their touch on the idol, they looked like gargoyles. Chief Jeff came out to tempt them with orange slices and glasses of water, yet they refused to step down and accept the offers, staying on their perches for one hour, then two.

Rich stepped down first, guessing correctly that he was going to the final two, no matter what. There was no sense burning in the sun when he could cool off with a swim. If Rudy won Immunity, he would vote Kelly off for loyalty reasons. If Kelly won Immunity she would gamble that Rich wasn't as popular as she was, and that she could beat him in a popular vote. Rich came back from his swim and lay down to sleep.

"How do you feel about that, Rudy?" Chief Jeff asked. "Rich leaves you up there to do the hard work while he takes a swim and a nap?"

Rudy was ticked. "I don't like it. You didn't say nothing about that Rich. I thought we were buddies."

But perhaps they weren't, really; perhaps they were just two good men stranded on an island together. Rudy made it clear that even if Richard sent him a Christmas card, his wife would be the one opening it. Felix and Oscar were no more. Rudy was on his own. If he fell he was gone.

And, eventually, he fell.

DAY THIRTY-NINE

Richard and Kelly spent a last day on Rattana Beach, picking up odds and ends, packing their clothes for the trip home. As a keepsake, Richard kept the "Rowdy Rudy's Diner" sign hanging in the cooking area.

There was a sadness and tension to the day. Not only was their time on

Pulau Tiga at an end, but only one would win the "Survivor" game. Both had played admirably—excellently, even. Through almost six weeks of intrigue and relentless compeition they proved themselves. But as the time came to march one last time through the jungle to the Tribal Council, their fates were out of their hands. The ultimate winner of "Survivor" would be decided by the seven-member jury of exiles: Rudy, Sue, Greg, Gervase, Sean, Jenna, and Colleen. Instead of voting someone off the island, though, they would be voting for a winner. Both Richard and Kelly had made both friends and enemies during their stay, so the outcome of the Tribal Council was definitely up in the air.

They began the march at dusk.

On the other side of the island, sequestered from the production crew, the jury debated their votes. Rudy kept to himself, but was aware of the simple fact that if he hadn't accidentally removed his hand and fallen from his log during "Hands on a Hard Idol," he would have won "Survivor." By winning "Hands on a Hard Idol" he would have enjoyed Immunity. Due to his pact with Richard, he would have selected Kelly to go home, instead of the other way around. Then, with the final vote down to just Rudy and Richard, the jury would have selected Rudy, if only because Richard's scheming had hurt more than a few feelings.

But Rudy hadn't won immunity. Instead of winning he settled for third place. A man of his word, he still intended to keep his bond with Richard by voting Rich the winner.

As the hour for Tribal Council drew near, the other castaways waffled. Sue prepared a speech she planned to give, telling why she was torn between Sue ("the rat") and Richard ("the snake").

Finally, darkness fell. The time had come for the thirteenth and final Tribal Council.

I stood to one side of the set as Richard and Kelly banged the gong and filed to their seats before the campfire. Neither looked too tense, though the few small jokes they exchanged with Jeff as the jury filed in sounded forced.

Things got underway with Jeff explaining the altered format: Richard and Kelly would deliver closing arguments, saying why they felt they should be declared the winner. Members of the jury had the right to ask questions and also, if they wished, deliver a summation of their own.

What transpired over the next thirty minutes was magical. In all my imaginings during the years I prepared "Survivor," I never once foresaw the drama and poetry unfolding on the set. These people were, literally, arguing for their very lives. Their very survival. It was primal and raw and harsh and painful and emotional.

Sue delivered a rambling five-minute diatribe against the rat and the snake, finally erring on the side of Richard, for Kelly's betrayal had deeply stung Sue. "If Kelly was lying in the street, dying, I'd walk past without giving her so much as a drink of water," she said solemnly.

Kelly spoke briefly, reminding everyone, in her level and uncomplicated way, that she had been their friend.

Richard, with all the elegance of a great trial lawyer, ticked off the reasons he should win: had great strategy, built the alliance, played the game.

As the moments passed, and the words flew, the tension was palpable, and made breathing difficult for me. All around me, the faces of production staff—Craig Piligian, Jamie Schutz, Ninja, Fed, Alicia, Biff—were riveted to the set. The drama couldn't have been better if it had been written by a top screenwriter.

Finally, Jeff rose and looked hard at Richard and Kelly, and then at the jury. "It's time," he intoned gravely, "to vote."

Richard and Kelly's votes would cancel one another out, so they didn't cast ballots. They could only sit quietly on their logs before the fire and watch as the jury filed into the voting booth, one by one.

When the voting was done, Jeff walked into the booth to count the seven votes.

He came back and slowly began reading the tally aloud, holding up the slips of paper for all to see. "Kelly."

"Richard."

"Kelly…"

After six votes it was tied: three for Richard, three for Kelly. The last vote would determine the winner of "Survivor."

Jeff slowly reached into the ballot box and pulled out the last ballot. He opened it, looked at it, then slowly turned it face out for jury and contestants to see. After thirty-nine long days and nights, "Survivor" had a winner.

"Richard."

DAY FORTY

"Survivor" is done. The production compound has the frantic energy of a world slowly being taken apart. The Big White Board lists no call schedule for today, just boat departure times and return flight schedules.

It's dawn, and the wrap party is just now winding down. I think the celebration was heard in KK. Castaways and crew finally mingled and talked openly, the dramality finally come full circle. Sue has been up all night, while Richard went to bed at midnight and is eager to catch a boat for home.

The breakdown will begin shortly. I will go home to supervise the creative portion of "Survivor"'s editing, but Craig Piligian will spend another week here, overseeing the removal of "Survivor." Some things will remain: Pagong's camp, Rattana's camp. The Malaysian owners of the production compound plan to spruce the island up a bit and rename it the Pulau Tiga Resort. Rich Hatch's fishing reefs will become prime tourist scuba diving.

The castaways' camps will become tourist attractions. (There is a precedent for this: When *South Pacific* was filmed on Kauai in 1957, a hotel was built specifically for cast and crew. The cast and crew of "Gilligan's Island" subsequently stayed there during the filming of their pilot in 1964.) In a perfect world, the Tribal Council set would be left to the jungle. Like remnants of a most bizarre civilization, the pillars and fire pit and voting booth would quickly be tangled in vines and leaves. Yellow-lipped kraits and reticulated pythons and monitor lizards would make homes in its lighting towers and rigging. The sound booth might make a nice hiker's refuge. But the Tribal Council set will be shipped home, too. Leaving Pulau Tiga pretty much as we found it has become a "Survivor" mission statement.

Of course, that cannot be. The island has changed us, just as we have changed the island. No doubt even the Pulau Tiga Resort (In the interests of full disclosure to future tourists: this is like no other resort you've ever been to. The roof's leak, the showers don't drain, and there is a singular absence of manicured walkways.) will someday be overgrown. But Pulau Tiga is paradise. It really is. Until you've waded waist deep in the South China Sea and gazed west to watch a sunset that gets more stunning with every passing instant, you have never known such blessed sanctuary. The jungle in the middle is as fierce and hostile and dense as anywhere in the world. But the outer fringes of this island will call to all of me long after the show has aired, then been rerun.

I will miss the macaques throwing wild olives and mango pits down on us as we walk through the compound, their errant shots bouncing off the corrugated metal bungalow roofs. I will miss the crashing waddle of monitors disappearing into the jungle. Back in dry Los Angeles I will grow wistful for the black beauty of an approaching South China Sea storm, then the hard fury of rain, thunder, and sheet lightning jolting tiny Pulau Tiga. And after, the sweet smell of drying rain.

For those of you wondering: every word of this book has been written on Pulau Tiga, as events occurred. Nothing has been added or deleted in hindsight, including the opening sentence of Evolution One.

Now, if you'll excuse me, it's time for me to go.

Q & A with Richard Hatch

What were your thoughts as you left Tagi Beach for one last Tribal Council?

When Kelly and I left the beach, I was feeling at peace. I was not certain by any stretch of the imagination that I would win, but I'd concluded that I'd done all I could to influence my winning. And losing meant winning one hundred thousand dollars—not terrible. There was also a nice feeling associated with knowing that this was the *last* time I had to make that trek to the island council. It was funny, because I was carrying all my stuff. I never took my stuff with me before, but this time we were both leaving after the council, so I had to bring all the things I wanted to bring home.

Did you and Kelly say anything about the Council to each other on the walk over?

Kelly and I had talked about the Council and she expressed her concern about the jury being able to ask questions. I was thrilled that they could—I welcomed the opportunity to address the concerns theyactually had rather than try to address concerns I thought they might have. Kelly was worried about anger and the situation becoming negative.

Were you surprised at Sue's impassioned speech? And did you think it had any effect on the final outcome?

Definitely. I thought I'd figured out everything on the island, but even I was surprised by Sue's animosity toward Kelly. I'm not sure about the

225

impact of Sue's speech on the jury. Personally, I felt for Sue. I didn't think the venom was appropriate and I felt her anger was misplaced. Sue's boldness and directness often come at the expense of accuracy and consideration. Rather than think through what she's faced with, Sue has learned to react immediately and I think she pays a price for that. She talked about my "whining" and since I believe she missed the mark with me, I can't assign much credibility to her attack of Kelly.

You were confident your entire time on the island. How did you feel during the Tribal Council with a million dollars on the line?

I actually enjoyed the Council that night. I felt relatively calm answering people's questions and listening to their statements. Even after the jury had finished questioning and Kelly and I had the opportunity to speak, I considered defending Kelly but felt that (particularly given my cocky attitude throughout) my defense might seem insincere or so selfishly motivated as to cause people to vote against me. Anyway, I decided to wait until after the vote to defend Kelly.

You weren't even a little nervous?

I did get nervous as Jeff was reading the votes. How much closer could it get? When he read my name first, I thought Kelly had won because Jeff had a habit of saving the winning name for later. When it was tied three to three and Jeff read my name as the tie breaker—that was a surreal moment for me. I tried to grasp all of what that would mean to me and my life and could quite get a comfortable grip on the reality of it. It was pleasantly overwhelming. My heart was pounding with excitement and, interestingly, disbelief. Even though all along I'd said I would win, when that final vote was read it was hard to believe. I was also feeling for Kelly who had had to deal with Sue's pretty irrational venom. Kelly was gracious and seemed genuinely happy for me. She had feared some reaction like Sue's and said something to the effect of "I told you what would happen," referring to Sue's animosity.

Going back to the days between your selection for the show and your arrival on the island, did you plan strategy beforehand?

I had begun thinking about and planning how best to approach winning "Survivor" long before I was even selected as a contestant. My friend, Tom, and I sat down and tried to strategize about who might be selected as contestants and why CBS would choose them. We realized early on that there was only so much planning that could be done until I knew who the other castaways were and what their personalities were like. However, as a corporate trainer, I'm faced with twenty to fifty people in a room at a time that I have to size up very quickly. Who are they? What do they want? How do they need to be treated? My undergraduate degree is in Applied Behavioral Sciences. I'm several months away from becoming a licensed counselor. And I've always enjoyed figuring people out and knowing how to approach and influence them and I've always felt particularly capable of doing so. So I felt quite comfortable that I would be able to decide how to manage the castaways shortly after meeting them.

OK, the gay thing. Do you think your sexuality hurt or helped you on the island?

I think being gay is the main reason for my success. I say that because as a result of growing up and learning who I am as a gay guy in this society, I have learned to decide for myself what's important to me, to love myself, and to interact assertively with people regardless of how they might misperceive who I am or what my motives are. I love myself and consider myself one of the most moral and ethical people I have ever met. I think a very important part of preparing to win involves coming to the island whole—knowing who you are before you get there. Add to that a certain general confidence and well-traveled experience and I felt well-prepared to win—which likely looked and will likely be perceived as cocky and arrogant.

How's it feel to be a millionaire?

The victory was an extraordinary feeling—I think mostly of relief but certainly of exultation as well. Its surrealness was increased by how utterly depleted I felt. I was exhausted, mentally and physically, and starving. I remember walking around the wrap party thinking that it was done. I'd done what I'd come to do and I could relax. I couldn't wait to go to bed. It felt great and I slept like a baby.

What are some good experiences you'll remember from the island?

Beyond the million dollars, which will certainly come in handy, I look back on my thirty-nine days on Pulau Tiga with extremely fond memories. Especially the time I spent naked and alone (off camera) exploring the coral reefs off this incredible deserted island in the middle of the South China Sea. Winning the mask, snorkel, and spear (I knew I would fare well after that), spear fishing, and catching my first stingrays and shark to feed the team. Reading journal entries and e-mail from my friend Val that came in the care package with Sean's father. Becoming engaged in a real and very personal conversation with Gretchen. And finally, the moment when Rudy learned I was gay at the first Tribal Council.

Will "Survivor" become part of your business now?

I'm not sure how my business might evolve as a result of my success on "Survivor" or how I might incorporate the experience. I've been facilitating seminars in the behavioral science arena for nearly fifteen years now and I can envision altering the way I earn a living. I imagine opportunity may knock as a result of my success on "Survivor" and I look forward to answering the door. I'm open to what comes and excited about the possibilities. As much as I tried to plan to win "Survivor," I haven't really planned for after-show. I'll play it by ear and look forward to suggestions.

Final thoughts?

You know, I thought I was challenged to be the Survivor on a deserted island in the middle of the South China Sea, but as I rejoin society, it seems I'm even more challenged to be the Survivor in a situation even less based on logic or rationality... real life.

Acknowledgments

"Survivor" could not have happened without help—lots of it. The list is long and international.

My co-writer, Martin Dugard, with whom I have had a long and interesting relationship, provided the backbone of this book. We have shared Adventures together in Madagascar, Sarawak, Utah, British Columbia, Queensland, and now Sabah. I hope we have many more. Conrad Riggs worked tirelessly for over a year to craft the "Survivor" deal for me at CBS. Charlie Parsons had the original idea—and sold me the rights!! Craig Piligian provided his long and incredible reality-television experience; without him we would not have had water, power, housing, wescam permits, and a hundred other production items... or stayed on schedule. Diane Winkler and Kelly Sutherland created a hundred production schedules and budget estimates. Peter Kaufman at TV Books agreed to publish this book after only one meeting. Ghen Maynard at CBS saw the vision and championed the cause. Leslie Moonves took the risk on such an outlandish idea and Nancy Tellem gave her continual guidance and support.

Also at CBS: Kelly Kahl, Chris Ender, Mike Naidus, Colleen Sullivan, Michelle Hooper, Ron Scalera, Marc Graboff, Deborah Barak, Lucy Cavallo, John Moczulski, Francis Cavanaugh, Monty Brinton, Paul Friedman, Bruce Gellman, Jonathan Shikora, Bill Cecil, Alix Jaffe, Deborah Marcus, Anne O'Grady, JoAnn Ross, George Schweitzer, Chris Simon,

Peter Golden, Jeff Nemerovski, Judy Bass, Mark Saks, Kevin Berg, Jerry Brandt, and Cindy Bedel Slaughter.

Lisa Hennessey, Amanda Harrell, Tricia Middleton, and all the other Eco-Challengers who pitched in without pay. Sabah Tourism, Sabah Parks, Sabah Air, and all the other entities in Sabah and Malaysia who passionately gave to "Survivor."

Mostly, I thank my wife Dianne Burnett and my boys James Burnett and Cameron Burnett for suffering through my continual "nutty" adventure escapades over the years. I wish I could promise it was the last one, but it's not. I love you all so much. Please understand.

Martin Dugard would like to separately acknowledge:

In Hong Kong: Craig Foster and Neil Gane—the lads. In Kuala Lumpur: Phil Kennington, for historical conversation, Monty Python, and instruction on proper delivery of the Royal Marine salute. In New York: Thanks to Peter Kaufman and Albert DePetrillo at TV Books, and the amazing Scott Waxman and the Scott Waxman Agency. Thanks also to Jason Kaufman. In San Francisco: Thanks to Fred Escarcega, a friend like no other. In Marin: The Dynamic Duo of Gordon Wright and Austin Murphy (Super Genius) for wit and perspective. In Orange County: The Orange County Survivor Crew: Calene riding herd on Devin, Connor, and Liam—none of the words happen without these four. Al and Rosemary Dugard, for lots of things, but patronage is right up there. Tom Silber, Gary Shutler, Mike Healy, Andrea Aldridge, and the AAA Yankees for letting their manager disappear for six weeks. Mark Johnson, for the e-mails. Kay and Milan Yerkovich for the insights and encouragement. Denny Bellesi, Rick Dunn, Eric Nachtrieb. Maureen and Bob Zehntner. Harry Lumb. And finally, for Marc Andrew Dugard, forest fire fighter and Survivor in every sense of the word: The tent stayed behind.

Survivor Crew List

Executive Producer Mark Burnett
Executive Producer Charlie Parsons
Co-Executive Producer Craig Piligian
Host Jeff Probst
Co-Producer Conrad Riggs
Supervising Producer Scott Messick
Senior Producer Brady Connell
Senior Producer Tom Shelley
Producer Maria Baltazzi
Producer Jay Bienstock
Producer John Feist
Coordinating Producer Kevin Greene
Line Producer Beth Holmes
Coordinating Field Producer Jamie Schutz
Associate Producer Gavin McCrary
Associate Producer Lucretia Miller
Associate Producer David Pritikin
Associate Producer Sara Tekula
Production Coordinator Ari Gottfried
Production Coordinator Shannon Owen
Production Coordinator Kristin Eichelberg
Exec. Pers. Asst. to Burnett, Piligian-Spencer
    Rosenberg
Executive Producer Coordinator Monica Ramone

Assistant to Craig Piligian- Meredith Rozbitsky
Production Office Manager Ariel Keefer
Production Secretary Carolyn Yamamoto

CASTING
Contestant Director Lynne Spiegel Spillman
Contestant Liaison Rosslynn Taylor
Contestant Associate Stephanie Furman
Contestant Associate Kristin Lane Prouty
Contestant Associate Fred Risher

ART DEPARTMENT
Production Designer Kelly Van Patter
Set Designer Wendell Johnson
Art Director Bruce Hollister
Construction Foreman Tim Zeug
Prop Master Corey Gomez
Asst. Prop Master Adam Picker
Prop Maker Ross Cairns
Prop Maker Jesse Jensen
Prop Maker Peter "Babylon" Owens
Prop Maker Mark Powell
Art. Dept. Coord. Pamela Fletcher
Art Dept. Asst. Zuhan Charuruks
Apprentice James Burnett

CHALLENGES
Challenges Producer John Kirhoffer
Segment Producer Fernando J. Mills
Associate Producer Seth Wellisch
Associate Producer Jude Weng
Associate Producer Christopher Damon

TECH CREW AND ELECTRIC
Lighting Director Tim Blair
Director of Photography Biff Bracht
Director of Photography Mark "Ninja" Lynch
Key Grip James Carol
BB Grip Michael Koepke

BB Electric Stephan Wassman
Swing Anthony Huljev
Cam/Audio Engineer Brett Wilmot
Avid Tech Bill Ball
Equipment Specialist Rich Desabatino

POST-PRODUCTION
Post Producer Kimberly Schaffer
Post Coord. Zoila A. Galeano
Associate Producer Junko Takeya
Offline Editor Brian Barefoot
Offline Editor James Smith
Offline Editor Sean Foley
Offline Editor Chris Simpson
Offline Editor Ivan Ladizinsky
Offline Editor Craig Serling
Offline Editor John Bergstesser
Offline Editor Jonathon Braun
Offline Editor Barry Gold
Offline Editor Michael Fendler
Offline Editor Rod C. Spence
Offline Editor Dan Morando
Offline Editor Clayton Halsey
Online Editor David Harris
First Assistant Editor Henry Harmon
Assistant Editor David Cutler
Assistant Editor Paul Westmacott
Assistant Editor Anne Marie Sisco
Post Prod. Asst. Laura Ambriz
Logger Glenn Arcaro
Logger Elio Chacon Jr.
Logger Andy King
Logger Tony Perez
Transcriber Echelle Avelar
Transcriber Sergio Gonzalez
Transcriber Cristina Versage
Transcriber James Woo
Re Recording Mixer Terry Dwyer
Re Recording Mixer John Morris

Sound Editor Ryan Owens
Sound Supervisor Derek Luff

CAMERA
Camera 1 Jeff Streich
Camera 2 – JIB Mark "Ninja" Lynch
Camera 3 Biff Bracht
Camera 4 Jim Harrington
Camera 5 Randall Einhorn
Camera 6 David Linstrom
Camera 7 Richard Dallett
Camera 8 Jimmy Garland
Camera 9 Michael Murray
Camera 10 Scott Sandman
Open Title Sequence Scott Duncan
35mm Camera Asst. Abe Martinez
Wescam Operator Mark Hyrma
Still Photos Scott Duncan

AUDIO
Audio 1 Libby Fernau
Audio 2 Le Fooks
Audio 3 Fed Wetherbee
Audio 4 Tom Wardan
Audio 5 Alicia Alexander
Audio 6 Pat Sielski
Audio 7 Derek Carver
Audio 8 Ian Vollmer
Audio 9 Rod Fox
Audio 10 Stacy Hruby

MUSIC
Composer Russ Landau
Composer David Vanacore
Music Editor Alison Tusan

MAKEUP/WARDROBE
Host Makeup and Hair/Wardrobe Shellie-Rae

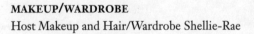

MALAYSIAN CREW
Location Manager Eric Thein
Island Advisor Gideon Abel Mosito
Island Site Manager Terence Lim
Island Guide James Chew
Island Guide Andrew Sani
Accountant Tham Yau Siong
Production Asst. James Wong

MEDICAL UNIT
Medical Director Dr. Adrian Cohen
Psychologist Dr. Gene Ondrusek
Psychologist Dr. Richard Levak
Medical Doctor(LA) Dr. Richard Horowitz
Paramedic Steve Martz
Nurse Heather Stewart

About the Authors

MARK BURNETT is the Executive Producer for the hit CBS series "Survivor!" and also for "Eco-Challenge" the six year old cable miniseries next scheduled to air in 2001 in primetime on USA Networks. He won an Emmy Award and Bannff Rockie Award for his work on the 1998 Eco-Challenge. He was previously Emmy-nominated for the 1996 Eco-Challenge and the show was nominated for an International Documentary Association Award for the 1997 Eco-Challenge. He has given motivational, leadership, and team-building speeches for such clients as IBM, Citibank, Sony, USA Networks, Discovery Channel, and AdWeek Asia. He recently concluded serving a second elected term on the Board of Directors of the British Academy of Film and Television Arts in Los Angeles. A former member of the famed British Army Parachute Regiment with active service medals in both the North Ireland and Argentina conflicts, Burnett is an open water certified SCUBA diver, Level A certified skydiver, has completed a white water guide course, and is Advanced Wilderness First Aid certified.

MARTIN DUGARD is an acclaimed sports and adventure writer who has written pieces for *Sports Illustrated, GQ, Esquire,* and other national publications. He is the author of *Knockdown: The Harrowing True Account of a Yacht Race Turned Deadly* and *Surviving the Toughest Race on Earth,* about his experience on the Raid Gauloises. He lives in California.